Anonymous

The Catholic's Manual of Instructions and Devotions

Anonymous

**The Catholic's Manual of Instructions and Devotions**

ISBN/EAN: 9783337331047

Printed in Europe, USA, Canada, Australia, Japan

Cover: Foto ©Lupo / pixelio.de

More available books at **www.hansebooks.com**

# The Catholic's Manual

OF

INSTRUCTIONS AND DEVOTIONS.

*Permissu Superiorum.*

LIVERPOOL:
PUBLISHED BY ROCKLIFF BROTHERS, CASTLE STREET.

MDCCCLXVII.

ENTERED AT STATIONERS' HALL.

# Explanatory Notice.

THE "usual conditions" for gaining a Plenary Indulgence, so often alluded to in the following pages, are to approach worthily the Sacraments of Penance and the Blessed Eucharist, and to pray for the intentions of the Sovereign Pontiff.

A further condition not unfrequently is required, that the prayers for the intention of the Sovereign Pontiff be recited in some church or public oratory; hence it is a useful and pious practice to comply with this condition before quitting the church or public oratory, after Holy Communion.

This Condition of visiting a church or public oratory is required in order to gain the Plenary Indulgence attached to the recital of the following prayers: Litany of Loretto (page 12); Memorare (page 19); Prayer to our Blessed Lady (page 19); Anima Christi (page 71); Ejaculatory Prayer to the Most Holy Trinity (page 143), and to the Blessed Virgin (page 146); For those in their Agony (page 355); Prayer for Peace (page 441); Praises of the Holy Name (page 475).

It is not necessary for those who go weekly to Confession, to confess on the day on which they propose to gain a Plenary Indulgence: their weekly Confession will suffice for all the Indulgences that may occur during the week, when confession of sins is required, provided the remaining conditions be complied with.

When the letter A is introduced in the following pages, it indicates that the Indulgence so marked is applicable, by way of suffrage, to the Souls in Purgatory.

STONYHURST COLLEGE,
Feast of the Nativity B. V. M.
Sept. 8, 1867.

# A Table of the Feasts

## OBSERVED BY THE CATHOLICS OF ENGLAND.

.The Days of Obligation are in Small Capitals. The Days of Devotion are in Italics.

ALL THE SUNDAYS IN THE YEAR.

### JANUARY.

1 The CIRCUMCISION, or New Year's Day.
6 The EPIPHANY, or Twelfth Day.

### FEBRUARY.

2 *The Purification, or Candlemas Day.*
24 *St. Matthias.*

### MARCH.

19 *St. Joseph, Spouse of the Blessed Virgin.*
25 *The Annunciation of the Blessed Virgin, or Lady Day.*

### APRIL.

23 *St. George the Martyr.*

### MAY.

1 *SS. Philip and James.*
3 *The Invention or Finding of the Cross.*

### JUNE.

24 *The Nativity of St. John the Baptist.*
29 SS. PETER and PAUL.

### JULY.

25 *St. James.*
26 *St. Ann, Mother of the Blessed Virgin.*

### AUGUST.

10 *St. Lawrence, Martyr.*
15 The ASSUMPTION of the Blessed Virgin.
24 *St. Bartholomew.*

### SEPTEMBER.

8 *The Nativity of the Blessed Virgin.*
21 *St. Matthew.*
29 *Michaelmas Day.*

### OCTOBER.

28 *SS. Simon and Jude.*

### NOVEMBER.

1 ALL SAINTS.
30 *St. Andrew.*

### DECEMBER.

8 *The Immaculate Conception of the Blessed Virgin.*
21 *St. Thomas.*
25 CHRISTMAS DAY.
26 *St. Stephen, Martyr.*
27 *St. John.*
28 *Holy Innocents.*
29 *St. Thomas of Canterbury.*

V.

## Moveable Feasts.

EASTER SUNDAY, *Monday* and *Tuesday*.

ASCENSION DAY, or the Thursday forty days after Easter.

WHITSUNDAY, *Monday* and *Tuesday*.

CORPUS CHRISTI, being the first Thursday after Trinity Sunday.

## Fasting Days.

THE forty days of Lent.

The Ember Days, at the four seasons, being the Wednesday, Friday, and Saturday of the first week in Lent, of Whitsun Week, of the third week in September, and of the third week in Advent.

The Vigils or Eves of Whitsunday, of Saints Peter and Paul, of the Assumption of the Blessed Virgin, of all Saints, and of Christmas day.

The Wednesdays and Fridays in Advent.

N.B.—When any fasting-day falls upon a Sunday, it is to be observed on the Saturday before. If the feast fall upon a Monday, the vigil is kept upon Saturday.

## Abstinence Days.

THE Sundays in Lent, unless leave be given to eat meat.

All the Fridays of the year, except when Christmas Day falls on a Friday.

N.B.—The Catholic Church commands all her children, upon Sundays and Holydays of Obligation, to be present at the great Eucharistic Sacrifice, which is called the Mass, and to rest from servile work on those days, and to keep them holy.

2ndly—She commands them to abstain from flesh on all days of fasting and abstinence; and on fasting days to eat but one meal.

3rdly—She commands them to confess their sins to their Pastors at least once a year.

4thly—She commands them to receive the blessed Sacrament at least once a year, and that at Easter, or thereabouts.

The fourth Council of Lateran, Can. 21, ordains, "That every one of the faithful of both sexes, after they come to the years of discretion, shall, in private, faithfully confess all their sins, at least once a year, to their Pastor: and take care to fulfil, to the best of their power, the penance enjoined them: receiving reverently, at least at Easter, the Sacrament of the Eucharist, unless perhaps by the counsel of their Pastor, for some reasonable cause, they judge it proper to abstain from it for a time; otherwise, let them be excluded from the Church whilst living, and when they die be deprived of Christian burial."

# A Table of Moveable Feasts.

| Year of our Lord. | Septuagesima. | Ash Wednesday. | Easter Sunday. | Ascension. | Whit Sunday. | Corpus Christi. | First Sunday in Advent. |
|---|---|---|---|---|---|---|---|
| 1867 | Feb 17 | Mar 6 | Apr 21 | May 30 | June 9 | Jun 20 | Dec 1 |
| 1868 | Feb 9 | Feb 26 | Apr 12 | May 21 | May 31 | Jun 11 | Nov 29 |
| 1869 | Jan 24 | Feb 10 | Mar 28 | May 6 | May 16 | May 27 | Nov 28 |
| 1870 | Feb 13 | Mar 2 | Apr 17 | May 26 | June 5 | Jun 16 | Nov 27 |
| 1871 | Feb 5 | Feb 22 | Apr 9 | May 18 | May 28 | June 8 | Dec 3 |
| 1872 | Jan 28 | Feb 14 | Mar 31 | May 9 | May 19 | May 30 | Dec 1 |
| 1873 | Feb 9 | Feb 26 | Apr 13 | May 22 | June 1 | Jun 12 | Nov 30 |
| 1874 | Feb 1 | Feb 18 | Apr 5 | May 14 | May 24 | June 4 | Nov 29 |
| 1875 | Jan 24 | Feb 10 | Mar 28 | May 6 | May 16 | May 27 | Nov 28 |
| 1876 | Feb 13 | Mar 1 | Apr 16 | May 25 | June 4 | Jun 15 | Dec 3 |
| 1877 | Jan 28 | Feb 14 | Apr 1 | May 10 | May 20 | May 31 | Dec 2 |
| 1878 | Feb 17 | Mar 6 | Apr 21 | May 30 | June 9 | Jun 20 | Dec 1 |
| 1879 | Feb 9 | Feb 26 | Apr 13 | May 22 | June 1 | Jun 12 | Nov 30 |
| 1880 | Jan 25 | Feb 11 | Mar 28 | May 6 | May 16 | May 27 | Nov 28 |
| 1881 | Feb 13 | Mar 2 | Apr 17 | May 26 | June 5 | Jun 16 | Nov 27 |
| 1882 | Feb 5 | Feb 22 | Apr 9 | May 18 | May 28 | June 8 | Dec 3 |
| 1883 | Jan 21 | Feb 7 | Mar 25 | May 3 | May 13 | May 24 | Dec 2 |
| 1884 | Feb 10 | Feb 27 | Apr 13 | May 22 | June 1 | Jun 12 | Nov 30 |
| 1885 | Feb 1 | Feb 18 | Apr 5 | May 14 | May 24 | June 4 | Nov 29 |
| 1886 | Feb 21 | Mar 10 | Apr 25 | June 3 | Jun 13 | Jun 24 | Nov 28 |
| 1887 | Feb 6 | Feb 23 | Apr 10 | May 19 | May 29 | June 9 | Nov 27 |
| 1888 | Jan 29 | Feb 15 | Apr 1 | May 10 | May 20 | May 31 | Dec 2 |
| 1889 | Feb 17 | Mar 6 | Apr 21 | May 30 | June 9 | Jun 20 | Dec 1 |
| 1890 | Feb 2 | Feb 19 | Apr 6 | May 15 | May 25 | June 5 | Nov 30 |

# Plenary Indulgences,

*Granted to the Faithful in the Dioceses of England.*

1. CHRISTMAS Day, and the twelve days following, to the day of the Epiphany, inclusively.

2. The first week of Lent, beginning with the first Sunday, and ending with the second Sunday, inclusively.

3. Easter, *i.e.* from Palm Sunday, inclusively, to Low Sunday, inclusively.

4. From Whitsunday, inclusively, to the end of the octave of Corpus Christi.

5. The feast of SS. Peter and Paul, and during the octave.

6. From the Sunday, inclusively, preceding the festival of the Assumption of the Blessed Virgin Mary to the twenty-second day of August, inclusively. But if the festival of the Assumption fall on a Sunday, the Indulgence begins on that day.

7. From the Sunday, inclusively, preceding the festival of St. Michael to the Sunday following, inclusively. But if the festival of St. Michael fall on a Sunday, the Indulgence begins on that day.

8. From the Sunday, inclusively, preceding the festival of All Saints to the eighth day of November, inclusively. But if the feast of All Saints fall on a Sunday, the Indulgence begins on that day.

ix.

*The Conditions of the 2nd, 4th and 8th are,*

1. That the faithful confess their sins, with sincere repentance, to a Priest approved by the Bishop.

2. That they worthily receive the Holy Communion.

3. That, if their state and condition allow it, they give some alms to the poor, either on the eve or on the day of their Communion.

4. That on the day of their Communion, they offer up some prayers to God, for the whole state of the Catholic Church throughout the world; for bringing back all straying souls to the fold of Christ, for the general peace of Christendom, and for the blessing of God upon this nation.

*The conditions of the 1st, 3rd, 6th and 7th are,*

1. That the faithful confess their sins, with sincere repentance, to a Priest approved by the Bishop.

2. That they worthily receive the Holy Communion.

3. That they visit some chapel or oratory where mass is celebrated, and pray to God for the peace of his Church.

4. That they be in readiness of mind to assist the poor with alms in proportion to their abilities; or to frequent catechisms and sermons when they can do it without great inconvenience; or to afford their assistance to the

sick, or to such as are near their end, out of the motive of Christian charity.

NOTE.—It is not required, for gaining these four indulgences granted by Pope Benedict XIV., that these works of mercy, corporal or spiritual, or the being present at catechism or sermons, be done on the same day with the communion; but only that persons be then in a disposition or readiness of mind to do these things, or some of them, at least, when they have an opportunity.

### The Conditions of the 5th are,

1. That the faithful confess their sins, with sincere repentance, to a Priest approved by the Bishop.
2. That they worthily receive the Holy Communion.
3. That, for some space of time, they pray to God, with a sincere heart, for the conversion of infidels and heretics, and for the free propagation of the holy faith.

## The manner of Lay Persons Baptizing an Infant in danger of Death.

TAKE common water, pour it on the head or face of the child, and while you are pouring it, say the following words:—

"I baptize thee in the name of the Father, and of the Son, and of the Holy Ghost. Amen."

N.B.—Any person, whether man, woman, or child, may baptize an infant in case of danger of death, that is, when there is reason to think that the child will not live till a Catholic Priest can come to baptize it.

# MANUAL

OF

# Instructions and Devotions.

### Instructions and Devotions on Rising.

IT is most important to commence the day well. The first thoughts of a Christian on rising are like those first fruits of which God in the Old Law was most jealous. Endeavour to contract the holy habit of raising your heart to God immediately on waking, to implore his protection and grace, that the day which, in his infinite goodness he adds to your life, may not add to the number of your sins, but, on the contrary, increase your merits and tend to his glory.

The first thoughts of the day are those the devil is most anxious to snatch from you; hence having made the sign of the cross, present your offering at once to God, and say, " *O my God, I offer thee my heart, and most earnestly beg of thee to take possession of it;*" or, "*In thee, O my God, and for thee, and from thee, and with thee, in union with the sacred hearts of Jesus and Mary, I will perform this action, and all the other actions of the day.*"

Have a fixed and early hour for rising, and let not sloth detain you in bed. Whilst dressing, entertain yourself with pious thoughts, and let all be done modestly and respectfully. If so much care is taken in adorning the body, and defending it from cold or heat, how much greater care should be taken in preparing the soul to appear in a becoming manner before God, and his Saints and Angels?

It is a pious and most useful practice to make a general intention in the morning, to gain those indulgences that are attached by the Church, to any actions you may perform during the day.

## Morning Prayers.

IN the name of the Father, and of the Son, and of the Holy Ghost. Amen.

Blessed be the Holy and undivided Trinity, now and for ever. Amen.

### THE LORD'S PRAYER.

OUR Father who art in heaven, hallowed be thy name: thy kingdom come: thy will be done on earth as it is in heaven. Give us this day our daily bread; and forgive us our trespasses, as we forgive them that trespass against us; and lead us not into temptation; but deliver us from evil. Amen.

## THE HAIL MARY.

HAIL Mary, full of grace, the Lord is with thee. Blessed art thou amongst women, and blessed is the fruit of thy womb, Jesus. Holy Mary, mother of God, pray for us sinners, now, and at the hour of our death. Amen.

## THE APOSTLES' CREED.

I BELIEVE in God the Father Almighty, Creator of heaven and earth. And in Jesus Christ his only Son our Lord, who was conceived by the Holy Ghost, born of the Virgin Mary; suffered under Pontius Pilate, was crucified, dead, and buried; he descended into hell, the third day he rose again from the dead; he ascended into heaven, sitteth at the right hand of God the Father Almighty; thence he shall come to judge the living and the dead. I believe in the Holy Ghost; the holy Catholic Church; the communion of Saints; the forgiveness of sins; the resurrection of the body, and life everlasting. Amen.

## THE CONFITEOR.

I CONFESS to Almighty God, to blessed Mary ever Virgin, to blessed Michael the Archangel, to blessed John the Baptist, to the holy Apostles Peter and Paul, and to all the Saints, that I have sinned exceedingly in thought, word, and deed, through my fault, through my fault, through my most grievous fault. Therefore I beseech the blessed Mary ever Virgin, the blessed Michael the Archangel, the blessed John the Baptist, the holy Apostles Peter and Paul, and all the Saints, to pray to the Lord our God for me.

May Almighty God have mercy on us and forgive us our sins, and bring us to life everlasting. Amen.

May the Almighty and merciful Lord give us pardon, absolution, and remission of our sins. Amen.

AN ACT OF FAITH IN THE PRESENCE
OF GOD.

O MY God, I firmly believe thou art here and perfectly seest me, and that thou observest all my actions, all my thoughts, and the most secret motions of my heart. Canst thou suffer in thy holy presence a sinner who has so often offended thee? It is thy goodness and liberality which invite and command my poverty to come to thee. Give me grace, therefore, to pray as I ought.

Come, O Holy Spirit, fill the hearts of thy faithful, and kindle in them the fire of thy love.

℣. Send forth thy Spirit, and our hearts shall be regenerated.

℟. And thou shalt renew the face of the earth.

PRAYER.

O GOD, who by the light of the Holy Ghost didst instruct the hearts of the faithful, give us by this same Holy Spirit, a love and relish of what is right and just, and the constant enjoyment of his comforts; through Jesus Christ our Lord thy Son, who with thee, in unity of the same Holy Ghost, liveth and reigneth God for ever. Amen.

AN ACT OF ADORATION AND THANKSGIVING.

O MY God, I adore thee as my Creator and my Sovereign Good: and with all possible thanksgiving I acknowledge the many benefits which thou hast conferred upon me, in relation both to body and soul. Thou hast created me out of nothing; redeemed me by the death of thy Son; sanctified me by the grace of thy Holy Spirit; preserved me from an infinity of dangers and from hell fire, which I have deserved by my sins. Thou knowest that I am an unprofitable and ungrateful servant, nevertheless thou hast all this time had patience with me; thou hast preserved me the night past, and given me this present day, that I may labour with more care and diligence than I have hitherto done, to obtain the crown of immortal glory, which thy goodness hath prepared for me. O my God, how good thou art towards me! What return can I make for such innumerable benefits? I will bless thy holy name, and serve thee all the days of my life.

Here let us renew our sorrow for the sins of our past lives, and make resolutions against the temptations and dangerous occasions we may meet with during the day.

### AN ACT OF CONTRITION WITH GOOD RESOLUTIONS.

O my God, how ill have I hitherto lived! How little have I done for thee! I am heartily sorry I have spent and lost that time in offending thee, which thine infinite goodness gave me to be employed in thy service, in advancing the good of my soul, and in purchasing everlasting life. I detest all the sins which I have committed against thy divine Majesty. I am sorry that I have offended thee, because thou art infinitely good, and sin is infinitely displeasing to thee: I love thee with my whole heart and soul, and I firmly purpose, by the help of thy grace, to serve thee more faithfully for the future. Receive, I beseech thee, the remainder of my life: I renew my promises made in baptism; I renounce the devil, his works, and all his pomps; I now begin and will endeavour to spend this day according to thy holy will, both as to the nature and circumstances of my actions, performing them so that they may be pleasing to thee. I will take particular care to avoid the failings to which I am subject, and to exercise the virtues which are most suitable to my state and employment.

### AN OBLATION.

I OFFER to thee, O my God! the life and death of thine only Son; and with them these my affections and resolutions, my thoughts, words, deeds, and sufferings of this day, and of all my life; in honour of thine adorable Majesty, in thanksgiving for all thy benefits, in satisfaction for my sins, and to obtain the assistance of thy grace; that persevering to the end in doing thy holy will, I may love and enjoy thee for ever in thy glory.

### A PETITION.

THOU knowest, O my God, how weak and unable I am to do good: leave me not to myself, but take me under thy protection, and give me grace faithfully to comply with these holy resolutions. Enlighten my understanding with a lively faith, raise up my will to a firm hope, and inflame it with an ardent charity.

Strengthen my weakness, and cure the corruption of my heart; grant that overcoming my enemies, both visible and invisible, I may make good use of thy grace; and vouchsafe to add to these blessings the inestimable gift of final perseverance.

℣. To thee, O Lord, I have lifted up my voice.

℟. And early in the morning my prayer shall come before thee.

℣. Let my mouth be ever filled with thy praises.

℟. That I may publish thy glory, and all the day thy greatness.

℣. Turn away thy face, O Lord, from my sins;
℟. And blot out all my iniquities.
℣. Create in me a clean heart, O God;
℟. And renew a right spirit within me.
℣. Cast me not out of thy sight;
℟. And take not thy Holy Spirit from me.
℣. Restore to me the joy of thy salvation;
℟. And strengthen me with a perfect spirit.
℣. Our help is in the name of our Lord.
℟. Who hath made both heaven and earth.
℣. Vouchsafe, O Lord, this day.
℟. To preserve us from all sin.
℣. Have mercy on us, O Lord.
℟. Have mercy on us.
℣. Let thy mercy, O Lord, be poured upon us;
℟. According to the hopes we have placed in thee.
℣. O Lord, hear my prayer.
℟. And let my cry come to thee.

### PRAYER.

ALMIGHTY Lord and God, who hast brought us to the beginning of this day, let thy powerful grace so conduct us through it, that we may not fall into any sin, but that all our thoughts, words, and actions may be regulated according to the rules of thy heavenly justice, and tend to the observance of thy holy law: through the merits of Jesus Christ our Lord. Amen.

### PRAYER.

LORD God, and King of heaven and earth, vouchsafe this day to rule and sanctify, to direct and govern our souls and bodies, our senses, words, and actions in conformity to thy law, and in strict obedience to thy commands; that by the help of thy grace, O Saviour of the world, we may be fenced and freed from all evils, both now and for ever. Amen.

### PRAYER.

O GOD, who out of thy unspeakable providence, art pleased to appoint the holy Angels for our guardians, give ear to the supplications which we make for a continuance of their protection, and that we may be added to their joyful number for all eternity. Amen.

O Angel of God, who, by divine appointment, art my guardian, to watch over me in all my ways, be pleased this day to enlighten, preserve, rule, and govern me, whom the goodness of our God has committed to thy charge, and to defend me from all the powers of darkness.

May our Lord bless us, and preserve us from all evils, and bring us to life everlasting.

And may the souls of the faithful, through the mercy of God, rest in peace. Amen.

## Litany of Loretto.

(300 days Indulgence for each recital. Plenary Indulgence on the Five Principal Feasts B.V.M., on usual Conditions. A.)

| | |
|---|---|
| Sᴜʙ tuum præsidium confugimus, sancta Dei Genitrix, nostras deprecationes ne despicias in necessitatibus nostris, sed a periculis cunctis libera nos, semper Virgo gloriosa et benedicta. | Wᴇ fly to thy patronage, O holy Mother of God, despise not our petitions in our necessities, but deliver us from all dangers, O ever glorious and blessed Virgin. |
| Kyrie eleison. | Lord, have mercy on us. |
| *Christe eleison.* | *Christ, have mercy on us.* |
| Kyrie eleison. | Lord, have mercy on us. |
| Christe audi nos. | Christ, hear us. |
| *Christe exaudi nos.* | *Christ, graciously hear us.* |
| Pater de cœlis Deus, *miserere nobis.* | God, the Father of heaven, *Have mercy on us.* |
| Fili, Redemptor mundi Deus, *miserere nobis* | God the Son, Redeemer of the world, *Have mercy on us.* |
| Spiritus Sancte Deus, *miserere nobis.* | God, the Holy Ghost, *Have mercy on us.* |
| Sancta Trinitas, unus Deus, *miserere nobis.* | Holy Trinity, one God, *Have mercy on us.* |
| Sancta Maria, | Holy Mary, |
| Sancta Dei Genitrix, | Holy Mother of God, |
| Sancta Virgo virginum, | Holy Virgin of virgins, |
| Mater Christi, | Mother of Christ, |
| Mater divinæ gratiæ, | Mother of divine grace, |

*Ora pro nobis.*     *Pray for us.*

LITANY OF LORETTO.   13

| | |
|---|---|
| Mater purissima, | Mother most pure, |
| Mater castissima, | Mother most chaste, |
| Mater inviolata, | Mother inviolate, |
| Mater intemerata, | Mother undefiled, |
| Mater amabilis, | Amiable Mother, |
| Mater admirabilis, | Admirable Mother, |
| Mater Creatoris, | Mother of our Creator, |
| Mater Salvatoris, | Mother of our Redeemer, |
| Virgo prudentissima, | Virgin most prudent, |
| Virgo veneranda, | Venerable Virgin, |
| Virgo prædicanda, | Renowned Virgin, |
| Virgo potens, | Powerful Virgin, |
| Virgo clemens, | Merciful Virgin, |
| Virgo fidelis, | Faithful Virgin, |
| Speculum justitiæ, | Mirror of justice, |
| Sedes sapientiæ, | Seat of wisdom, |
| Causa nostræ lætitiæ, | Cause of our joy, |
| Vas spirituale, | Spiritual vessel, |
| Vas honorabile, | Honourable vessel, |
| Vas insigne devotionis, | Singular vessel of devotion, |
| Rosa mystica, | Mystical rose, |
| Turris Davidica, | Tower of David, |
| Turris eburnea, | Tower of ivory, |
| Domus aurea, | House of gold, |
| Fœderis arca, | Ark of the covenant, |
| Janua cœli, | Gate of heaven, |
| Stella matutina, | Morning star, |
| Salus infirmorum, | Health of the weak, |
| Refugium peccatorum, | Refuge of sinners, |
| Consolatrix afflictorum, | Comforter of the afflicted, |
| Auxilium Christianorum, | Help of Christians, |

*Ora pro nobis.*   *Pray for us.*

Regina Angelorum, — Queen of Angels,
Regina Patriarcharum, — Queen of Patriarchs,
Regina Prophetarum, — Queen of Prophets,
Regina Apostolorum, — Queen of Apostles,
Regina Martyrum, — Queen of Martyrs,
Regina Confessorum, — Queen of Confessors,
Regina Virginum, — Queen of Virgins,
Regina Sanctorum omnium, — Queen of all Saints,
Regina sine labe originali concepta, — Queen conceived without original sin,

*Ora pro nobis.* — *Pray for us.*

Agnus Dei, qui tollis peccata mundi, *parce nobis, Domine.*

Lamb of God, who takest away the sins of the world, *Spare us, O Lord.*

Agnus Dei, qui tollis peccata mundi, *exaudi nos, Domine.*

Lamb of God, who takest away the sins of the world, *Graciously hear us, O Lord.*

Agnus Dei, qui tollis peccata mundi, *miserere nobis.*

Lamb of God, who takest away the sins of the world, *Have mercy on us.*

*Ant.* Sub tuum præsidium confugimus, sancta Dei Genitrix, nostras deprecationes ne despicias in necessitatibus nostris, sed a periculis cunctis libera nos, semper Virgo gloriosa et benedicta.

*Ant.* We fly to thy patronage, O holy Mother of God, despise not our petitions in our necessities, but deliver us from all dangers, O ever glorious and blessed Virgin.

## LITANY OF LORETTO.

℣. Ora pro nobis, sancta Dei Genitrix.
℞. Ut digni efficiamur promissionibus Christi.

℣. Pray for us, O holy Mother of God.
℞. That we may be made worthy of the promises of Christ.

### ORATIO.

GRATIAM tuam quæsumus, Domine, mentibus nostris infunde; ut qui, Angelo nuntiante, Christi Filii tui incarnationem cognovimus, per passionem ejus et crucem, ad resurrectionis gloriam perducamur. Per eumdem Christum Dominum nostrum. Amen.

### PRAYER.

POUR forth, we beseech thee, O Lord, thy grace into our hearts; that we, to whom the incarnation of Christ thy Son was made known by the message of an angel, may, by his passion and cross, be brought to the glory of his resurrection, through the same Christ our Lord. Amen.

℣. Divinum auxilium maneat semper nobiscum. ℞. Amen.
℣. Et fidelium animæ per misericordiam Dei, requiescant in pace. ℞. Amen.

℣. May the divine assistance remain always with us. ℞. Amen.
℣. And may the souls of the faithful, through the mercy of God, rest in peace. ℞. Amen.

## Angelus Domini.

To be said morning, noon, and night, in memory of our Saviour becoming man for our salvation.

(100 days Indulgence for each recital as above.—Plenary Indulgence once a month, on the usual conditions. A.)

ANGELUS Domini nuntiavit Mariæ;

Et concepit de Spiritu Sancto.
*Ave Maria, &c.*
Ecce ancilla Domini;

Fiat mihi secundum verbum tuum.

*Ave Maria, &c.*
Et Verbum caro factum est;
Et habitavit in nobis.

*Ave Maria, &c.*
℣. Ora pro nobis, Sancta Dei Genitrix.
℟. Ut digni efficiamur promissionibus Christi.

ORATIO.

GRATIAM tuam, quæsumus Domino, mentibus nostris infunde: ut qui, Angelo nuntiante, Christi Filii tui incarnationem cogno-

THE Angel of the Lord declared unto Mary;
And she conceived of the Holy Ghost.
*Hail Mary, &c.*
Behold the handmaid of the Lord:
May it be done to me according to thy word.

*Hail Mary, &c.*
And the Word was made flesh:
And dwelt amongst us.

*Hail Mary, &c.*
℣. Pray for us, O holy Mother of God.
℟. That we may be made worthy of the promises of Christ.

PRAYER.

POUR forth, we beseech thee, O Lord, thy grace into our hearts, that we, to whom the incarnation of Christ thy Son was

vimus, per passionem ejus et crucem ad resurrectionis gloriam perducamur. Per eumdem Christum Dominum nostrum. Amen.

made known by the message of an Angel, may, by his passion and cross, be brought to the glory of his resurrection. Through the same Christ our Lord. Amen.

## Regina Cœli.

Instead of the "Angelus Domini," the Anthem "Regina Cœli" is said from Easter Eve till Trinity Sunday.
(Indulgences the same as for the "Angelus Domini.")

REGINA cœli lætare; Alleluia.
Quia quem meruisti portare; Alleluia.

Resurrexit sicut dixit; Alleluia.
Ora pro nobis Deum. Alleluia.
℣. Gaude et lætare, Virgo Maria: Alleluia.

℞. Quia surrexit Dominus vere. Alleluia.

ORATIO.

DEUS, qui per resurrectionem Filii tui Domini nostri Jesu Christi mundum laeti-

QUEEN of heaven rejoice; Alleluia.
Because he whom thou hast deserved to bear; Alleluia.
Has risen, as he said; Alleluia.
Pray to God for us. Alleluia.
℣. Rejoice and be glad, O Virgin Mary: Alleluia.

℞. Because the Lord hath truly risen. Alleluia.

PRAYER.

O GOD, who through the resurrection of thy Son Jesus Christ our Lord, hast vouchsafed

ficare dignatus es; praesta quaesumus, ut per ejus Genitricem Virginem Mariam, perpetuæ capiamus gaudia vitæ. Per eumdem Christum Dominum nostrum. Amen.

to give joy to the world: grant, we beseech thee, that by the intercession of the Virgin Mary, his Mother, we may receive the joys of eternal life. Through the same Christ our Lord. Amen.

## Act of Consecration to our Blessed Lady.

SANCTA Maria, Mater Dei et Virgo, ego N. N., te hodie in Dominam, Patronam, et Advocatam eligo: firmiterque statuo ac propono me nunquam te derelicturum, neque contra te aliquid unquam dicturum aut facturum, neque permissurum ut a meis subditis aliquid contra tuum honorem unquam agatur. Obsecro te igitur, suscipe me in servum perpetuum, adsis mihi in actionibus omnibus meis, nec me deseras in hora mortis. Amen.

HOLY Mary, Mother of God and Virgin, I, N. N., choose thee this day for my Queen, my Patroness, and my Advocate, and I firmly resolve and purpose never to abandon thee, and never to say or do anything against thee, nor allow anything to be done against thy honour by those subject to me. I beseech thee, therefore, receive me as thy servant for ever, assist me in all my actions, and abandon me not at the hour of death. Amen.

### Memorare.

(300 days Indulgence for each recital.—Plenary Indulgence once in the month, on usual conditions. A.)

MEMORARE, O piissima Virgo Maria, non esse auditum a sæculo quemquam ad tua currentem præsidia, tua implorantem auxilia, tua petentem suffragia, esse derelictum. Ego tali animatus confidentia, ad te, Virgo virginum, Mater, curro, ad te venio, coram te gemens peccator assisto; noli, Mater Verbi, verba mea despicere, sed audi propitia, et exaudi. Amen.

REMEMBER, O most Holy Virgin Mary, that no one ever had recourse to thy protection, implored thy help, or sought thy mediation, without obtaining relief. Confiding therefore in thy goodness, behold me a miserable sinner before thee, groaning under my sins, beseeching thee to adopt me for thy child, and to take upon thee the care of my eternal salvation. Despise not, O Mother of Jesus, the petition of thy humble client, but hear and grant my prayer. Amen.

### Prayer to our Blessed Lady.

MY Queen and my Mother! to thee I offer myself without any reserve; and to give thee a mark of my devotion, I consecrate to thee during this day, my eyes, my ears, my mouth, my heart, and my whole person. Since I belong to thee, O my good Mother, preserve and defend me as thy property and possession.

EJACULATION IN TIME OF TEMPTATION.

My Queen and my Mother! remember that I belong to thee; preserve and defend me as thy property and possession.

By a decree, *Urbi et orbi* (August 5, 1851), our Holy Father Pope Pius IX. grants: 1° 100 days Indulgence, to be gained once a day for the above prayer, if recited morning and evening after a "Hail Mary." 2° A Plenary Indulgence once a month, on the ordinary conditions. 3° 40 days for using the Ejaculation in time of temptation.

## Dedication to St. Joseph.

Holy Joseph, nursing Father of my Lord Jesus, and Spouse of the Blessed Virgin Mary, I, N., choose thee for my special patron and director, and since God has appointed thee to be the head of his holy family, I pray and beseech thee to look kindly upon my vocation, and to help me in it by thy intercession. Teach me, I implore thee, to honour Mary as my Queen, and to love her as my Mother. Under thy guidance let me walk in the way of virtue and devotion, and so deserve by thy patronage always to live and to die a true son of Mary and a faithful companion of Jesus. Amen.

## Prayer to St. Joseph.

O HOLY Joseph, father and protector of virgins, to whose faithful keeping Innocence itself, Christ Jesus, and Mary the Virgin of virgins, were committed, by these dearest pledges, Jesus and Mary, I beseech and conjure thee to preserve me from all impurity, that I may always serve Jesus and Mary in perfect chastity, with a mind unpolluted, a clean heart and a chaste body. Amen.

## Prayer to our Guardian Angel.

(100 days Indulgence for each devout recital.
Pius VI.—Pius VII. A.)

O ANGEL of God, who art appointed to be my Guardian, enlighten and protect me, direct and govern me. Amen.

## Prayer to St. Aloysius for Purity.

(100 days Indulgence once a day if recited with the Our Father and Hail Mary.—Pius VII. A.)

O BLESSED Aloysius! adorned with angelic graces, I, thy most unworthy servant, recommend specially to thee the chastity of my soul and body; praying thee by thy angelical purity, to plead for me with Jesus Christ, the Immaculate Lamb, and his most holy Mother, Virgin of virgins, that they would vouchsafe to keep me from all grievous sin. O never let me be defiled with any stain against my chastity; but when thou seest me in temptation, or in danger of falling, remove far from me all bad thoughts and wicked desires; and awaken in me the memory of an eternity to come, and of Jesus crucified. Impress deeply in my heart a holy fear of God, and thus kindling in me the fire of thy divine love, enable me to follow thy footsteps here on earth, that in heaven with thee, I may be made worthy to enjoy the sight of our God for ever. Through our Lord Jesus Christ. Amen.

One Our Father and Hail Mary.

## Instruction upon Meditation.

MEDITATION, or Mental Prayer, is a devout and fruitful consideration of Divine things, and of all that is conducive to the acquirement of virtue and of eternal salvation. By meditation we dispose ourselves to receive the gifts of God, and obtain his aid to overcome ourselves, and to remove from our hearts every evil affection. Thus we enable ourselves either to ascertain more securely and embrace more readily the state of life to which we are called by God, or to improve ourselves in the one we have chosen, by animating ourselves to the more perfect accomplishment of the duties imposed upon us.

Meditation, when made according to the method proposed by St. Ignatius in his book of the "Spiritual Exercises," consists of four parts, the Preparatory Prayer, the Preludes, the Points of the Meditation, and the Colloquies.

1° THE PREPARATORY PRAYER.—This is the same in all meditations, and is some short prayer directed to Almighty God, in which we ask, through his grace, that all the powers and operations of our mind may be directed to his greater honour and glory. The following may be used:

" Prevent, we beseech thee, O Lord, our
" actions by thy holy inspirations, and carry
" them on by thy gracious assistance, that
" every prayer and work of ours may always
" begin from thee, and by thee be happily
" ended."

2° THE PRELUDES.—There are two or three, according to the subject matter of the meditation. When we meditate upon some historical event in the life of Christ or his Saints, there are three Preludes; in all other meditations two will suffice. When there are but two preludes, the first consists in what is called the Composition of Place, or in forming, in our mind as best we can, a picture or image of some place or scene that has reference to the subject upon which we wish to meditate. If it be hell, we may imagine some obscure and horrible dungeon full of fire, and souls burning there: if upon sin, we may picture to ourselves the miserable condition we should be in, were we wandering as prisoners in the midst of the brute creation, living and eating with them, unable and unworthy to fare better. This first prelude or picture helps much to recall our thoughts when, during the meditation, they wander from the subject. The second prelude consists of some short prayer, in which we ask of God to grant us that particular fruit we desire to obtain from our meditation.

When three preludes are made, the first consists in briefly recalling to the memory the mystery in the life of Christ or of his Saints, on which we are about to meditate. This is done without proceeding to make reflections or considerations upon it. The second prelude is the Composition of Place as explained above. The third prelude is a petition for that special virtue which we need, and to attain which, our meditation is directed.

3° THE POINTS OF THE MEDITATION.— There are usually three. In each of them we are to apply our memory, understanding, and will. The memory presents to the understanding a truth to be considered; the understanding examines it, studies it, dwells upon its meaning, weighs the advantages of fulfilling what it enjoins, and the evil of doing what it forbids. The will, enlightened by God's grace, determines to carry out in practice what the understanding shows to be conformable to God's will or pleasure.

4°. THE COLLOQUIES.—At the end of each point, and more especially before the close of the meditation, the soul addresses herself with earnestness to God, to beg for grace and strength to keep most exactly the good resolutions she has made. We may, at one time, address our prayers to God the Father, at another to the Divine Word, or to the Holy Ghost. We may also ask the powerful intercession of Mary, our Mother, or of the saint on whose virtues we have been meditating. Each colloquy may be ended by reciting some short prayer, according to the Person to whom we have addressed ourselves; if it be to God the Father, the "Our Father;" if to Jesus Christ, the "Anima Christi;" if to the Blessed Virgin, the "Hail Mary."

N.B.—For persons who are deterred from attempting meditation through inability to find matter for serious and continued reflexion, the following suggestion will be very serviceable. In each point one or more of these questions may be considered :—

(1.) What practical conclusion should I draw from the mystery or truth contained in this point?

(2.) What motives have I to apply this truth to myself? Is the conclusion right and just, necessary or useful for me in my daily conduct?

(3.) What has been my conduct hitherto?
(4.) What shall I do for the future?
(5.) What obstacles are to be removed? What means must I employ, in order to carry out my good resolutions?

The short meditations that follow are drawn up so that they may serve for each day of the month.

## First Day.

### ON THE END OF MAN.

1°. MAN is created like unto God: he is created to know God, to glorify him, and to enjoy him. Therefore the end of man is not to acquire riches or reputation: he is not created to attend to the comforts or the follies of life.. This is a fundamental truth which we all know and profess to believe; but do we show by our lives that we are practically convinced of it?

2°. Consider the sublimity of the end for which we are created. God is his own end, and can have no other; he knows, glorifies, loves, and enjoys himself; he forms plans for his own glory in eternity, and executes them in time. In this, Almighty God has made me like unto himself, that I can love, glorify, and enjoy him. God even places his glory in being loved by me, and receiving my actions as a tribute from my free choice.

3°. Man is created solely to enjoy God: he cannot find any true and lasting happiness out of God: if the heart of man is created solely for the love of God, it cannot remain satisfied until God alone be the centre of all its affections. "O Lord, thou hast made us for thyself, and our heart cannot rest until it rests in thee!"—(St. Augustine.)

## Second Day.

### ON THE NECESSITY OF SAVING OUR SOULS.

1°. SALVATION is the most important of all concerns which regard man: it is the end of his creation. Almighty God, in bestowing life upon me, wills that I should spend it in saving my soul, and without this I cannot honour him. Should I lose my soul, creation is to me a curse instead of a blessing. Had I not been created, there would have been one man less in the world; but if I am lost, there will be one soul more in hell. If I save my soul, I may lose everything else without regret; but if I lose my soul, what will everything else avail me at the hour of my death?

2°. We must spare nothing to save our souls. Most men act as if they thought salvation easy to be obtained; but it is not so: the way is rough and narrow, and no man can pursue it without difficulty and great struggles. To obtain this treasure, much prayer, much interior and exterior self-denial are absolutely necessary. Should the salvation of our soul cost fortune, reputation, or life, all is a trifle when compared with this all-important issue.

3°. We must then, never risk our salvation. No man of sense risks his health, fortune, or life, unless for the attainment of some greater good: then how can we risk the loss of that which is everything to us for eternity, and of which alone God will require a strict account? Every interrogation at the day of judgment may be reduced to this: Hast thou saved thy soul?

## Third Day.

### ON THE GRIEVOUSNESS OF MORTAL SIN.

1°. CONSIDER the sin of the rebel Angels: this was the first of all sins. These Angels were created in a state of grace, but refusing in the time of trial what was required for the consummation of their happiness, (being unwilling to yield reverence and obedience to their Creator,) they were changed from the state of grace to that of sin, and from heaven were precipitated into hell. Good God! what a dreadful example. For one sin, and that in thought only, heaven is lost for ever, angels are changed into devils, they are removed for ever from the face of God, and "reserved under darkness, in everlasting chains, unto the judgment of the great day."—(St. Jude i. 6.)

2°. Consider the sin of our first Parents in the garden of Paradise. Call to mind their state: what a state of happiness, what prospects for the future! But seduced by Satan, they eat of a fruit whereof God had commanded them not to eat: this was their sin. O God, how very different are thy ways from ours, how different are thy judgments! In an instant, they are cast out of Paradise, they are forced to clothe themselves in the skins of beasts, they are deprived of original justice, and must spend the rest of their days in labour and penance. One sin is committed, and more than nine hundred years of weeping and toil must follow, and then bitter death.

3°. Consider that there are some souls in Hell, suffering in atonement for one mortal sin, and many who have been condemned for fewer sins than I have committed. O God, send down thy light and thy truth. Give me to see and to understand the grievousness and malice of mortal sin, which so much offends thee, the Creator and Lord of all things. Yes, the infliction of eternal banishment and pain is justly assigned to sin committed against a God whose goodness has neither end nor measure; for were it otherwise, how could Infinite Majesty have deigned to become a creature for my sake, to rescue me from sin and hell?

## Fourth Day.

### ON HELL.

1°. CONTEMPLATE what the damned souls suffer in hell. Descend alive into that pit of fire, as the Holy Scripture advises. Enter that prison of God's justice, that furnace of fire never to be extinguished, lighted up by the breath of an angry God. It is truly a lake of fire and brimstone, a land of misery, darkness and horror, where there is no light, no order, but everlasting confusion, wailing, and despair. Can I, so sensible of pain, even the least, believe all this and still be so mad as to commit mortal sin?

2°. In hell every sense will be exquisitely tormented. The sight, by the presence of devils: the ears, by shrieks and howlings, by curses and blasphemies: the smell, by insupportable stench and rottenness: the taste, by raging hunger and thirst, nor will the damned obtain one drop of water: the touch, by glowing fire that will search their inmost parts, and penetrate them throughout. It is said of the joys of heaven, that "neither eye hath seen, nor ear heard what things God hath prepared for those who love him;" (1 Cor. ii. 9.) may not the same words be applied to the justice of God!

3°. Great are the torments the damned endure in their senses, but far greater is their interior suffering, the worm of conscience that gnaws and yet never consumes, "for the worm dieth not." (Mark ix. 47.) Bound as they are, unable to do the smallest act, or move a single step either to ease themselves or end their torments, deprived of all the goods of fortune, of grace, and of glory, what a prospect is before them, and how bitterly must they not regret the opportunities that were offered them whilst in life, of saving their immortal souls!

4°. The thought of the eternity of their torments also racks and tortures the damned souls. The dreadful torments of hell would be in some sort tolerable if they were at last to end: but no, God's hatred must for ever pursue the wretched sinner : after millions of years the fire of hell will be as active and raging as ever, the body and soul as much disposed to suffer, and God as much irritated and irreconcileable as at the first moment of their imprisonment. And yet, with this terrible thought before them, men will still sin, and make little or no account of it! How grateful ought I to be to God, who has spared me from hell, which I have so often deserved by my sins?

## Fifth Day.

### ON DEATH.

1°. DEATH is an eternal and entire separation from this lower world. You must then leave the world, and everything in it, and the world will leave you. At your death, you must resign at once, life, pleasure, amusements, studies, prospects, goods, honours, friends, business, all, in a word, that constitutes the life and occupation of men upon earth. Withdraw then your affections from all earthly things, while yet you may do it freely, that at your last hour you may leave all these things without regret. See to what things you retain an attachment ; detachment from all things is the strict duty of a true Christian, and without it there is no happiness for him at the hour of death.

2°. At your death, the world will also quit you. The great bulk of mankind will be completely unconcerned respecting your death. The few who inherit the spoils of the deceased are easily comforted; perhaps they rejoice. Perhaps on the very day of his burial, his surviving friends seek to recreate themselves, in order to efface the melancholy image of death. Others fill his place; a few months pass away, and he is no longer missed among the living.

3°. The awful uncertainty of death is well calculated to make an impression on our minds. Death is uncertain as to its time, manner, and place. It steals upon us like a thief in the night. God alone knows when or how we shall die. Our blessed Lord commands us to watch and pray. Nothing but constant fervour in God's service can obtain for us that grace which we do not deserve, but which Almighty God will not refuse to grant us, the grand grace of final perseverance, and a happy death.

## Sixth Day.

### ON THE PARTICULAR JUDGMENT.

1°. At the instant in which the soul quits the body, she is presented before the tribunal of God to be judged, and condemned or rewarded, according to her works. Stripped of everything she had in the world, she will stand before an omniscient Judge, who sees all things as they are—a Judge infinitely just, whom nothing can influence; and infinitely great and powerful, from whom there is no appeal. What dread will seize the soul at that awful moment, when she will have nothing to rely upon but her own works! There will be no room then for prayer, repentance, or forgiveness. Inexorable justice will then decide her lot for eternity.

2°. In one instant, a most strict account will be taken of our every thought, word, and deed, from the first use of reason to our last breath. Nothing can escape the infinite knowledge of our Judge, before whom every thing will be brought into judgment, and who will render to every man according to his works. God will take an account not only of our evil deeds, but of our omissions of the good we ought to have done. Nay, our good actions, our best virtues, will be rigorously scrutinized, to see if they have full weight. The greater the graces we have received, the stricter will be the account we shall have to render. But what a severe account will be demanded of those *special* graces attached to each particular state of life!

3°. This examination being ended, our Judge will pronounce upon us the definitive sentence to eternal glory, or to reprobation. What sentence will be ours? If we were told that in the course of an hour we should be judged, what would we not do to obtain one year of life, to prepare for our last end? Oh, then, let us make the same use of the time which may still be ours.

## Seventh Day.

### ETERNITY.

1°. I AM made for eternity. Lately I began an existence that will never end. I now inhabit a perishable world, but I am made for a world that is eternal. The sun, the stars, the earth and sea will pass away; years and ages will go by, and cease to exist; but my years, like those of God, shall not fail. My soul was created immortal, and therefore nothing that is perishable is worthy of taking up my thoughts and affections. We have not here a lasting dwelling or a permanent city, therefore we seek a better.

2°. We are at the very entrance of eternity; for the longest life is a mere point when compared with it. "The number of man's days is at most a hundred years," and "as a drop of water unto the sea, and as one grain unto the sand on the sea shore, so are a thousand years unto the days of eternity." In the course of the few thousand years which have elapsed since the creation of the world, what myriads of immortal souls have passed into the bosom of eternity! I am still awaiting my turn: it is coming, it may perhaps come before I lie down to rest this night; but if it is delayed, it must inevitably come within a few years.

3°. Almighty God has given me the power of choosing for myself a happy or a miserable eternity. Do I endeavour to secure to myself eternal happiness, or do I leave to chance to decide whether I shall enjoy God for ever, or whether I shall suffer with the damned as long as eternity lasts? Alas! I have often risked my eternity; but I will do so no more. Do thou, O Lord, give me thy grace, that I may serve thee here, and be thou my portion for ever!

## Eighth Day.
### VENIAL SINS.

1°. VENIAL sin is an offence against God, and is therefore to be avoided, and dreaded more than any temporal evil whatsoever. We ought rather to suffer death than incur the guilt of one known and deliberate venial sin; it can never be authorised by any pretext of doing a greater good.

By every wilful venial sin, we "grieve the Holy Spirit of God," according to the words of the Apostle St. Paul (Ephes. iv. 30); and yet of what numberless sins have we been guilty in the course of our lives! May we not truly exclaim with the Psalmist, "My sins are multiplied above the hairs of my head." (Ps. xxxix. 13.) What numbers of faults proceed from dissipation, from sloth, from freedom of speech, from hastiness of temper, from dislike to others, &c.; and how many of these do we commit with deliberation and full knowledge!

2°. Consider the danger of venial sin. By it, the horror of mortal sin is lost or weakened in the soul. And moreover, as the distinction between mortal and venial sin is in some cases difficult to discern, we may, by custom, and carelessness in avoiding those faults which we consider venial, be led into the dreadful evil of mortal sin.

3°. The consequences and punishment of venial sin are also well worthy of our attention. The most usual effects of it are a disrelish for spiritual things, a disgust for prayer, and the withholding of the special graces which Almighty God bestows upon those who are faithful to him. Whoever dies in venial sin must remain separated from God in penal fire, until the last debt be paid. What a thought is this for a soul that loves God!

## Ninth Day.

### ON PURGATORY.

1°. WE are taught by faith, that nothing defiled can enter into the kingdom of heaven; and therefore, those who depart this life defiled with the stain of venial sin, or owing some satisfaction for mortal sin which has been remitted by penance, cannot enjoy the presence of God until "the last farthing" be paid to Divine justice. When the soul appears before Jesus Christ to be judged, she then clearly understands the horror and deformity of sin, the least degree of which she sees to be more dreadful than every calamity that we can imagine: at the same time she comprehends the infinite perfection of Almighty God, in whose presence the slightest shadow of sin cannot exist; and if she is defiled with any imperfection, she instantly flies from his presence, and rushes willingly and with gratitude, into a place of expiation, by means of which she may be fitted to see God; and were there no such means for effacing the rust of sin, she would suffer far more grievous torments from the grief she would feel at the impossibility of removing this obstacle to the enjoyment of God.

2°. Though it be not a defined article of faith that fire is the punishment of purgatory, still it is the common belief; and St. Gregory says, the same fire purifies the elect and burns the reprobate. The pains of purgatory differ immensely, it is true, from the torments of hell, inasmuch as these are eternal, while those are temporary, and the souls there detained have the consolation of hope; but still the sufferings of purgatory exceed all that we can imagine in this world. Yet the pain of sense endured by these suffering souls is far more tolerable than the pain of loss. This torments them by the languishing of intense desire and deferred hope; nor is it possible for us in our imperfect state, to imagine in any just degree, the anguish they feel till they can be united to God, whom they now love with perfect charity, and whom they know and feel to be the only centre of their happiness.

3°. It is still in our power to escape these dreadful sufferings, by making our lives a purgatory of love, which we may substitute for a purgatory of fire. Let us imitate, by a religious life, the holy souls who are expiating their guilt in the other world. They sin not there; they are always suffering, always submissive; they suffer without impatience or reluctance: they earnestly sigh for the possession and enjoyment of God, who is the supreme object of their love.

## Tenth Day.
### OF THE CAUSE OF THE SUFFERINGS OF PURGATORY.

1° THE fuel that feeds the fire of purgatory is the multitude of venial sins which we so easily commit, or satisfaction due to the justice of God for mortal sin, the guilt of which has been remitted by the sacrament of penance. The fuel of this fire consists in idle words; in breaches of good resolutions; in voluntary negligence in prayer; in indulging sentiments of disobedience, impatience, aversion, &c. Let us search our own hearts, and see if there is nothing there which will be matter for the fire of purgatory.

2°. It is not only our sins of commission, and the evil we have done, which will be punished hereafter; it is also the good we have omitted to do, or done amiss. We shall also be punished for the bad example we have given others, and the sins we may have caused them to commit, or neglected to prevent.

3°. If we saw temporal flames lighted up to torment us, having the power to quench them, should we forbear to do it, and madly rush into the devouring element? And yet we see by the light of faith, that Almighty God has prepared a purgatory for imperfect souls after death; we know the means of avoiding it, and still we refuse or delay to make use of those means. But what are those means? Contrition and penitential tears, love of God, self-denial, purity of conscience; in a word, serious efforts at perfection. Let us consider for a moment, how we employ these means. Do we not find in ourselves, on the contrary, a great reluctance to bear pain, and an eagerness to avoid everything inconvenient? Do we not endeavour to avoid humiliations, privations, heat, cold, hunger, thirst; in a word, all those things which we should joyfully embrace, if we desired to substitute the slight sufferings of this life for the pains of purgatory? Let us ponder well these words of our blessed Lord; "Whosoever will save his life, shall lose it; and he that shall lose his life for my sake, shall find it." (Matt. xvi. 25.) To offer up our prayers and good works for the deliverance of the holy souls suffering in purgatory is a very charitable practice, and also very advantageous to us. Ingratitude cannot exist in heaven; and if we are so happy as to procure or hasten for them the enjoyment of supreme beatitude, they will surely not be unmindful of us, but will intercede in our behalf with God.

## Eleventh Day.
### ON THE NECESSITY OF PENANCE.

1°. FROM voluntary sin results the necessity of doing penance. Though we may have returned seriously to God, we have still great debts to discharge to his justice; for no sin committed after baptism can be remitted without satisfaction proportioned to the offence. Every mortal sin which we may have had the misfortune to commit, requires long and severe penance and great mortification. We may, and ought to endeavour to gain the indulgences of the church; but a sincere penitent will not wish to defraud God's justice. If we gain indulgences, this ought to increase our gratitude and love for God, and excite in us a holy hatred of sin, which will only increase our desire to lead a penitential life.

2°. Works of penance and mortification are very necessary, in order to subdue our former bad habits. We may perhaps have overcome some defects, but how many evil inclinations have we still to combat with? Every one of these must be mortified, if we would subdue them; and our will, which is prone to offend God, must be forcibly curbed, and brought into complete subjection to the holy will of God, and conformity with it.

3°. To regain the lost favour of Almighty God, is also a powerful incitement to fervent acts of penance. By the sacrament of penance our sins are remitted; but we do not thereby immediately regain the affection of God, with all the tenderness he had for us before our fall. This grace was granted to the penitent Magdalen, but this was "*because she loved much.*"

Let us add to these reflections, the consideration of the voluntary sufferings of our blessed Lord, who for our sake became "a man of sorrow, and acquainted with infirmity." Let us contemplate at the foot of our crucifix the agonies of our dying Saviour, and who among us will dare to complain of the rigours of a penitential life?

## Twelfth Day.

### ON THE PRODIGAL SON.

1°. THIS thoughtless youth, seduced by a flattering notion of liberty, and a desire of doing his own will, foolishly left his father's house for a foreign land. This represents the conduct of a Christian, who having been educated in piety, grows weary of restraint, indulges his own corrupt inclinations, and resolves to gratify them in the follies of a dissipated world. It is also the image of a soul, which having been favoured with great graces, gradually sinks into tepidity, by sloth in spiritual duties, by forgetfulness of God, &c.; hence arise a fondness for independence, frequent venial sins, and imminent danger of mortal.

2°. The perverted youth wasted his fortune in a life of luxury, and being reduced to penury, he sold the very liberty which he had so much coveted, by hiring himself to feed swine. This portrait resembles that of a Christian, who having received excellent instructions in the Catholic Church, mingles with the worldly crowd, adopts their fashionable notions, and quickly wastes the religious principles which were once his delight; other objects fill his thoughts, practices of piety are omitted, fear of God perishes. The voice of conscience is stunned.

3°. Most deplorable is this perversion of a Christian soul, who, stifling the noble sentiments of his profession, becomes a slave to inordinate pursuits which can never bring happiness. The natural appetite of the soul seeks the food proportioned to its heavenly substance. The world may amuse with empty pleasures, but it cannot satisfy the cravings of an immortal soul; nothing but God can give it content. Acknowledge your dignity, deplore your past transgressions, and resolve, like the prodigal, to arise, and go home to the most indulgent of Fathers, who will be more rejoiced at your repentance than he has hitherto been grieved by your multiplied offences.

## Thirteenth Day.
### ON THE PRODIGAL SON.

1°. THE penitent prodigal no sooner had resolved to go home to his father, than he hastens to execute his generous resolution without delay. Full of contrition and confidence, trusting to the goodness of an affectionate father, he throws himself at his feet, and in the anguish of his heart exclaims, "Father, I have sinned against heaven and before thee; I am not worthy to be called thy son, rank me among thy servants:" here is the true model of a sincere penitent; excite within yourself similar sentiments of deep contrition, self-accusation, and confidence in the love and goodness of God. Rest all your hopes of pardon on the humility and sincerity of your confessions, your desire of doing penance, and above all, on the goodness and mercy of your heavenly Parent.

2°. The prodigal son wished and asked for the lowest place in his father's house. Do you imitate him in his humility? Offer yourself to God to be the meanest in his service. Reflect on the expressions of love and tenderness with which the father received his penitent son. He goes forth to meet him; he raises him from the earth; he folds him in his arms; he presses him to his breast; no reproach, no reprimand; he clothes the penitent with a rich robe; he gives him a ring, the mark of liberty. He prepares a banquet, that all may share his joy for the recovery of his lost child. Such was the conduct of this good father, but what were the feelings of the son? My soul, thou shouldst know them from thine own; thou hast sinned; but Jesus has given thee a will to repent, and has stretched out his hand to assist thy return, and receive thee, not only into his arms, but even into his Sacred Heart.

3°. Before you began to return to God, it was God himself who touched your heart; and as soon as you wished to correspond with his grace, he came to meet you. He gives you the robe of innocence; he forgets your sins, he invites you to rejoice in union with his angels and saints, who rejoice in your conversion; he admits you to the banquet of his precious body. Can your confidence in such a

Father, your gratitude, your love for him ever abate? Remember that the penitent prodigal never relapsed; make him your model, and reflect that it was your sins that crucified your Saviour, and that by his merits you are pardoned.

## Fourteenth Day.

### ON THE KINGDOM OF CHRIST.

1°. By the vows of baptism, you enrol yourself a soldier of Jesus Christ, in order to conquer the kingdom of heaven by violence. Listen to the words of your king: "If any one will come after me, let him deny himself, take up his cross, and follow me." You must then deny yourself by refusing your senses the indulgences that withdraw you from the thoughts of heaven; by refusing your will and understanding every gratification that nourishes pride, lust, vanity, or self-ease. You must take up your cross by suffering willingly the corporal and mental hardships of your state of life; the contradictions which may come from superiors and others; and you must besides, practise voluntary exterior penance. You must imitate and follow Christ: he loved poverty; he practised humility, patience, meekness; his zeal extended to save the whole world. A generous soldier would blush to behold his king enduring the whole toil of the combat, of which he himself was to enjoy the glory and profit, and not wish to share his toils.

2°. "A man's own enemies are those of his household." Victory in this intestine war is your object: it will facilitate the conquest of external enemies. You must first attack your own passions; above all, the predominant one which most frequently betrays you into faults. You must overcome sloth in spiritual exercises, which stops you in the way of virtue; self-love, which shuns all hardships; self-will, that destroys obedience; vanity, that seeks esteem; love of superfluities, that disgraces poverty, &c. Examine these enemies, and renew your fidelity to your king, whose kingdom is not of this world.

3°. Consider the means by which these enemies are vanquished. Your king has taught you by his own practice and in his gospel. He teaches humility in his incarnation; in his birth from a poor mother; in living unnoticed in a lowly station of life. He particularly requires of you to learn from all his outward actions the inward meekness of his heart. He teaches poverty in his birth. He canonizes it in his lessons, and promises the kingdom of heaven as its reward. He teaches mortification in every instant of his life, from his birth to his tomb. He teaches obedience to persons of every sort, from his nativity to his death on the cross. He teaches the love and practice of prayer; love of God and our neighbour; and entire forgiveness of enemies. What an armoury of virtues! Resolve to imitate them, and remember St. Bernard used to say, "A delicate member, under a thorny head, was a scandal to religion."

## Fifteenth Day.

### ON THE INCARNATION OF JESUS CHRIST.

1°. CONSIDER the dismal condition of mankind before the Incarnation of Jesus Christ, plunged in the abyss of sin, excluded from heaven, daily filling hell. In this multitude of slaves of Satan, contemplate yourself, and think how dismal would have been the lot which you deserved by your sins. Sentiments of deep humility, and ardent gratitude to your Divine Deliverer must here fill your soul; and to imprint them indelibly in it, contemplate the astonishing humility, the excessive love of your Redeemer, which brought him down from the seat of his Divinity to the lowest degradation among sinners, in order to rescue you. Follow him in thought and affection from the bosom of his Father to his sepulchre: you will find no room for pride. Humility and gratitude must penetrate your soul.

2°. Consider the exalted dignity to which the humility of the Incarnation of Jesus has raised you. Rescued from the abyss of misery, " you are raised to the participation of the Divine Nature," (St. Leo,) by sanctifying grace, you are become an adopted son of God. Measure, if you can, the distance between heaven and hell, between a reprobate sinner and a just soul predestined to reign in heaven: conceive the greatness of the favour, and ask your soul, if it can ever forget such a benefactor as Jesus Christ. Can you forbear to consecrate yourself to serve him with your whole might? Deplore the blind insensibility of men, who treat him as a stranger, with coldness and indifference, even with insult: perhaps you have yourself been thus guilty. But all that you have done has not frustrated the effects of his love for you.

3°. Consider the means by which your Deliverer conferred upon you such astonishing favours. To raise you, he communicated his Divinity to your degraded nature, because, being impassible in his own essence, he could not otherwise be humbled, suffer and die for you. He would not have been less happy, if you had perished with the mass of mankind; and he acts as if his own happiness could not be complete, unless yours were secure. If you had the powers of all the angels, you could not discharge the immense debt of gratitude you owe to Jesus Christ. What have you hitherto done to repay him? What will you do henceforth? Reflect on these two points; the first will produce some imitation of your Redeemer, by unfeigned humility: the second will animate you to generous sentiments, purposes, and resolutions.

## Sixteenth Day.

### ON THE NATIVITY OF JESUS CHRIST.

1°. CONSIDER the principal virtues of Jesus in his nativity, and first his obedience. He submits to the edict of a temporal prince, and inspires his blessed Mother and St. Joseph to repair to Bethlehem, where he would be born far from home and destitute of human succour.

In obedience to the will of his Heavenly Father, announced by the ancient prophets, he would be born in Bethlehem and laid in a manger between two beasts. Though he is the Eternal Wisdom of the Father, he submits to be swathed by his Virgin Mother, to be handled as an infant by her, and by St. Joseph. The Son of God, because he came to be our model, regards not whom, nor in what things he obeys; he seeks only to fulfil his Father's will. You cannot offer anything more acceptable to your Infant Saviour, than a truly obedient soul.

2°. Reflect on the example of humility given by Jesus Christ in his Nativity. The heir of the royal house of David chooses a stable for his palace, a manger for his throne. He conceals himself from the great ones of the earth, and reveals his birth to poor shepherds. He created the world from nothing, and he weeps and exhibits every mark of infirmity common to other infants. Reflect how you follow this example, and remember that you cannot enter the kingdom of heaven, unless you become like that little One, who came down from heaven to make you great by his humility.

3°. Consider the example of poverty given by Jesus Christ in his Nativity. Excluded by the inhabitants of Bethlehem from the hospitality of a convenient lodging, he is born in a cold and comfortless stable, laid on straw, and warmed, in the coldest season of winter, at midnight, by the breath of beasts. And this is the Lord of all, who provides for us every necessary we want. Can we repine when we have not all we wish for? Contemplate all you have, and compare these with what Jesus reserved for himself and his blessed Mother at Bethlehem. O Jesus! my Infant Lord, give me thy love and thy grace, and with that I am sufficiently rich, I desire no more.

## Seventeenth Day.
### ON THE HIDDEN LIFE OF JESUS CHRIST.

1°. Contemplate Jesus Christ in the house at Nazareth. The hidden life of our Redeemer is an admirable mystery. Though he came from heaven to spread the gospel throughout the world, yet of 33 years which he spent on earth he passed 30 in solitude and retirement. He meant to check in us that vanity and fondness of notice which poisons so many virtues. No religious soul can belong to God, if he does not live an interior life, and learn to love God in retirement. The example of Jesus Christ annihilates all our specious pretexts for seeking dissipation. All virtues quickly perish in a dissipated Christian.

2°. Consider the occupations of Jesus at Nazareth. They were low, ordinary, even servile; but they honoured God as much as his greatest miracles, because they were performed with a spirit of submission to God, and pure intention to please him. Jesus had performed no other actions than these, when God said, "This is my beloved Son, in whom I am well pleased." (Matt. iii. 7.) What a source of confidence for a pious religious Christian! His life may easily be the "Life hidden with Christ in God." (Colos. iii. 3.) It is condemned by the world, but prized by God, because different are the thoughts of God and man.

3°. Reflect on the happiness of such a life. The holy family at Nazareth were unknown to the world, but they heard nothing of its follies and vices. They conversed with God and found perpetual peace. Peace is not found out of God, nor God out of the path of self-denial. The world is like a raging sea. He who leads a "life hidden in God," confines himself to his own duty; he talks much to God about it, but meddles not with the business of others. Happy he who thus lives! He cuts off by it an endless source of uneasiness. Why should he seek happiness abroad, when with God, he is sure of finding it within himself?

## Eighteenth Day.
### ON THE PRESENCE OF GOD.

1°. "Walk before me, and be perfect." (Gen. xvii. 1.) This is the foundation of a spiritual life, or rather, as we are taught by Holy Scripture, it is the very completion and perfection of it; for as forgetfulness of God is the main source of sin, so the remembrance of his presence is the general remedy against it. Who would venture to sin if he considered and felt God present in his heart? At the very thought of this, every temptation must vanish; and every difficulty in the pursuit of virtue will be diminished or disappear. He who has God present in his mind, passes through all dangers without dismay: he exclaims with the prophet, "In the midst of the shades of death I will fear no evil, for thou art with me!" (Ps. xxii. 4.)

2°. A man cannot be truly religious, unless he study to be perfect; and the abridgment of perfection is the habitual presence of God. Whoever feels this divine presence in his heart, will find God in all created objects; he does every action for God, and therefore seriously endeavours to do them well: thus everything he does becomes an act of homage to the Divinity, and enables him to anticipate in this life the occupation of the blessed in heaven. In order to discover whether we have made progress in a spiritual life within any given time, it is useful to examine whether we have improved or failed in this holy exercise.

3°. To acquire this blessed habit, we must carefully avail ourselves of the numerous opportunities presented to us by our state of life; and in the observance of our daily duties, we must frequently think of God, and we shall find that every action rightly performed will help us in this exercise. The practice of very frequently directing our thoughts and affections to God, will, with perseverance, produce an habitual state of soul, in which the heart naturally, as it were, turns to God; and no effort is required to recall the remembrance of him to the mind, but rather some sort of violence is necessary to withdraw the attention to outward things. This happy state is not to be acquired without much patience, watchfulness over the senses, and persevering labour to control and check the imagination; but when once it is acquired, it subsists quietly, and without exertion. O how truly desirable is this happy state!

## Nineteenth Day.
### ON PURITY OF INTENTION.

1°. Motive and intention form the soul and merit of our actions, and by these they are entirely influenced; and if they are performed without intention, they are void of value, like the actions of brutes. If we have a bad motive, our actions become bad; but if our intention is pure and upright, even our indifferent actions become pleasing to Almighty God, and will be rewarded. What treasures of merit may be lost or gained, by attending to, or by neglecting a good intention in performing them! We must therefore be on our guard against blank actions, which are performed without any particular motive; for if we have not in view the intention of pleasing God, some sinister motive will very probably creep in and spoil our very best deeds.

2°. It is just that all our actions should be directed to please God; for we are his creatures, and the work of his hands; and as we are entirely his, so our every thought, word, and action belong to him; nor can we in justice refuse to employ to his honour the faculties of mind and body with which, in his goodness, he has endowed us. But another very pressing motive for us to be punctual in the practice of purity of intention is, that Almighty God is so good as to accept graciously our poor endeavours, and to take complacency in them. Who, then, can refuse to this merciful and loving Lord the small tribute of his actions? actions which he would necessarily perform, and which are, in many cases, gratifying even to nature.

3°. The ultimate end of all our actions should be the glory of God; and this end must be kept in view, not only in our state of life in general, but also in every particular action. This is the very end God proposes to himself in all his operations. What an honour, therefore, is it to us to be allowed to imitate this perfection of God! And since God may be honoured by our actions, to direct them to any other end is to rob him of his glory.

## Twentieth Day.

### ON THE PERFECTION OF OUR DAILY ACTIONS.

1°. The perfection of our state of life does not consist in doing many things, nor yet in doing great things, for many great saints have done nothing that is extraordinary in the eyes of men; but humility, recollection, regularity, and an ardent desire of pleasing God, made them saints in the performance of small things. Perfection requires not that singular and extraordinary actions shall be done, such opportunities seldom occur; but it is attainable by every one of us, by the exact performance of the duties of our state of life. Thus, we do the will of God; and in this all sanctity ultimately consists.

2°. In order to attain perfection by ordinary actions, they must be well done; that is, they must be performed with exactitude, fervour, and perseverance. Exactitude requires attention to time, place, and manner. Fervour implies readiness of will and purity of intention, even when the action is irksome and distasteful to nature. Perseverance is the continuance of fervour, which must therefore be continually renewed and refreshed. He who perseveres in the fervent and exact discharge of many small duties, does something very great, and will undoubtedly attain perfection, because he is constantly engaged in the exercise of self-denial, by which he continually combats sloth, levity, caprice, human respects, natural inclination, and passion.

3°. The perfection of our ordinary actions depends upon the interior spirit with which they are performed. Exterior exactitude is but the body of sanctity; this is the soul. All actions performed through interest, inclination or self-love, are dead and void of merit; for the one thing that gives any worth, either to great or small actions, is the purity of our intention in performing them, and this intention should be frequently renewed, lest vanity or any unworthy motive creep in.

## Twenty-first Day.

### ON THE CHARITY OF JESUS CHRIST IN HIS ACTIVE LIFE.

1°. The charity of Jesus Christ was meek. The precept of mutual charity is closely connected with that of evangelical self-denial, because we continually afford one another occasions of exercising charity by overcoming ourselves. Study the unalterable meekness of Jesus amidst the sharpest provocations from the malice of the carnal Jews; from the ignorance, selfishness, and inattention, &c., of his own Apostles. Truly he might say, "Learn of me, for I am meek." (Matt. xi. 29.) Have you studied this lesson? How do you bear the tempers, the faults of others, who are obliged to bear yours? Their imperfections are designed to perfect our charity. If we cannot alter them entirely, we may gain them by condescension. Do we not, on the contrary, express disdain and contempt by hasty or harsh words? What a source of division among disciples of Christ, who profess mortification and humility.

2°. The charity of Christ was kind. Raising the dead, healing the sick, comforting the afflicted, &c. We cannot imitate his miracles, but we have frequent opportunities of doing little services, of sacrificing our wishes, conveniences, and opinions, to the cause of charity. We can share the joys and sorrows of others; we can serve them as we would Christ himself, who has transferred his claims upon us to our neighbour. Do we not rather feel jealousy at their success, joy at their disappointments, &c. ? Jesus has said, that his Father will treat us, as we shall have treated our brethren. Can we expect his best graces now and hereafter, if our hearts are not expanded and tender to one another ?

3°. The charity of Jesus was universal. Being the Redeemer of all men, he made no exception of persons: all were objects of his charity. Hence to confine charity to a few, is to destroy the virtue. If our charity does not comprehend our worst enemies, it will not be acknowledged by Jesus Christ. How do we fulfil this duty ? Examine seriously on what occasions self-denial is requisite to save the rights of charity, and conclude with an earnest prayer for this double spirit.

## Twenty-second Day.

### ON THE GENEROUS THOUGHTS OF THE TRUE CHILDREN OF GOD.

1°. From Jesus Christ only can we learn to have high thoughts like those of God. Upon his cross he draws to himself the hearts, the thoughts and affections of all who belong to God. Our thoughts then, that is, the acts of our understanding and will, must rise up to the cross of Jesus, if we mean to be sons of God. They must be active, and full of energy; such as to excite in us strong desires of suffering injuries, contempt, &c., so that we reckon ourselves honoured when we are despised, wrongfully accused, &c. These were the thoughts of the twelve favourite sons of God, who "rejoiced that they were found worthy to suffer reproach for the sake of Christ." (Acts v. 41.) To feel an affection for enemies and disagreeable persons, to pray for the choicest graces for them, to show them special kindness, this would be to copy Jesus on the cross.

2°. A second class of exalted thoughts, usual with the sons of God, may be called passive: such are to bear in silence, and without repining, whatever Almighty God permits: temptations, loss of goods, loss of reputation, sickness, affronts, and injuries; to endure all these things without a desire of revenge. Consider what Jesus Christ endured in mortal flesh, and arm yourself with the same thoughts. He is your model, you are pledged to strive to imitate him.

3°. A third class of exalted thoughts familiar to the sons of God may be said to consist in omissions, that is to say, not to wish for any praise, any gratitude, nor to desire any respect or regard from superiors or equals, on account of age or past services; not to wish that your advice or opinions be heard or adopted; to seek no favour, no compassion; never to relate your afflictions; never to wish your innocence to be known, &c.; to quit the most serious business at the first sign of obedience; never to speak to your own praise, &c. All this is observable in Jesus Christ, who for us and for our example, not only was neglected, but reduced himself to nothing, "taking the form of a slave." (Phil. ii. 7.) Do not, then, fall away from the high thoughts of the sons of God.

## Twenty-third Day.

**ON THE SUFFERINGS OF JESUS CHRIST.**

1°. *Consider the multitude of his afflictions.* This Man of dolours suffered in every part of his body, in all the faculties of his soul; he suffered from all people, Jews, Pagans, his judges, his accusers, and his apostles of whom one sold him, and another denied him. He felt in his own soul all that his blessed Mother suffered under the cross. His eternal Father seemed to abandon him, he treated him as a sinner, as St. Paul strongly expresses it. View him sinking beneath his cross, and know that your sins give it all its weight; view him fastened to it in agonies of pain, and reflect that your sins point the nails; weep not for him, but for yourself.

2°. Contemplate his sacred body mangled to one wound, his hands and feet pierced, his head crowned with thorns, his beautiful face swollen with blows. His sinking eyes see nothing but an enraged multitude around him, his timid disciples retiring from him, his afflicted Mother at the foot of the cross with one disciple and the tender Magdalen. His ears are shocked with the blasphemies and cries of his enemies who demand his blood.

3°. Enter into his soul: it is pierced with the foresight of the loss of thousands for whom he dies. He carries all our sins; he carries yours, mine, and those of all the world; he agonizes for them in the garden; he bears for them ignominy without comfort, and torments without relief; he shows us they cannot be expiated without humiliations, contrition, and penance. O Jesus, teach me to court and cherish the little humiliations and crosses which thy kind hand dispenses; let me kiss the hand that strikes me; permit me not to increase my afflictions by murmuring, impatience, and reluctance. I desire to share thy sufferings, and from the sincerity of my heart to repeat with you, *"Father, thy will be done."*

## Twenty-fourth Day.

### ON THE SUFFERINGS OF JESUS CHRIST.

1°. *Consider the greatness of the sufferings of Jesus.* God defies us by the mouth of the prophet, to find elsewhere pains and grief equal to those of Jesus. *" See if there be sorrow like unto my sorrow."* (Lam. i. 12.) Because he took upon himself the guilt of all our sins, a murderer is preferred before him; for this cause his flesh is mangled, his blood flows, his very bones are uncovered by the scourging inflicted on him, as if he had been the greatest criminal in the world; his diadem of thorns pierces his brow and temples, &c. His soul is wrung with mortal grief and agony at the sight of my sins and ingratitude. He drinks the chalice to the very dregs. And shall I not desire to lighten his cross, by bearing all my afflictions for his sake with love and resignation? Enable me, O Jesus, to do so.

2°. *Consider the duration of his sufferings.* Christ's passion lasted longer than a few days or hours; his life was a continual martyrdom.

His sufferings were ever present to his mind, by his foreknowledge of them; they were the frequent subject of his conversations and predictions. He suffered in mind every instant of his life what he was to suffer in detail at Jerusalem; his soul was always in the Garden of Olives, although he did not always show, by a sweat of blood, the agony he suffered.

3°. If St. Paul was penetrated with continual grief at the obstinacy of the Jews, how much more was the soul of Jesus Christ wrung, at the sight of the numerous sins that had been committed and would be committed till the end of time, notwithstanding all he had done to purchase for us pardon and peace. I beseech thee, O Jesus, make me grateful for all thou hast suffered, and teach me to show my gratitude by fidelity to the cross in whatever way thou mayest appoint.

## Twenty-fifth Day.

### ON THE SACRIFICES OF CHRIST IN HIS PASSION.

1°. Meditation on the passion is sterile if it do not incline you to self-denial. Consider how Jesus Christ sacrificed all his interior comforts, seeking no relief in his desolation but in short interviews with three of his most perfect friends, in redoubled prayer and acts of perfect resignation. Reflect on your own uneasiness, and in imitation of Jesus Christ, bring yourself to renounce all human relief, and desire only the comfort that comes from conformity to God's will, and from love of suffering for his sake.

2°. The voluntary, entire, public, and ignominious sacrifice which Jesus Christ made of his liberty for man. Think how the true followers of Christ have gloried in the title of servants and bondsmen of Jesus Christ. Offer yourself generously to wear the triple bond which will presently fasten you to the cross of Christ, by destroying your own will and all its corrupt inclinations. Renounce every wish of relaxing this bond. The more tightly it binds you now, the more amply it will give you hereafter the liberty of the sons of God. The Apostle St. Paul assures us that the Spirit of God is a spirit of liberty.

3°. The sacrifice which Jesus Christ made of his friends. Some betrayed him, others forsook him in his distress: all abandoned him. Only his holy Mother and a few of her special clients followed to the cross, and the sight of their distress only served to increase his grief. Try to imitate this great sacrifice, and choose only for friends those who will lead you most zealously to Jesus Christ. Pray earnestly for grace to comprehend and imitate the sacrifices which Jesus Christ made in his passion.

## Twenty-sixth Day.

### ON THE SACRIFICES OF CHRIST IN HIS PASSION.

1°. The sacrifice Jesus Christ made of his reputation. No other man's reputation was ever so universally established as was that of

Jesus Christ; none other was ever so completely overthrown in the last week of his life. Begin early to imitate this sacrifice; opportunities of renewing it will be multiplied as you advance in life and in perfection. Contemplate the sacrifice which Jesus Christ made of his honour. He, who was the King of kings, the Holy of holies, is treated in the house of Caiphas as a slave, in the palace of Herod as a fool, in the court of Pilate as a robber and felon. This despised man is your God, your Redeemer, your Master, and he will be your Judge; and can you desire worldly honours? If you do, will not the humiliations of Jesus condemn you?

2°. The complete sacrifice which Jesus Christ made of his body, especially in the three stages of his flagellation, crowning with thorns, and crucifixion. Recollect that Jesus, speaking of his future sufferings, said, "With desire I have desired to drink this chalice, &c." (Luke xxii. 15.) Examine and enliven your desires of imitating him in these sacrifices; review your actual practice; and interrogate your own heart what change you ought to make in it.

3°. The last sacrifice of Jesus Christ: it was that of his life. What else have you to do, but to learn to die? Alas how few have learned this necessary science! Study the great lesson given on Mount Calvary. Jesus Christ dies perfectly disengaged from the love of this world and of everything in it. He dies with the most wonderful patience in the greatest tortures, and full of the most unshaken confidence in his Heavenly Father. All the Saints die in these holy dispositions. These must be yours through life, to support you at the hour of death. You will imitate Jesus Christ in death, if, like St. Paul, you "die daily."

## Twenty-seventh Day.

### ON THE INGRATITUDE OF MEN TO JESUS IN THE BLESSED SACRAMENT.

1°. The ingratitude of men. They know by faith, that the body of Jesus Christ is their food in this divine sacrament, his blood their drink; that he has an immense desire to be their daily food, that he promises eternal life to those who receive it; but they are disgusted with the manna of heaven. What an outrage to the Heart of Jesus Christ! And what withholds them from it? It is commonly a trifle, a temporal concern, more frequently it is the dread of interior abnegation, the distaste of piety, the love of sin; they will not sacrifice their passions to possess all the treasures of heaven. Oh, if they reject Jesus in life, must they not be rejected by him after death!

2°. Others receive Jesus Christ, but without preparation, by custom and habit: they hardly distinguish the bread of heaven from ordinary corporal food; they receive Jesus Christ not with the affection of Mary and Martha, but with the malice of Judas; their conscience stained with sins, their treachery consummated. Oh, in that instant the Angels of the sanctuary would exterminate these sacrilegious prevaricators, if the love of Jesus Christ did not suspend the vengeance!

3°. After he is received, how is he again treated? Instead of loving him, alas! some fall into dissipation of mind: Jesus Christ is hardly thought of. Instead of exposing their wants, and deploring their sins, they begin again to commit new ones; the same resistance to grace, the same tepidity in prayer, the same sins are continued. O what patience in the amiable Jesus! What ingratitude in men! Humbled and contrite for my innumerable irreverences towards thy holy Sacrament, O Jesus! I sink with confusion and shame; but above all I dread the misery of being deprived of it. O give thyself to me, penitent and humbled, but give me also thy holy love; a continual increase of love be my nourishment, my comfort here, and the pledge of my future enjoyment of thee in heaven.

## Twenty-eighth Day.

### ON THE RESURRECTION OF JESUS CHRIST.

1°. JESUS CHRIST is in all things your model. As you have proposed to imitate his virtues, so you must also imitate his Resurrection. "If you be risen with Christ," says the Apostle, "seek the things that are above." (Col. iii. 1.) You cannot rise in this manner by your own strength, but Jesus Christ invites you: he calls you from the grave, and you must co-operate with his call. Your resurrection must be real, as is that of Christ, with whom you rise. "Risen with Christ." It must be said of you as of him, "He is risen indeed, and hath appeared." (Luke xxiv. 34.)

2°. You must not impose upon yourself or others. You must be truly risen in the infallible judgment of Christ himself. It will be, according to St. Paul, a strong presumption of the reality of your resurrection, if you henceforward seek and relish "the things above," if you grow fond of prayer, recollection, and pious conversation; if you experience more ease and agility in serving God; more courage in surmounting temptations and passions; more desire of mortification; more caution in guarding your senses; more willingness to suffer for Jesus. Persons who are practically ignorant of these things, are yet dead to Christ.

3°. See if you have these marks of a new life in you; for, if you have not truly risen with Christ, you will show nothing to prove this resurrection. Whereas, if your interior become what you have so often purposed to make it, you may say with holy Job: "I know that my Redeemer liveth, and in the last day I shall rise out of the earth, and shall be clothed again with my skin, and in my flesh I shall see God, whom I myself shall see, and my eyes shall behold, and not another: this my hope is laid up in my bosom." (Job xix. 25, 27.) To merit this happy destiny, you must lay aside all sin, even the slightest attachment to the least wilful offence, and you must assume a new life in and with Jesus Christ.

## Twenty-ninth Day.
### ON THE ASCENSION OF JESUS CHRIST.

1°. Jesus Christ rising in glory from the summit of Mount Olivet, in sight of his disciples. By the grace of redemption, heaven has become the term of your hopes and wishes. The Ascension of Jesus Christ leads you to the contemplation of heaven, of which he now takes possession for you. Jesus is there, "seated at the right hand of God," (Mark xvi. 19,) and "of his kingdom there shall be no end." (Luke i. 33.) He has earned this kingdom for himself, and for the imitators of his humility; he invites you to consider its beatitude. It is the square city of God, described in the Apocalypse. (chap. xxi.) Its foundations, walls, gates, and pavement, are jasper, pearls, adamant, and lucid gold; and the brightness of God enlightens it, and in it there is no night.

2°. The happiness you will enjoy in this blessed abode, from which all evil of labour, sickness, pain, treachery, sorrow, grief, doubt, &c., is eternally banished. Your soul will rest in the bosom of consolation, vested in a body impassible, subtle, active, and resplendent like that of Jesus Christ, "who will reform the body of our lowness, made like to the body of his glory." (Phil. iii. 21.) What a comforting prospect will this be to you, at the time of your humiliations, persecutions, and death! What a consolation, in present sufferings, to know, with the certainty of divine faith, "that we have a building of God, a house not made with hands, eternal in heaven." (2 Cor. v. 1.) With what joy will you then sing, "O death, where is thy victory? O death, where is thy sting?" (1 Cor. xv. 55.)

3°. You must awaken your minds to these precious hopes, and cease to sin; "for sin is the sting of death." "Awake, ye just, and sin not." (1 Cor. xv. 34.) Next to the absence of all evil, Christ invites you to contemplate the enjoyment of every good. There you will behold the majesty of the Divine Nature, the sacred mystery of the Blessed Trinity, all the attributes of God, his almighty power, wisdom, goodness, &c., together with the various beauties of heaven and of all created things, which you will see, know, and love in the essence of God as in a clear mirror. Can any pains or sufferings be too great to secure a place in such an abode of bliss?

## Thirtieth Day.

### ON THE LOVE OF GOD.

1°. You should propose to yourself, as the first motive, *Gratitude*. Love God, because he has first loved you. Supernatural love is not merely the bent of our affections towards God, it moreover excites a promptitude in the will, to do whatever is pleasing to him. Call to mind the signal blessings of creation, redemption, vocation to the true faith, to a perfect life, &c. Why has God preferred you? Why has he favoured you more than others? In his love alone can an answer be found to the question. What then, does justice, what does gratitude demand of you? Nothing less than an entire surrender of yourself to his Divine Majesty.

2°. God contains within himself every perfection capable of exciting our affections, and fixing them upon him. His beauty, his goodness, his wisdom, his power, his mercy, have no bounds. He displays these perfections in his works for your sake and service: "The heavens show forth the glory of God." (Ps. xviii. 2.) His power appears in the structure of the heavens and of the earth: whatever is beautiful and grand in the sun, moon, and stars, or in the productions of the earth, manifests his wisdom and his bounty. In the midst of creatures designed for your use, he has placed you (says St. Ignatius) like a temple dedicated to his glory, and he has made you to his own image and likeness. Raise your thoughts from the visible wonders of creation, to admire, glorify, and love the invisible Creator; he will not always be invisible. In every creature that he has made, he thought of you: he gives them all to you as means to help you to rise to him and to eternal happiness. Will you always enjoy his gifts, and never think of the Giver? Remember that besides all external gifts, he has given you understanding, memory, and will, that you may know him, never forget him, and always love him.

3°. Consider that all moral qualities which promote your happiness on earth, all power, justice, knowledge, wisdom, prudence, all authority, strength, skill, &c., are little streams derived from God himself; all human revolutions prove the eternity of his kingdom, which sees all things pass, but itself shall never pass. All sanctity arising from supernatural virtues is an expression of God's sanctity, an immediate production of his grace, a gratuitous gift of his Holy Spirit. Can you refuse to labour for him, even in your smallest actions? Learn, from St. Ignatius, to rise from creatures to the pure love of the Creator; and say with St. Paul, "Neither death, nor life, nor any other creature, shall separate us from the love of God which is in Christ Jesus our Lord." (Rom. viii.)

## Thirty-first Day.
### ON THE LOVE WE OUGHT TO BEAR TO THE BLESSED VIRGIN.

1°. Consider that she is our Mother, and let us have recourse to her as such. The last thing our dear Saviour recommended on the cross to us, in the person of St. John, was, to look to Mary as our Mother. Let us ever do so, especially when it pleases God to send us sufferings. What an honour it is to have the Mother of Jesus for our Mother! We must endeavour not to render ourselves unworthy of it, and therefore must avoid sin; for that alone can make us unworthy of her adoption and love. O most dear Lady! show thyself a Mother to me, for the sake of thy dear Son, and then my salvation will be secure.

2°. Consider that our Lady loves us with all tenderness and affection. She remembers that she is our Mother, left us as such by the will and testament of her dying Son; and that to comply with the duty of a mother, favours alone are not sufficient. Love and affection must be the principle from which they proceed. If, then, her heart, now she reigns in heaven, is a furnace of divine love, far surpassing that of all the other saints, what may we not hope from the love which burns in the breast of this heavenly Mother for us? No doubt, she makes use of it for our advantage; and, though at present we know not the number of the favours we receive by her intercession, yet, after this life we shall see the many graces she has obtained for us from the Divine Mercy. Can we ever cease to love this Mother?

3°. Consider that we cannot doubt of our Lady's seeing all our necessities in the Divine Word, as in a clear and spotless mirror; for if Almighty God makes them known to our Guardian Angels, that they may help and assist us, it cannot be supposed he would keep them secret from the Mother to whom he has recommended all mankind in the person of St. John. If she then sees all our necessities, who can think that the sight of so much misery in creatures so helpless of themselves, does not move her compassion to implore her divine Son's mercy for us, that we may find speedy relief in all wants and miseries? Let us then, fly with confidence and love to the feet of this tender Mother, we are sure to find aid in her maternal love, for her dear Son never refuses the petitions of his Mother, to whom he was so obedient here on earth.

SHORT EXAMEN AT THE END OF EACH
MEDITATION.

(1°.) Did I, before my Meditation, place myself in the presence of God?

(2°.) Did I make the Preparatory Prayer, and the Preludes?

(3°.) Did I preserve a becoming posture in Prayer? Was I attentive?

(4°.) Did I make good resolutions for the coming day?

## Anima Christi.

Soul of Christ, sanctify me.
Body of Christ, save me.
Blood of Christ, inebriate me.
Water from the side of Christ, wash me.
Passion of Christ, strengthen me.
O good Jesus, hear me;
Within thy wounds hide me;
Never permit me to be separated from thee;
From the wicked enemy defend me;
At the hour of my death call me,
And bid me come to thee;
That with thy Saints I may praise thee,
For ever and ever. Amen.

(300 days Indulgence for each recital.—Plenary Indulgence once a month, on usual conditions. A.)

## Acts of Faith, Hope, Charity, and Contrition.

(Seven years and seven forty days Indulgence for each devout recital of the Acts of Faith, Hope, and Charity.—Plenary Indulgence once a month on the usual conditions. A.)

A PRAYER TO BE SAID BEFORE THESE ACTS.

O ALMIGHTY and eternal God, grant to us the increase of Faith, Hope, and Charity, and that we may deserve to obtain what thou promisest, make us to love what thou commandest. Through Christ our Lord. Amen.

AN ACT OF FAITH.

I FIRMLY believe there is one God; and that in this one God there are three Persons, the Father, the Son, and the Holy Ghost: that the Son took to himself the nature of man, from the Virgin Mary's womb, by the power of the Holy Ghost; and that in this our human nature he was crucified and died for us; that afterwards he rose again and ascended into heaven, thence he shall come to repay the just everlasting glory, and the wicked everlasting punishment. Moreover I believe whatsoever else the Catholic Church proposes to be believed, and this because God who is the Sovereign Truth, who can neither deceive nor be deceived, has revealed all these things to this his Church.

A. *Grant, O God, that we may humbly receive, and firmly hold fast all those truths which thou hast revealed, and thy Church has proposed to our belief.*

AN ACT OF HOPE.

O MY God, relying on thy almighty power and thy infinite mercy and goodness, and because thou art faithful to thy promises, I trust in thee that thou wilt grant me forgiveness of my sins, through the merits of Jesus Christ thy Son; and that thou wilt give me the assistance of thy grace, with which I may labour to continue to the end in the diligent exercise of all good works, and may deserve to obtain the glory which thou hast promised in heaven.

A. *This hope thus grounded on thy mercy, thy power, and thy promises, still more, O God, confirm and strengthen in us.*

AN ACT OF CHARITY.

O LORD, my God, I love thee with my whole heart, and above all things, because thou, O God, art the Sovereign Good, and for thy own infinite perfections art most worthy of all love; and for thy sake, I also love my neighbour as myself.

A. *Thus only, O Lord, can we satisfy our duty, and thy commandment of loving thee above all things, and our neighbour as ourselves.*

### AN ACT OF CONTRITION.

O MY God, who art infinitely good, and always hatest sin, I beg pardon from my heart for all my offences against thee; I detest them all and am heartily sorry for them, because they offend thy infinite goodness, and I firmly resolve by the help of thy grace never more to offend thee, and carefully to avoid the occasions of sin.

A. *Wherefore, O God, we come before thee this day, to beg pardon for all our transgressions, and to implore thine assistance for the time to come.*

# The most holy Sacrifice of the Mass.

THE most holy Sacrifice of the Mass is the highest act of worship and of praise that can be offered to the Supreme Majesty of God. It is a memorial and mystical renewal of the great Sacrifice of Mount Calvary, and in it Jesus Christ is both the High Priest and the Victim. He offered himself once in a bloody manner upon the cross, and thus reconciled man with his offended Creator : but in order to apply to our souls the fruits of his bitter sufferings and death, he continues to offer himself daily upon the altar, in an unbloody manner, by the ministry of his Priests in the Mass.

This great Sacrifice of the New Law is offered up for four great ends : 1°, for the greater honour and glory of God : 2°, in thanksgiving for all the benefits which, in his goodness, God has bestowed upon us : 3°, for obtaining pardon of our sins : 4°, for procuring for ourselves and for others graces and favours, through the merits of Jesus Christ.

In order to assist profitably at the holy Sacrifice of the Mass, 1°, show great devotion and respect in your outward deportment : 2°, strive to enter into those holy sentiments that this great Mystery so forcibly suggests. Never lose sight of the truth, that you are assisting at the same Sacrifice as that which Jesus Christ offered upon the cross. Every thing about the altar is intended to remind us of the Passion and death of our Saviour. The "Altar," with the "Crucifix" upon it, is a figure of Mount

Calvary, and of Christ crucified: the "Candles lighted" are emblematic of the light of faith that was revealed to the Jews and Gentiles, by Him who came into this world, "to enlighten them that sit in darkness, and in the shadow of death." (Luke i. 79.) The "Priest" who celebrates, represents the person of Christ, and the "Vestments" worn by him recall to our minds the garments with which Jesus was ignominiously clothed during his passion. The "Amice," an oblong piece of linen the Priest puts over his head and then on his shoulders, signifies the rag with which Jesus was blindfolded by the Jews, when in mockery they smote and buffeted him, saying : " prophecy unto us, Christ, who is he that struck thee." (Matt. xxvi. 68.) The "Alb," a long white linen garment reaching almost to the feet, reminds us of the robe of derision, in which Herod clothed Jesus, when having jeered him as a fool, he sent him back to Pilate. (Luke xxiii.) The "Girdle," with which the Priest girds his loins, the "Maniple," anciently made of linen, but now of the same material and colour as the vestment, and which is worn on the left arm, and the "Stole" crossed over the breast of the Priest, represent the cords and fetters with which the officers of the Jews bound our Saviour, and dragged him from one tribunal to another. (John xviii.) The "Chasuble" or "Vestment" is a figure of the purple garment with which Jesus was clothed, when in mockery of royalty, the soldiers "platting a crown of thorns, put it upon him, and began to salute him: Hail, King of the Jews!" (Mark xv. 17, 18.) The various parts and ceremonies of the Mass correspond with the different stations of the passion, and bring back to the mind all that took place from the bitter agony in the garden, to the last scenes in the life of Jesus.

Enter into these thoughts and sentiments, and you will hear Mass, both devoutly and profitably.

## Prayers before Mass on Sundays.

IN the name of the Father, and of the Son, and of the Holy Ghost. Amen.

Come, O Holy Spirit! fill the hearts of thy faithful, and kindle in them the fire of thy love.

Send forth thy Spirit, and our hearts shall be regenerated.

*And thou shalt renew the face of the earth.*

### LET US PRAY.

O ALMIGHTY and eternal God, who hast appointed us six days in which we may labour, and hast consecrated the seventh to thyself; grant, we beseech thee, that according to what thou hast commanded, we may sanctify this day, by devoting it entirely to thy love and service. Mercifully forgive us all our past neglect; pardon the sins of which we have been guilty during the course of the week; and give us grace to avoid them for the future. Through Jesus Christ our Lord. Amen.

O Lord, open thou our lips,
*And our mouth shall declare thy praise.*
Let us adore the Lord of glory.
*Let us adore the God of our salvation.*

The King of heaven invites and graciously calls us into his sacred presence; to him we owe all the days of our lives; let us give this day at least to his service.

*Let us adore the Lord of Glory.*

Always are the Angels assembled in their choirs above; always are the Saints ready with their hymns; behold now the Church also prepares her solemn offices, and summons all her children to bring in their tribute of prayer and praise.

*Let us adore the God of our Salvation.*

Come, let us rejoice before the Lord; let us sing joyfully to God our Saviour! let us make haste to approach his presence, and proclaim his praises; for the Lord is a great God, and a great King above all gods: in his hands are all the ends of the earth.

*Let us adore the God that made us.*

Let us adore and fall down before the Lord, who created us; for he is the Lord our God, and we are his people and the sheep of his pasture.

*Let us adore and fall down before him.*

To-day, if you shall hear his voice, harden not your hearts, but listen with awe to his word, and bend your knees before his holy altars.

*We will adore the Lord of glory; we will worship the God of our salvation.*

Glory be to the Father, &c.

*As it was in the beginning, &c.*

Our Father, who art in heaven, hallowed be thy name: thy kingdom come: thy will be done on earth as it is in heaven.

*Give us this day our daily bread; and forgive us our trespasses, as we forgive them that trespass against us; and lead us not into temptation, but deliver us from evil. Amen.*

---

ACTS OF FAITH, HOPE, CHARITY AND CONTRITION.—PAGE 72.

---

PRAYERS FOR THE QUEEN.

O Lord save the Queen,
*And hear us in the day that we shall call upon thee.*

## PRAYERS BEFORE MASS.

**LET US PRAY.**

O God, by whom kings reign, and the princes of the earth exercise their power; O God, who art the strength and support of those kingdoms that serve thee, mercifully hear our prayers, and defend thy servant *N.* our queen from all dangers; and grant that her safety may conduce to the peace and welfare of thy people. Through, &c.

**PRAYERS FOR THE SICK.**

Let us offer up our prayers for those who are visited with sickness, for those especially who are members of this congregation.

Heal thy servants, O Lord, who are sick, and who put their trust in thee.

*Send them help, O Lord, and comfort from thy holy place.*

**LET US PRAY.**

O Almighty and everlasting God, the eternal salvation of those who believe in thee, hear us in behalf of thy servants who are sick, for whom we humbly crave the help of thy mercy; that their health, if thou seest good, being restored to them, they may render thanks to thee in thy Church, through Jesus Christ our Lord. Amen.

## PRAYERS FOR THE DEAD.

LET us offer up our prayers for the repose of the souls of the faithful departed, particularly for those of our deceased parents, relations, and friends, and for those who have been members of this congregation.

*Psalm cxxix. De Profundis.*

OUT of the depths I have cried to thee, O Lord. Lord, hear my voice.

*Let thine ears be attentive to the voice of my supplication.*

If thou, O Lord, wilt mark iniquities, Lord, who shall stand it?

*For with thee there is merciful forgiveness, and by reason of thy law I have waited for thee, O Lord.*

My soul hath relied on his word; my soul hath hoped in the Lord.

*From the morning watch even until night, let Israel hope in the Lord.*

Because with the Lord there is mercy, and with him plentiful redemption.

*And he shall redeem Israel from all his iniquities.*

Eternal rest give to them, O Lord,

*And may perpetual light shine upon them.*

LET US PRAY.

O GOD, the Creator and Redeemer of all the faithful, grant to the souls of thy servants departed, the remission of all their sins, that through pious supplications they may obtain that pardon which they have always desired; who livest and reignest with God the Father, in the unity of the Holy Ghost, God, world without end. Amen.

To thee, O Lord, we recommend the soul of thy servant *N*., that being dead to this world he may live to thee; and whatever sins he has committed in this life, through human frailty, do thou, in thy most merciful goodness, pardon. Through our Lord Jesus Christ. Amen.

### AN OBLATION.

AND now, O almighty Father, behold we thy people presume to appear before thee this day, to offer up to thee by the hands of thy Minister, and by the hands of our great High Priest, Jesus Christ thy Son, the unbloody sacrifice of his Body and Blood, as a perpetual commemoration of his passion and death. United, therefore, with this our great Mediator, and with his whole Church of heaven and earth, we offer to thee, O holy Lord, Almighty Father, and Eternal God, this pure Sacrifice, and spotless Victim.

*First.* For thy own honour, praise, adoration, and glory. Prostrate before thee, sensible of our own unworthiness, and conscious of our absolute dependence on thee, we hereby acknowledge thee as the great Disposer of life and death: we adore thee as the supreme Ruler of us and of all things.

*Secondly.* Calling to mind with the greatest gratitude, the innumerable benefits we have received from thy bounty, in our creation, redemption, and preservation, we here offer thee in return this pure oblation, as a sacrifice of thanksgiving for all thy mercies and blessings bestowed upon us, and upon all thy creatures.

*Thirdly.* O God, the consciousness of our manifold crimes, forces us to confess our unworthiness to appear before thee. But is not Jesus the propitiation not only for our sins, but for those of the whole world? Him then we offer to thee who has cancelled the hand-writing that was against us, and whose blood is sufficient to wash away the sins of a thousand worlds, that through him we may obtain mercy, pardon, and full remission of all our sins.

*Fourthly.* Acknowledging that nothing is granted by thee to man, but through the merits of the passion and death of thy Son; we here offer thee this same victim of our redemption, for obtaining all those graces and blessings of which we stand so much in need.

For these ends, O eternal Father, graciously accept of the offering which we are preparing to make unto thee. Oh, be thou pleased to assist us in such a manner by thy grace, that we may conduct ourselves this day as we ought to do, in thy divine presence, and that we may so commemorate the death and passion of thy divine Son, as to partake most plentifully of the fruits of this holy sacrifice. Through our Lord Jesus Christ, thy Son; who, with thee and the Holy Ghost, liveth and reigneth, world without end. Amen.

A PRAYER TO BE SAID BY THE PRIEST IMMEDIATELY BEFORE MASS.

And now, O God, calling to mind with the greatest gratitude, the blessed passion of thy Son Christ our Lord, as also his resurrection from the dead, and his glorious ascension into heaven; we prepare to offer to thy divine Majesty a pure, holy, and spotless Victim; for so thou hast ordained it, the holy bread of eternal life, and the cup of our salvation. Look down, therefore, upon them, O Lord, and accept them, as thou wast pleased to accept the offerings of thy righteous servant Abel, and the sacrifice of our father Abraham, and that which thy high priest Melchisedech offered to thee, a holy sacrifice, and a spotless Victim. Amen.

SHORT PREPARATORY PRAYER BEFORE MASS.

Prostrate in spirit at the foot of thy holy altar, I adore thee, O almighty God; and firmly believe that the Mass at which I am going to assist is the Sacrifice of the body and blood of thy Son Christ Jesus. Oh, grant that I may assist thereat with the attention, respect, and awe due to such august mysteries; and that, by the merits of the Victim there offered for me, I myself may become an agreeable sacrifice to thee, who livest and reignest with the same Son and Holy Ghost, one God, world without end. Amen.

## A Devout Method of Hearing Mass.

✝

*Make the sign of the cross with the Priest, and say as follows:*

IN the name of the Father, and of the Son, and of the Holy Ghost. Amen.

I will draw near to thy altar, O my God, there to gain new strength and vigour for my soul; by thy grace separate me from those unbelievers, who have no trust in thee. Give me that grace which comforts me, when the remembrance of my sins afflicts and casts me down; that grace which lets me know there is an everlasting refuge in thy goodness, and that thou art ready to forgive even our greatest sins, upon a sincere repentance.

The Psalm "Judica me Deus," as also the "Gloria in Excelsis Deo," and "Creed," are not said by the Priest in Masses for the Dead.

*At the* CONFITEOR, *say*,

I CONFESS to Almighty God, to blessed Mary ever Virgin, to blessed Michael the Archangel, to blessed John the Baptist, to the holy Apostles Peter and Paul, and to all the Saints, that I have sinned exceedingly in thought, word, and deed, through my fault, through my fault, through my most grievous fault. Therefore I beseech the blessed Mary ever Virgin, the blessed Michael the Archangel, the blessed John the Baptist, the holy Apostles Peter and Paul, and all the Saints, to pray to the Lord our God for me.

*After the* CONFITEOR, *say,*

O MY God, who hast commanded us to pray for one another, and in thy holy Church hast given even to sinners the power of absolving from sin, receive with equal goodness the prayers of thy people for the Priest, and those of thy Priest for the people.

We beseech thee, O Lord, by the merits of those Saints, whose relics are here, and of all the Saints, that thou wouldst vouchsafe to forgive us all our sins. Amen.

*At the* INTROIT, *say,*

GRANT, O Lord, that we may be truly prepared to offer this great Sacrifice to thee this day; and because our sins alone can render us displeasing to thee, we call aloud to thee for mercy.

*At the* KYRIE ELEISON, *say,*

HAVE mercy on me, O Lord, and forgive me all my sins.

Have mercy on me, O Lord, have mercy on me.

*At the* GLORIA IN EXCELSIS DEO, *say,*

GLORIA in excelsis Deo, et in terra pax hominibus bonæ voluntatis. Laudamus te, benedicimus te, adoramus te, glorificamus te, gratias agimus tibi propter magnam gloriam tuam. Domine Deus, Rex cœlestis, Deus Pater omnipotens, Domine Fili unigenite Jesu Christe, Domine Deus, Agnus Dei, Filius Patris, qui tollis peccata mundi, miserere nobis ; qui tollis peccata mundi, suscipe deprecationem nostram; qui sedes ad dexteram Patris, miserere nobis ; quoniam

GLORY be to God on high, and peace on earth to men of good will. We praise thee, we bless thee, we adore thee, we glorify thee, we give thee thanks for thy great glory. Lord God, heavenly King, God the Father almighty ; Lord Jesus Christ, the only begotten Son, Lord God, Lamb of God, Son of the Father, who takest away the sins of the world, have mercy on us ; who takest away the sins of the world, receive our prayer ; who sittest at the right hand of the Father,

tu solus sanctus, tu solus Dominus, tu solus altissimus, Jesu Christe, cum Sancto Spiritu, in gloria Dei Patris. Amen.

have mercy on us; for thou only art holy, thou only art the Lord, thou only art most high, O Jesus Christ, together with the Holy Ghost, in the glory of God the Father. Amen.

*At the* DOMINUS VOBISCUM, *say,*

BE thou always with us, O my God, and let thy grace never depart from us.

*At the* COLLECTS, *or Prayers for the Day, say,*

O ALMIGHTY and eternal God, we humbly beseech thee mercifully to give ear to the prayers of thy servant, which he offers to thee in the name of thy people. Accept them to the honour of thy name, and the good of our souls; and grant to us all those blessings which may contribute to our salvation. Through our Lord Jesus Christ. Amen.

*At the* EPISTLE, *say,*

BE thou, O Lord, eternally praised and blessed for having communicated thy spirit to the holy Prophets and Apostles, disclosing to them admirable secrets redounding to thy glory and our greater good. We

tertia die, secundum Scripturas; et ascendit in cœlum; sedit ad dexteram Patris; et iterum venturus est cum gloria, judicare vivos et mortuos; cujus regni non erit finis. Et in Spiritum Sanctum, Dominum et vivificantem; qui ex Patre Filioque procedit; qui cum Patre et Filio simul adoratur et conglorificatur; qui locutus est per Prophetas. Et unam, sanctam, Catholicam, et Apostolicam Ecclesiam. Confiteor unum Baptisma in remissionem peccatorum; et expecto resurrectionem mortuorum, et vitam venturi sæculi. Amen.

And the third day he rose again according to the Scriptures; and he ascended into heaven; sits at the right hand of the Father; and is to come again with glory, to judge the living and the dead; of whose kingdom there will be no end. And in the Holy Ghost the Lord and Giver of life; who proceeds from the Father and the Son, who together with the Father and the Son is adored and glorified; who spoke by the Prophets. And one holy, Catholic, and Apostolic Church. I confess one Baptism for the remission of sins; and I look for the resurrection of the dead, and the life of the world to come. Amen.

*At the* OFFERTORY, *or when the Priest uncovers the Chalice, say,*

ACCEPT, O holy Father, almighty and eternal God, this unspotted host, which I thy unworthy servant now offer to thee, my living and true God, for my innumerable sins, offences, and negligences, and for all present, and for all faithful Christians, living and dead, that it may avail me and them to life everlasting. Amen.

*At the offering of the* CHALICE, *say,*

WE offer thee, O Lord, the Chalice of salvation, beseeching thy clemency, that it may ascend before thy divine Majesty, as a sweet perfume for our salvation and for that of the whole world.

Accept this offering, O Lord, that we make in the spirit of humility, and a contrite heart; and so may our sacrifice be made this day in thy sight, that it may be pleasing to thee, O Lord God.

*When the Priest washes his fingers, say,*

THOU, O Lord, who once vouchsafedst to wash thy disciples' feet before their invitation to the holy table, wash us also, we beseech thee, O Lord, and wash us again; not only our feet and hands, but our hearts, our desires, our souls, that we may be made innocent and pure.

Receive, O holy Trinity, this oblation we make to thee, in memory of the passion, resurrection, and ascension of our Lord Jesus Christ; and in honour of the ever blessed Virgin Mary, of blessed John Baptist, of the holy apostles Peter and Paul, of these, and of all the Saints, that it may be available to their honour and our salvation; and may they vouchsafe to intercede for us in heaven, whose memory we celebrate on earth. Through the same Christ our Lord. Amen.

*At the* ORATE FRATRES, *say,*

MAY our Lord receive this sacrifice from thy hands, to the praise and glory of his name, for our good, and the benefit of his whole church.

*At the* SECRET PRAYERS, *say,*

MERCIFULLY hear our prayers, O Lord, and graciously accept this oblation, which we, thy servants, are making to thee, that, as we offer it to the honour of thy name, so it may be to us here, a means of obtaining thy grace, and in the next life, everlasting happiness. Amen.

*At the* PREFACE, *say,*

IT is verily meet and just, right and helpful to salvation, that we always, and in all places, give thanks to thee, O holy Lord, Father almighty, eternal God, through Christ our Lord; through whom the Angels praise thy Majesty, the Dominations adore it, the Powers tremble before it, the Heavens and the heavenly Virtues and blessed Seraphim with common jubilee glorify it, together with whom we beseech thee, that we may be admitted to join our voices, saying, in a most humble manner,

Holy, holy, holy, Lord God of Sabaoth; the heavens and earth are full of thy glory.

Hosanna in the highest. Blessed is He that cometh in the name of the Lord. Hosanna in the highest.

*At the* CANON *of the Mass, say,*

MOST merciful Father, who hast given us thy only Son to be our daily sacrifice, incline thine ear to our prayers, and favour our desires; protect, unite, and govern thy holy church throughout the whole world; pour forth thy blessing on his present Holiness, our chief Pastor, on our Bishop, and on all true professors of the Catholic Faith.

*At the* MEMENTO *or* COMMEMORATION FOR THE LIVING, *say,*

I OFFER thee, O eternal Father, with this thy Minister at the altar, this oblation of the Body and Blood of thy only Son, to thy honour and glory, in remembrance of my Saviour's passion, in thanksgiving for all thy benefits, in satisfaction for all my sins; and for the obtaining thy grace, whereby I may be enabled to live virtuously and die happily. I desire thee likewise to accept it, O God, for my parents, [*if alive,*] friends, and benefactors; grant them all blessings, spiritual and temporal. I offer it up also, [*Here name the particular intention you would offer it up for; as for obtaining this virtue, overcoming that vice; for blessings, such as health, &c.,*] likewise for all that are in distress; for those I have in any ways injured in word or deed; for all my enemies; for the conversion of sinners, and for enlightening all that sit in darkness. Pour forth thy blessings on all, according to their different necessities; through the merits of thy only Son, our Lord.

GIVE ear, we beseech thee, to the prayers of thy servant who is here appointed to make this oblation in our behalf; and grant that it may be effectual for obtaining all those blessings he asks for us. Behold, O Lord, we all here present to thee, in this bread and wine, the symbols of our perfect union. Grant, O Lord, that they may be made for us the true Body and Blood of thy dear Son, that being consecrated to thee by this holy Victim, we may live in thy service, and depart this life in thy grace.

*At the* ELEVATION OF THE HOST, *say,*

MOST adorable Body, I adore thee with all the powers of my soul. O Lord, who hast given thyself entirely to us, grant that we may become entirely thine. I believe, O Lord; help my unbelief. Most merciful Saviour, be thou my protector; strengthen and defend me by thy heavenly grace, now, and especially at the hour of my death. Amen.

*At the* ELEVATION OF THE CHALICE, *say,*

MOST adorable Blood, by which all our sins are washed away, I adore thee. Happy we, if we can return our life and blood for thine! O Jesus, do thou cleanse, sanctify, and preserve our souls to eternal life. Do thou, O Jesus, live in us, and we in thee.

F

*After* THE ELEVATION, *say*,

It is now, O Lord, with grateful hearts we call to mind the sacred mysteries of thy passion and death, thy resurrection and ascension. Here is thy Body that was broken, here is thy Blood that was shed for us, of which these exterior signs are but the figures, and yet in reality contain the substance. It is now we truly offer thee, O Lord, that pure and holy Victim, which thou hast been pleased to give us, of which all the other sacrifices were but so many types and figures.

*At the* MEMENTO FOR THE DEAD, *say*,

I offer thee again, O Lord, this holy sacrifice of the Body and Blood of thy only Son, in behalf of the faithful departed; and in particular for the souls of [*Here name those for whom you chiefly propose to pray*] my parents, [*If dead,*] relations, benefactors, and friends; likewise of such as I have in any ways injured, or to whom I have been the occasion of sin; of such as have injured me and been my enemies; of such as have died in war, or have none to pray for them. To these, O Lord, and to all that rest in Christ, grant, we beseech thee, a place of refreshment, light, and peace; through the same Christ our Lord.

*At the* NOBIS QUOQUE PECCATORIBUS, *say,*

VOUCHSAFE to grant the same grace one day to us poor miserable sinners, and judge us not according to our demerits; but through the infinite multitude of thy mercies in which we hope, liberally extend to us thy grace and pardon.

We ask it of thee, in the name of thy dear Son, who liveth and reigneth eternally with thee, and in that form of prayer which he himself has taught us.

*At the* PATER NOSTER, *join with the Priest, and say:*

OUR Father, who art in heaven, hallowed be thy name; thy kingdom come; thy will be done on earth, as it is in heaven; give us this day our daily bread; and forgive us our trespasses, as we forgive them that trespass against us; and lead us not into temptation; but deliver us from evil. Amen.

Deliver us, we beseech thee, O Lord, from all those evils which we labour under at present; from past evils, which can be nothing but our manifold sins; and from the evils to come, which will be the just chastisement of our offences, if our own prayers, and those more powerful ones of thy Saints, who intercede for us, intercept not thy justice, or excite not thy bounty.

*At the* BREAKING OF THE HOST, *say*,

THY Body was broken, and thy Blood was shed for us. Grant that the commemoration of this holy Mystery may obtain for us peace, and that those who receive it may find everlasting rest.

*At the* AGNUS DEI, *say*,

LAMB of God, who takest away the sins of the world, have mercy on us.

Lamb of God, who takest away the sins of the world, have mercy on us.

Lamb of God, who takest away the sins of the world, grant us peace.

*At the* PRAYERS BEFORE COMMUNION,
*say*,

IN saying to thy Apostles, " Peace I leave you, my peace I give you," (John xiv. 27,) thou hast promised, O Lord, to all thy church, that peace which the world cannot give, peace with thee, and peace with ourselves.

Let nothing, O Lord, ever interrupt this holy peace; let nothing separate us from thee, to whom we heartily desire to be united, through this blessed Sacrament of peace and reconciliation; let this food of Angels strengthen us in every Christian duty, so that we may never more yield under temptations, or fall into our common weaknesses.

*At the* DOMINE NON SUM DIGNUS,
*say thrice,*

LORD, I am not worthy thou shouldst enter under my roof; say only the word, and my soul shall be healed.

At the Communion of the Priest, those who do not receive sacramentally, may do so in spirit and desire by a Spiritual Communion, so much recommended and practised by the saints. This consists in a fervent desire of receiving this heavenly bread; and that this desire may be efficacious, it must be accompanied with a lively faith, a firm confidence in the efficacy of this Sacrament, and an ardent love of Jesus Christ: above all, there must be a hearty sorrow for sin, without which sorrow a spiritual Communion would be an insult to Jesus Christ. This devotion may be practised not only at Mass, but at any hour of the day.

*At the* SPIRITUAL COMMUNION, *say*,

MOST loving Jesus, I adore thee with a lively faith, who art present in this Sacrament by virtue of thy infinite power, wisdom and goodness. All my hope is in thee. I love thee, O Lord, with all my heart, who hast so loved me; and therefore I desire to receive thee now spiritually. Come therefore, O Lord, to me in spirit, and heal my sinful soul. Feed me who am hungry; comfort me who am weak; enliven and sanctify me with thy sacred Body and Blood; free me from all sin, and make me always obedient to thy commands; and let me never be separated from thee, my Saviour, who with the Father and the Holy Ghost liveth and reigneth one God for ever. Amen.

*At the* ABLUTION, *and* WIPING OF THE CHALICE, *say*,

GIVE us, O Lord, a part of the fruit of thy passion and death, the sacred memory of which we have commemorated in this present Sacrifice and Communion. Happy those who sit at thy table to partake of the bread of life! O Jesus, my soul sighs after thee. I long with thy Apostle to be dissolved and be with thee. My heart and my whole body, with transports of joy, seek the living God.

My soul languishes with an ardent desire of entering into the house of our Lord. I love thee, O my God, with all my heart. O that I could always enjoy the presence of thy adorable Body, which is the pledge of our eternal happiness! I adore thy goodness, and return thee grateful thanks, O gracious Lord, for thy inestimable favour and mercy, in admitting me to be present this day at the dread Sacrifice, where thou art both Priest and Victim. Make me, O God, always sensible of this great blessing, and let not my unworthiness put an obstacle to the effects of thy mercy and goodness.

*At the* COMMUNION, *say,*

MAY thy mercy, O Lord, grant that we, who have been present at this holy mystery, may find the benefit of it in our souls.

*At the* POST-COMMUNION, *say,*

WE give thee thanks, O God, for thy mercy, in admitting us to have a part in offering this Sacrifice to thy holy Name.

Accept it now to thy glory, and be for ever mindful of our weakness.

Most gracious God, Father of mercy, grant, I beseech thee, that the adorable Sacrifice of the blessed Body and Blood of thy Son our Lord Jesus Christ, may obtain for us, at thy hands, mercy, and the remission of all our sins.

Defend also from all adversity thy servants, Pope *N*., our Bishop *N*.; grant peace in our days, and drive from thy Church all wickedness, through our Lord Jesus Christ, thy Son, who liveth and reigneth with thee in the unity of the Holy Ghost, one God, world without end.   Amen.

*When the* PRIEST BLESSES THE PEOPLE,
*say,*

THE blessing of God Almighty, Father, Son, and Holy Ghost, descend upon us, and dwell in our hearts for ever.   Amen.

*The* BEGINNING OF THE GOSPEL OF
ST. JOHN.

IN the beginning was the Word, and the Word was with God, and the Word was God.  The same was in the beginning with God.  All things were made by him, and without him was made nothing that was made. In him was life, and the life was the light of men; and the light shineth in darkness, and the darkness did not comprehend it. There was a man sent from God, whose name was John. This man came for a witness, to give testimony of the light, that all men might believe through him. He was not the light, but was to give testimony of the light. That was the true light, which enlighteneth every man that cometh into the world. He was in the world, and the world was made by him, and the world knew him not. He came unto his own, and his own received him not. But as many as received him, he gave them power to be made the sons of God; to them that believe in his name. Who are born not of blood, nor of the will of the flesh, nor of the will of man, but of God. *And the Word was made flesh* and dwelt among us, and we saw his glory, the glory as of the only begotten of the Father, full of grace and truth.

## The Asperges.

*Ant.* Asperges me, Domine, hyssopo, et mundabor: lavabis me, et super nivem dealbabor.

*Ps.* Miserere mei Deus, secundum magnam misericordiam tuam.
℣. Gloria, &c.
*Ant.* Asperges, &c.

*Ant.* Thou shalt sprinkle me with hyssop, O Lord, and I shall be cleansed; thou shalt wash me, and I shall be made whiter than snow.

*Ps.* Have mercy on me, O God, according to thy great mercy.
℣. Glory, &c.
*Ant.* Thou shalt, &c.

The Priest returning to the foot of the Altar, says:

Ostende nobis, Domine, misericordiam tuam.
℟. Et salutare tuum da nobis.
℣. Domine exaudi orationem meam.
℟. Et clamor meus ad te veniat.
℣. Dominus vobiscum.
℟. Et cum spiritu tuo.

Shew us, O Lord, thy mercy.
℟. And grant us thy salvation.
℣. O Lord, hear my prayer.
℟. And let my cry come unto thee.
℣. The Lord be with you.
℟. And with thy spirit.

OREMUS.

EXAUDI nos, Domine sancte, Pater omnipotens, æterne Deus:

LET US PRAY.

GRACIOUSLY hear us, O holy Lord, Father Almighty, Eternal

et mittere digneris sanctum Angelum tuum de cœlis, qui custodiat, foveat, protegat, visitet atque defendat omnes habitantes in hoc habitaculo. Per Christum Dominum nostrum.

℟. Amen.

God: and vouchsafe to send thy holy Angel from heaven, who may keep, cherish, protect, visit and defend all who dwell in this place. Through Christ our Lord.

℟. Amen.

In Paschal time, instead of the above *Antiphon* the following is sung, and *Alleluia* is added to the first *V.* and *R.*

*Ant.* Vidi aquam egredientem de templo, a latere dextro, Alleluia: et omnes ad quos pervenit aqua ista, salvi facti sunt, et dicent, Alleluia.

*Ps.* Confitemini Domino, quoniam bonus: quoniam in sæculum misericordia ejus.

℣. Gloria, &c.

*Ant.* Vidi aquam, &c.

*Ant.* I saw water coming forth from the temple, on the right side, Alleluia: and all those to whom this water came were saved, and shall say, Alleluia.

*Ps.* Give praise to the Lord for he is good: for his mercy endureth for ever.

℣. Glory, &c.

*Ant.* I saw water, &c.

## The Ordinary of the Mass.

In nomine Patris, et Filii, et Spiritus Sancti. Amen.

*Ant.* Introibo ad altare Dei.

M. Ad Deum qui lætificat juventutem meam.

*Psalm* XLII.

JUDICA me Deus, et discerne causam meam de gente non sancta: ab homine iniquo et doloso erue me.

M. Quia tu es Deus, fortitudo mea: quare me repulisti? et quare tristis incedo, dum affligit me inimicus?

S. Emitte lucem tuam, et veritatem tuam: ipsa me deduxerunt, et adduxerunt in montem sanctum tuum, et in tabernacula tua.

M. Et introibo ad altare Dei: ad Deum qui lætificat juventutem meam.

S. Confitebor tibi in cithara, Deus, Deus meus: quare tristis es anima mea? et quare conturbas me?

M. Spera in Deo, quoniam adhuc confitebor illi, salutare vultus mei, et Deus meus.

S. Gloria Patri, et Filio, et Spiritui Sancto.

M. Sicut erat in principio, et nunc, et semper, et in sæcula sæculorum. Amen.

S. Introibo ad altare Dei.

M. Ad Deum qui lætificat juventutem meam.

S. Adjutorium nostrum in nomine Domini.

M. Qui fecit cœlum et terram.

S. Confiteor, &c.

M. Misereatur tui omnipotens Deus, et dimissis peccatis tuis, perducat te ad vitam æternam.

S. Amen.

M. Confiteor Deo omnipotenti, beatæ Mariæ semper Virgini, beato Michaeli Archangelo, beato Joanni Baptistæ, sanctis Apostolis Petro et Paulo, omnibus Sanctis, et tibi, Pater, quia peccavi nimis cogitatione, verbo, et opere, mea culpa, mea culpa, mea maxima culpa. Ideo precor beatam Mariam semper Virginem, beatum Michaelem Archangelum, beatum Joannem Baptistam, sanctos Apostolos Petrum et Paulum, omnes Sanctos, et te Pater, orare pro me ad Dominum Deum nostrum.

S. Misereatur vestri, &c.

M. Amen.

S. Indulgentiam, absolutionem, et remissionem peccatorum nostrorum, tribuat nobis omnipotens et misericors Dominus.

M. Amen.

S. Deus, tu conversus vivificabis nos.

M. Et plebs tua lætabitur in te.

S. Ostende nobis, Domine, misericordiam tuam.

M. Et salutare tuum da nobis.

S. Domine, exaudi orationem meam.

M. Et clamor meus ad te veniat.

S. Dominus vobiscum.

M. Et cum spiritu tuo.

*Sacerdos, ascendens ad altare, dicit secreto.*

AUFER a nobis, quæsumus, Domine, iniquitates nostras: ut ad Sancta Sanctorum puris mereamur mentibus introire. Per Christum Dominum nostrum. Amen.

*Deinde inclinatus dicit.*

ORAMUS te, Domine, per merita Sanctorum tuorum, quorum reliquiæ hic sunt, et omnium Sanctorum: ut indulgere digneris omnia peccata mea. Amen.

*Celebrans incipit Introitum, quo finito, dicit:*

S. Kyrie eleison.
M. Kyrie eleison.
S. Kyrie eleison.
M. Christe eleison.
S. Christe eleison.
M. Christe eleison.
S. Kyrie eleison.
M. Kyrie eleison.
S. Kyrie eleison.

GLORIA in excelsis Deo, et in terra pax hominibus bonæ voluntatis. Laudamus te, benedicimus te, adoramus te, glorificamus te. Gratias agimus tibi propter magnam gloriam tuam, Domine Deus, Rex cœlestis, Deus Pater omnipotens. Domino Fili unigenite Jesu Christe. Domine Deus, Agnus Dei, Filius Patris, qui tollis peccata mundi, miserere nobis. Qui tollis peccata mundi, suscipe deprecationem nostram. Qui sedes ad dexteram Patris, miserere nobis. Quoniam Tu solus sanctus. Tu solus Dominus, Tu solus altissimus, Jesu Christe, cum Sancto Spiritu, in gloria Dei Patris. Amen.

S. Dominus vobiscum.
M. Et cum spiritu tuo.

*Deinde dicit orationes. Sequitur Epistola, Graduale, et Tractus.*

*In fine Epistolæ respondet Minister.*

M. Deo gratias.

*Deinde Sacerdos dicit:*

MUNDA cor meum, ac labia mea, omnipotens Deus, qui labia Isaiæ Prophetæ calculo mundasti ignito: ita me tua grata miseratione dignare mundare, ut sanctum Evangelium tuum digne valeam nuntiare. Per Christum Dominum nostrum. Amen.

S. Dominus vobiscum.
M. Et cum spiritu tuo.

Initium (vel sequentia) Sancti Evangelii secundum &c.
R. Gloria tibi, Domine.

*In fine Evangelii:*
M. Laus tibi, Christe.

CREDO in unum Deum, Patrem omnipotentem, factorem cœli et terræ, visibilium omnium et invisibilium.
Et in unum Dominum Jesum Christum, Filium Dei unigenitum, et ex Patre natum ante omnia sæcula; Deum de Deo, Lumen de lumine; Deum verum de Deo vero; genitum non factum; consubstantialem Patri, per quem omnia facta sunt. Qui propter nos homines, et propter nostram salutem descendit de cœlis; et incarnatus est de Spiritu Sancto, ex Maria Virgine, ET HOMO FACTUS EST. Crucifixus etiam pro nobis, sub Pontio Pilato, passus et sepultus est. Et resurrexit tertia die, secundum Scripturas, et ascendit in cœlum; sedet ad dexteram Patris; et iterum venturus est cum gloria, judicare vivos et mortuos: cujus regni non erit finis.
Et in Spiritum Sanctum, Dominum et vivificantem, qui ex Patre Filioque procedit: qui cum Patre et Filio simul adoratur, et conglorificatur; qui locutus est per Prophetas. Et unam sanctam Catholicam et Apostolicam Ecclesiam. Confiteor unum Baptisma in remissionem peccatorum. Et expecto resurrectionem mortuorum, et vitam venturi sæculi. Amen.

Dominus vobiscum.
R. Et cum spiritu tuo.

*Dicit Sacerdos Offertorium; deinde Hostiam offert.*

SUSCIPE, sancte Pater, omnipotens æterne Deus, hanc immaculatam Hostiam, quam ego indignus famulus tuus offero tibi Deo meo vivo et vero, pro innumerabilibus peccatis, offensionibus et negligentiis meis, et pro omnibus circumstantibus; sed et pro omnibus fidelibus Christianis, vivis atque defunctis; ut mihi et illis proficiat ad salutem in vitam æternam. Amen.

*Deinde vinum et aquam in calicem infundit, dicens.*

DEUS, qui humanæ substantiæ dignitatem mirabiliter condidisti, et mirabilius reformasti; da nobis per hujus aquæ et vini mysterium, ejus divinitatis esse consortes, qui humanitatis nostræ fieri dignatus est particeps, Jesus Christus Filius tuus Dominus noster; qui tecum vivit et regnat, in unitate Spiritus Sancti, Deus, per omnia sæcula sæculorum. Amen.

*Calicem offerens, dicit:*

OFFERIMUS tibi, Domine, calicem salutaris, tuam deprecantes clementiam, ut in conspectu divinæ majestatis tuæ, pro nostra et totius mundi salute, cum odore suavitatis ascendat. Amen.

*Deinde aliquantulum inclinatus dicit:*

IN spiritu humilitatis, et in animo contrito suscipiamur a te, Domine; et sic fiat sacrificium nostrum in conspectu tuo hodie, ut placeat tibi, Domine Deus.

*Benedicit Oblata.*

VENI, sanctificator, omnipotens æterne Deus, et benedic hoc sacrificium tuo sancto nomini præparatum.

*Lavat manus, dicens:*

LAVABO inter innocentes manus meas: et circumdabo altare tuum, Domine.

Ut audiam vocem laudis: et enarrem universa mirabilia tua.

Domine, dilexi decorem domus tuæ: et locum habitationis gloriæ tuæ.

Ne perdas cum impiis, Deus, animam meam: et cum viris sanguinum vitam meam.

In quorum manibus iniquitates sunt: dextera eorum repleta est muneribus.

Ego autem in innocentia mea ingressus sum: redime me, et miserere mei.

Pes meus stetit in directo: in ecclesiis benedicam te, Domine.

Gloria Patri, et Filio: et Spiritui Sancto.

Sicut erat in principio, et nunc et semper: et in sæcula sæculorum. Amen.

*Inclinatus in medio altaris, dicit Celebrans:*

Suscipe sancta Trinitas hanc oblationem, quam tibi offerimus, ob memoriam passionis, resurrectionis, et ascensionis Jesu Christi Domini nostri: et in honore beatæ Mariæ semper Virginis, et beati Joannis Baptistæ, et sanctorum Apostolorum Petri et Pauli, et istorum et omnium Sanctorum: ut illis proficiat ad honorem, nobis autem ad salutem: et illi pro nobis intercedere dignentur in cœlis, quorum memoriam agimus in terris. Per eumdem Christum Dominum nostrum. Amen.

*Versus ad populum dicit:*

Orate, Fratres, ut meum ac vestrum sacrificium acceptabile fiat apud Deum Patrem omnipotentem.

M. Suscipiat Dominus sacrificium de manibus tuis ad laudem et gloriam nominis sui, ad utilitatem quoque nostram, totiusque Ecclesiæ suæ sanctæ.

*Orationibus secretis finitis, dicit:*

S. Per omnia sæcula sæculorum.

M. Amen.

S. Dominus vobiscum.

M. Et cum spiritu tuo.

S. Sursum corda.

M. Habemus ad Dominum.

S. Gratias agamus Domino Deo nostro.

M. Dignum et justum est.

cœli cœlorumque Virtutes, ac beata Seraphim, socia exultatione concelebrant. Cum quibus et nostras voces, ut admitti jubeas deprecamur, supplici confessione dicentes:

Sanctus, Sanctus, Sanctus, Dominus Deus Sabaoth. Pleni sunt cœli et terra gloria tua. Hosanna in excelsis. Benedictus qui venit in nomine Domini. Hosanna in excelsis.

*In omnibus Feriis et Festis ubi propria non habetur, et in omnibus Missis Defunctorum.*

VERE dignum et justum est, æquum et salutare, nos tibi semper, et ubique gratias agere, Domine sancte, Pater omnipotens, æterne Deus. \*Per Christum Dominum nostrum ; per quem majestatem tuam laudant Angeli, adorant Dominationes, tremunt Potestates ;

*In festo S.S. Trinitatis, et in Dominicis propriam non habentibus.*

\*QUI cum unigenito Filio tuo, et Spiritu Sancto unus es Deus, unus es Dominus: non in unius singularitate personæ sed in unius Trinitate substantiæ. Quod enim de tua gloria, revelante te, credimus, hoc de Filio tuo, hoc de Spiritu Sancto, sine differentia discretionis sentimus. Ut in confessione veræ, sempiternæque Deitatis, et in personis proprietas, et in essentia unitas, et in majestate adoretur æqualitas. Quam laudant Angeli, atque Archangeli, Cherubim quoque ac Seraphim ; qui non cessant clamare quotidie, una voce dicentes, Sanctus. &c.

*A Nativitate Domini usque ad Epiphaniam; in festo Corporis Christi, et in Transfiguratione Domini, ac in Festo S. S. Nominis Jesu, necnon in Missis votivis de S.S. Sacramento, et in Festo Purificationis B. Mariæ.*

\*Quia per incarnati Verbi mysterium, nova mentis nostræ oculis lux tuæ claritatis infulsit; ut dum visibiliter Deum cognoscimus, per hunc in invisibilium amorem rapiamur. †Et ideo cum Angelis et Archangelis, cum Thronis et Dominationibus, cumque omni militia cœlestis exercitus, hymnum gloriæ tuæ canimus sine fine dicentes, Sanctus, &c.

*In Epiphania Domini et per octavam.*

\*Quia cum Unigenitus tuus in substantia nostræ mortalitatis apparuit, nova nos immortalitatis suæ luce reparavit. †Et ideo, cum angelis, &c.

*A feria IV. Cinerum usque ad Sabbatum ante Dominicam Passionis.*

\*Qui corporali jejunio vitia comprimis, mentem elevas, virtutem largiris et prœmia. \*Per Christum, &c.

*A Dominica Passionis usque ad feriam v. in Cœna Domini, et in Missis de Cruce et de Passione.*

\*Qui salutem humani generis in ligno Crucis constituisti ; ut unde mors oriebatur, inde

vita resurgeret, et qui in ligno vincebat, in ligno quoque vinceretur. *Per Christum, &c.

*A Vigilia Paschæ usque ad Ascensionem.*

VERE dignum et justum est æquum et salutare, te quidem Domine, omni tempore, sed [in hac potissimum nocte, *vel* die, *vel*] in hoc potissimum gloriosius prædicare, cum Pascha nostrum immolatus est Christus. Ipse enim verus est Agnus, qui abstulit peccata mundi, qui mortem nostram moriendo destruxit, et vitam resurgendo reparavit. †Et ideo, cum Angelis, &c.

*A die Ascensionis usque ad vigiliam Pentecostes.*

*Per Christum Dominum nostrum. Qui post resurrectionem suam omnibus discipulis suis manifestus apparuit, et ipsis cernentibus est elevatus in cœlum, ut nos divinitatis suæ tribueret esse participes. †Et ideo, &c.

*A vigilia Pentecostes usque ad sequens Sabbatum inclusive, et in Missis votivis de Spiritu Sancto.*

*Per Christum Dominum nostrum. Qui ascendens super omnes cœlos sedensque ad dexteram tuam, promissum Spiritum Sanctum [hodierna die] in filios adoptionis effudit. Quapropter profusis gaudiis totus in orbe terrarum mundus exultat. Sed et supernæ Virtutes atque angelicæ Potestates, hymnum gloriæ tuæ concinunt, sine fine dicentes, Sanctus, &c.

*In Festis B. Mariæ excepto Festo Purificationis.*

* Et te in N. Beatæ Mariæ semper Virginis collaudare, benedicere, et prædicare. Quæ

et Unigenitum tuum Sancti Spiritus obumbratione concepit, et virginitatis gloria permanente, lumen æternum mundo effudit, Jesum Christum Dominum nostrum. *Per quem, &c.

*In Festis Apostolorum.*

VERE dignum et justum est, æquum et salutare, te Domine suppliciter exorare, ut gregem tuum, Pastor æterne, non deseras, sed per beatos Apostolos tuos continua protectione custodias. Ut iisdem rectoribus gubernetur, quos operis tui vicarios eidem contulisti præesse pastores. *Et ideo, cum Angelis, &c.

---

CANON MISSÆ.

TE igitur, clementissime Pater, per Jesum Christum Filium tuum Dominum nostrum, supplices rogamus ac petimus, uti accepta habeas, et benedicas, hæc dona, hæc munera, hæc sancta sacrificia illibata, imprimis quæ tibi offerimus pro Ecclesia tua sancta Catholica, quam pacificare, custodire, adunare, et regere digneris toto orbe terrarum; una cum famulo tuo Papa nostro N. et Antistite nostro N. et omnibus orthodoxis atque catholicæ et apostolicæ fidei cultoribus.

*Commemoratio pro vivis.*

MEMENTO, Domine, famulorum, famularumque tuarum N. et N.

Et omnium circumstantium, quorum tibi fides cognita est, et nota devotio: pro quibus tibi offerimus, vel qui tibi offerunt hoc sacrificium laudis, pro sè suisque omnibus, pro redemptione animarum suarum, pro spe salutis et incolumitatis suæ, tibique reddunt vota sua æterno Deo, vivo et vero.

Communicantes, et memoriam venerantes, imprimis gloriosæ semper Virginis Mariæ, Genitricis Dei et Domini nostri Jesu Christi: sed et beatorum Apostolorum ac Martyrum tuorum, Petri et Pauli, Andreæ, Jacobi, Joannis, Thomæ, Jacobi, Philippi, Bartholomæi, Matthæi, Simonis et Thaddæi, Lini, Cleti, Clementis, Xysti, Cornelii, Cypriani, Laurentii, Chrysogoni, Joannis, et Pauli, Cosmæ et Damiani, et omnium Sanctorum tuorum: quorum meritis precibusque concedas, ut in omnibus protectionis tuæ muniamur auxilio. Per eumdem Christum Dominum nostrum. Amen.

*Tenens manus expansas super Oblata dicit:*

Hanc igitur oblationem servitutis nostræ, sed et cunctæ familiæ tuæ, quæsumus, Domine, ut placatus accipias; diesque nostros in tua pace disponas, atque ab æterna damnatione nos eripi, et in electorum tuorum jubeas grege numerari. Per Christum Dominum nostrum. Amen.

Quam oblationem tu, Deus, in omnibus, quæsumus, benedictam, adscriptam ratam, rationabilem, acceptabilemque facere digneris; ut nobis corpus et sanguis fiat dilectissimi Filii tui Domini nostri Jesu Christi.

Qui pridie quam pateretur, accepit panem in sanctas et venerabiles manus suas, et elevatis oculis in cœlum, ad te Deum Patrem suum omnipotentem, tibi gratias agens, benedixit, fregit, deditque discipulis suis, dicens: Accipite et manducate ex hoc omnes, Hoc est enim corpus meum.

*Hostiam consecratam genuflexus adorat, et ostendit populo: tunc dicit:*

Simili modo, postquam cœnatum est, accipiens et hunc præclarum Calicem in sanctas ac venerabiles manus suas, item tibi gratias agens benedixit, deditque discipulis suis, dicens: Accipite et bibite ex eo omnes, Hic est enim calix sanguinis mei novi et æterni testamenti, mysterium fidei: qui pro vobis et pro multis effundetur in remissionem peccatorum.

Hæc quotiescumque feceritis, in mei memoriam facietis.

*Genuflexus Calicem adorat, et ostendit populo. Deinde dicit:*

Unde et memores, Domine, nos servi tui, sed et plebs tua sancta, ejusdem Christi Filii tui Domini nostri tam beatæ passionis, necnon et ab inferis resurrectionis, sed in cœlos gloriosæ ascensionis, offerimus præclaræ majestati tuæ, de tuis donis ac datis, Hostiam puram, Hostiam sanctam, Hostiam immaculatam, panem sanctum vitæ æternæ, et Calicem salutis perpetuæ.

Supra quæ propitio ac sereno vultu respicere digneris, et accepta habere, sicuti accepta habere dignatus es munera pueri tui justi Abel, et sacrificium Patriarchæ nostri Abrahæ, et quod tibi obtulit summus sacerdos tuus Melchisedech, sanctum Sacrificium, immaculatam Hostiam.

Supplices te rogamus, omnipotens Deus, jube hæc perferri per manus sancti Angeli tui in sublime altare tuum, in conspectu divinæ majestatis tuæ; ut quotquot ex hac altaris participatione sacrosanctum Filii tui corpus et sanguinem sumpserimus, omni benedictione cœlesti et gratia repleamur. Per eumdem Christum Dominum nostrum. Amen.

*Commemoratio pro Defunctis.*

MEMENTO etiam, Domine, famulorum famularumque tuarum N. et N. qui nos præcesserunt cum signo Fidei, et dormiunt in somno pacis. *Ipsis Domine, et omnibus in Christo quiescentibus, locum refrigerii, lucis et pacis, ut indulgeas deprecamur : per eumdem Christum Dominum nostrum. Amen.

*Manu dextra percutit sibi pectus, dicens :*

NOBIS quoque peccatoribus famulis tuis, de multitudine miserationum tuarum sperantibus, partem aliquam et societatem donare digneris, cum tuis sanctis Apostolis et Martyribus ; cum Joanne, Stephano, Matthia, Barnaba, Ignatio, Alexandro, Marcellino, Petro, Felicitate, Perpetua, Agatha, Lucia, Agnete, Cæcilia, Anastasia, et omnibus Sanctis tuis; intra quorum nos consortium, non æstimator meriti, sed veniæ quæsumus largitor admitte. Per Christum Dominum nostrum.

Per quem hæc omnia, Domine, semper bona creas, sanctificas, vivificas, benedicis, et præstas nobis. Per ipsum, et cum ipso, et in ipso, est tibi Deo Patri omnipotenti, in unitate Spiritus Sancti, omnis honor et gloria.

S. Per omnia sæcula sæculorum.
M. Amen.

## THE ORDINARY OF THE MASS.

OREMUS.

PRÆCEPTIS salutaribus moniti, et divina institutione formati, audemus dicere:

Pater noster, qui es in cœlis, sanctificetur nomen tuum; adveniat regnum tuum; fiat voluntas tua sicut in cœlo, et in terra; panem nostrum quotidianum da nobis hodie; et dimitte nobis debita nostra, sicut et nos dimittimus debitoribus nostris; et ne nos inducas in tentationem.

M. Sed libera nos a malo.

S. Amen.

Libera nos, quæsumus, Domine, ab omnibus malis, præteritis, præsentibus, et futuris; et intercedente beata et gloriosa semper Virgine Dei Genitrice Maria, cum beatis Apostolis tuis Petro et Paulo, atque Andrea, et omnibus Sanctis, da propitius pacem in diebus nostris, ut ope misericordiæ tuæ adjuti, et a peccato simus semper liberi, et ab omni perturbatione securi. Per eumdem Dominum nostrum Jesum Christum Filium tuum, qui tecum vivit et regnat, in unitate Spiritus Sancti, Deus.

S. Per omnia sæcula sæculorum.

M. Amen.

S. Pax Domini sit semper vobiscum.

M. Et cum spiritu tuo.

*Hostiam frangit et particulam in calicem immittit, dicens:*

HÆC commixtio et consecratio Corporis et Sanguinis Domini nostri Jesu Christi, fiat accipientibus nobis in vitam æternam. Amen.

*Deinde inclinatus et ter pectus percutiens, dicit:*

AGNUS Dei, qui tollis peccata mundi, miserere nobis.

G

Agnus Dei, qui tollis peccata mundi, miserere nobis.

Agnus Dei, qui tollis peccata mundi, dona nobis pacem.

*In Missis pro Defunctis non dicitur* Miserere nobis, *sed ejus loco,* dona eis requiem; *et in tertio additur,* sempiternam.

DOMINE Jesu Christe, qui dixisti Apostolis tuis, pacem relinquo vobis, pacem meam do vobis, ne respicias peccata mea, sed fidem Ecclesiæ tuæ; eamque secundum voluntatem tuam pacificare et coadunare digneris; qui vivis et regnas Deus, per omnia sæcula sæculorum. Amen.

*In Missis Defunctorum non dicitur Oratio præcedens.*

DOMINE Jesu Christe, Fili Dei vivi, qui ex voluntate Patris, co-operante Spiritu Sancto, per mortem tuam mundum vivificasti, libera me per hoc sacro-sanctum Corpus et Sanguinem tuum ab omnibus iniquitatibus meis, et universis malis; et fac me tuis semper inhærere mandatis, et a te nunquam separari permittas; qui cum eodem Deo Patre et Spiritu Sancto vivis et regnas Deus in sæcula sæculorum. Amen.

Perceptio Corporis tui, Domine Jesu Christe, quod ego indignus sumere præsumo, non mihi proveniat in judicium et condemnationem; sed pro tua pietate prosit mihi ad tutamentum mentis et corporis, et ad medelam percipiendam; qui vivis et regnas cum Deo Patre, in unitate Spiritus Sancti, Deus, per omnia sæcula sæculorum. Amen.

*Genuflectit, surgit, et dicit:*

PANEM cœlestem accipiam, et nomen Domini invocabo.

*Deinde accipit Hostiam in manum sinistram, et dextera percutiens pectus, dicit ter devote et humiliter.*

DOMINE, non sum dignus ut intres sub tectum meum; sed tantum dic verbo, et sanabitur anima mea.

*Sumit reverenter ambas partes Hostiæ, dicens:*

CORPUS Domini nostri Jesu Christi custodiat animam meam in vitam æternam. Amen.

*Accipit Calicem et dicit:*

QUID retribuam Domino pro omnibus quæ retribuit mihi? Calicem salutaris accipiam, et nomen Domini invocabo. Laudans invocabo Dominum, et ab inimicis meis salvus ero.

*Sumit Sanguinem.*

SANGUIS Domini nostri Jesu Christi custodiat animam meam in vitam æternam. Amen.

*Ablutionem primam sumit, dicens:*

QUOD ore sumpsimus, Domine, pura mente capiamus, et de munere temporali fiat nobis remedium sempiternum.

*Abluit digitos et sumit ablutionem, dicens:*

CORPUS tuum, Domine, quod sumpsi, et Sanguis quem potavi, adhæreat visceribus meis; et præsta, ut in me non remaneat scelerum macula, quem pura et sancta refecerunt sacramenta. Qui vivis et regnas in sæcula sæculorum. Amen.

*Communionem dicit.*

S. Dominus vobiscum.

M. Et cum spiritu tuo.

S. Oremus.

*Postcommunionem dicit.*

S. Dominus vobiscum.

M. Et cum spiritu tuo.

S. Ite, missa est, *vel*, Benedicamus Domino.

M. Deo gratias.

*In Missis Defunctorum.*

S. Requiescant in pace.

M. Amen.

*Sacerdos inclinat se ante medium altaris et dicit:*

PLACEAT tibi, sancta Trinitas, obsequium servitutis meæ; et præsta, ut Sacrificium, quod oculis tuæ Majestatis indignus obtuli, tibi sit acceptabile, mihique, et omnibus pro quibus illud obtuli, sit, te miserante, propitiabile. Per Christum Dominum nostrum. Amen.

*Deinde versus ad populum, dat benedictionem.*

BENEDICAT vos omnipotens Deus, ✠ Pater, et Filius, et Spiritus Sanctus.

M. Amen.

S. Dominus vobiscum.

M. Et cum spiritu tuo.

S. Initium sancti Evangelii secundum Joannem.

M. Gloria tibi, Domine.

In principio erat Verbum, et Verbum erat apud Deum, et Deus erat Verbum. Hoc erat in principio apud Deum. Omnia per ipsum facta sunt, et sine ipso factum est nihil, quod factum est. In ipso vita erat, et vita erat lux hominum; et lux in tenebris lucet, et tenebræ eam non comprehenderunt.

Fuit homo missus a Deo, cui nomen erat Joannes. Hic venit in testimonium, ut testimonium perhiberet de lumine, ut omnes crederent per illum. Non erat ille lux; sed ut testimonium perhiberet de lumine. Erat lux vera, quæ illuminat omnem hominem venientem in hunc mundum.

In mundo erat, et mundus per ipsum factus est, et mundus eum non cognovit. In propria venit, et sui eum non receperunt. Quotquot autem receperunt eum, dedit eis potestatem filios Dei fieri; his qui credunt in nomine ejus, qui non ex sanguinibus, neque ex voluntate carnis, neque ex voluntate viri, sed ex Deo nati sunt. ET VERBUM CARO FACTUM EST, et habitavit in nobis; et vidimus gloriam ejus, gloriam quasi Unigeniti a Patre, plenum gratiæ et veritatis.

M. Deo gratias.

## Prayers to be said after Mass.

### LET US PRAY.

WE give thee thanks, almighty and gracious Father, that thou hast permitted us this day to offer our homage to thy divine majesty, and especially that thou hast allowed us to be present at the most holy Sacrifice of the body and blood of thy beloved Son. If we have been wanting in attention and devotion, pardon us, we beseech thee, in pity to our weakness. For the sake of Him whose sufferings and death we have commemorated, grant the petitions which we have made in his name, and send down upon us thy blessing, which may remain with us for ever. Through the same Jesus Christ our Lord. Amen.

---

In Lent and Advent the Miserere is said instead of the Te Deum.

---

## Te Deum.

Te Deum laudamus:* te Dominum confitemur.

We praise thee, O God: we acknowledge thee to be the Lord.

Te æternum Patrem* omnis terra veneratur.

All the earth doth worship thee, the Father everlasting.

Tibi omnes Angeli,* tibi Cœli, et universæ Potestates:

To thee all Angels cry aloud, the Heavens and all the Powers therein.

Tibi Cherubim et Seraphim,* incessabili voce proclamant,

To thee Cherubim and Seraphim continually do cry,

Sanctus, Sanctus, Sanctus,* Dominus Deus Sabaoth.

Holy, Holy, Holy, Lord God of Sabaoth.

Pleni sunt cœli et terra* majestatis gloriæ tuæ.

Heaven and earth are full of the majesty of thy glory.

Te gloriosus* Apostolorum chorus,

The glorious choir of the Apostles praise thee.

Te Prophetarum * laudabilis numerus,

Te Martyrum candidatus* laudat exercitus.

Te per orbem terrarum* sancta confitetur Ecclesia,

Patrem * immensæ Majestatis,

Venerandum tuum verum* et unicum Filium,

Sanctum quoque* Paraclitum Spiritum.

Tu Rex gloriæ,* Christe.

Tu Patris * sempiternus es Filius.

Tu ad liberandum suscepturus hominem,* non horruisti Virginis uterum.

Tu, devicto mortis aculeo,* aperuisti credentibus regna cœlorum.

Tu ad dexteram Dei sedes,* in gloria Patris.

The admirable company of the Prophets praise thee.

The white-robed army of Martyrs praise thee.

The Holy Church throughout all the world doth acknowledge thee,

The Father of infinite Majesty;

Thy adorable, true, and only Son;

Also the Holy Ghost the Comforter.

Thou, O Christ, art the King of Glory.

Thou art the everlasting Son of the Father.

When thou didst take upon thee to deliver man, thou didst not abhor the Virgin's womb.

When thou hadst overcome the sting of death, thou didst open the kingdom of Heaven to believers.

Thou sittest at the right hand of God, in the glory of the Father.

| | |
|---|---|
| Judex crederis* esse venturus. | We believe that thou shalt come to be our Judge. |
| Te ergo, quæsumus, tuis famulis subveni,* quos pretioso sanguine redemisti. | We pray thee, therefore, help thy servants whom thou hast redeemed with thy precious blood. |
| Æterna fac cum Sanctis tuis,* in gloria numerari. | Make them to be numbered with thy Saints, in glory everlasting. |
| Salvum fac populum tuum, Domine,* et benedic hæreditati tuæ. | O Lord, save thy people, and bless thine inheritance. |
| Et rege eos, et extolle illos,* usque in æternum. | Govern them, and exalt for ever. |
| Per singulos dies,* benedicimus te. | Day by day, we magnify thee. |
| Et laudamus nomen tuum in sæculum,* et in sæculum sæculi. | And we praise thy name for ever: yea, for ever and ever. |
| Dignare, Domine, die isto,* sine peccato nos custodire. | Vouchsafe, O Lord, this day, to keep us without sin. |
| Miserere nostri, Domine,* miserere nostri. | Have mercy on us O Lord, have mercy on us. |
| Fiat misericordia tua, Domine, super nos:* quemadmodum speravimus in te. | Let thy mercy, O Lord, be upon us, as we have hoped in thee. |
| In te, Domine, speravi;* non confundar in æternum. | In thee, O Lord, have I hoped, let me not be confounded for ever. |
| ℣. Benedictus es, | ℣. Blessed art thou, |

Domine Deus, Patrum nostrorum.
℟. Et laudabilis, et gloriosus in sæcula.

℣. Benedicamus Patrem et Filium, cum Sancto Spiritu.
℟. Laudemus et superexaltemus eum in sæcula.

℣. Benedictus es, Domine Deus, in firmamento cœli.
℟. Et laudabilis, et gloriosus, et superexaltatus in sæcula.

℣. Benedic, anima mea, Domino.
℟. Et noli oblivisci omnes retributiones ejus.

℣. Domine, exaudi orationem meam.
℟. Et clamor meus ad te veniat.

℣. Dominus vobiscum.
℟. Et cum spiritu tuo.

OREMUS.

DEUS, cujus misericordiæ non est numerus, et bonitatis infinitus est thesaurus, piissimæ Majestati tuæ pro

O Lord, the God of our Fathers.
℟. And worthy to be praised, and glorious for ever.

℣. Let us bless the Father, and the Son, with the Holy Ghost.
℟. Let us praise and magnify him for ever.

℣. Blessed art thou, O Lord, in the firmament of heaven.
℟. And worthy to be praised, glorious and exalted for ever.

℣. Bless the Lord, O my soul.
℟. And forget not all his benefits.

℣. O Lord, hear my prayer.
℟. And let my cry come unto thee.

℣. The Lord be with you.
℟. And with thy spirit.

LET US PRAY.

O GOD, whose mercies are without number, and the treasure of whose goodness is infinite: we render

collatis donis gratias agimus, tuam semper clementiam exorantes: ut qui petentibus postulata concedis, eosdem non deserens, ad præmia futura disponas.

Deus, qui corda fidelium Sancti Spiritus illustratione docuisti; da nobis in eodem Spiritu recta sapere, et de ejus semper consolatione gaudere.

Deus, qui neminem in te sperantem nimium affligi permittis, sed pium precibus præstas auditum: pro postulationibus nostris, votisque susceptis gratias agimus, te piissime deprecantes, ut a cunctis semper muniamur adversis. Per Christum Dominum nostrum.

℞. Amen.

thanks to thy most gracious Majesty, for the gifts thou hast bestowed upon us, evermore beseeching thy clemency, that as thou grantest the petitions of those that ask thee, thou wilt never forsake them, but wilt prepare them for the rewards to come.

O God, who hast taught the hearts of the faithful by the light of the Holy Spirit: grant us, by the same Spirit, to relish what is right, and evermore to rejoice in his consolation.

O God, who sufferest none that hope in thee to be afflicted above their strength, but dost afford a gracious ear unto their prayers: we render thee thanks that thou hast heard our supplications and vows; and we most humbly beseech thee, that we may evermore be protected from all adversities. Through Christ our Lord.

℞. Amen.

## Miserere.

Miserere mei, Deus,\* secundum magnam misericordiam tuam.
Et secundum multitudinem miserationum tuarum,\* dele iniquitatem meam.
Amplius lava me ab iniquitate mea\*; et a peccato meo munda me.

Quoniam iniquitatem meam ego cognosco\*; et peccatum meum contra me est semper.
Tibi soli peccavi, et malum coram te feci\*; ut justificeris in sermonibus tuis, et vincas cum judicaris.

Ecce enim in iniquitatibus conceptus sum\*; et in peccatis concepit me mater mea.

Ecce enim veritatem dilexisti\*: incerta et occulta sapientiæ tuæ manifestasti mihi.

Have mercy on me, O God, according to thy great mercy.
And according to the multitude of thy tender mercies, blot out my iniquity.
Wash me yet more from my iniquity: and cleanse me from my sin.
For I know my iniquity: and my sin is always before me.

To thee only have I sinned and have done evil before thee; that thou mayest be justified in thy words, and mayest overcome when thou art judged.
For behold I was conceived in iniquities; and in sins did my mother conceive me.
For behold thou hast loved truth: the uncertain and hidden things of thy wisdom thou hast made manifest to me.

Asperges me hyssopo, et mundabor*: lavabis me, et super nivem dealbabor.

Auditui meo dabis gaudium et lætitiam*; et exultabunt ossa humiliata.

Averte faciem tuam a peccatis meis*; et omnes iniquitates meas dele.

Cor mundum crea in me, Deus*; et spiritum rectum innova in visceribus meis.

Ne projicias me a facie tua*; et spiritum sanctum tuum ne auferas a me.

Redde mihi lætitiam salutaris tui*; et spiritu principali confirma me.

Docebo iniquos vias tuas*; et impii ad te convertentur.

Libera me de sanguinibus, Deus, Deus salutis meæ*; et exultabit lingua mea justitiam tuam.

Thou shalt sprinkle me with hyssop and I shall be cleansed: thou shalt wash me and I shall be made whiter than snow.

To my hearing thou shalt give joy and gladness; and the bones that have been humbled shall rejoice.

Turn away thy face from my sins, and blot out my iniquities.

Create a clean heart in me, O God; and renew a right spirit within my bowels.

Cast me not away from thy face; and take not thy Holy Spirit from me.

Restore unto me the joy of thy salvation; and strengthen me with a perfect spirit.

I will teach the unjust thy ways; and the wicked shall be converted to thee.

Deliver me from blood, O God, thou God of my salvation; and my tongue shall extol thy justice.

Domine, labia mea aperies*; et os meum annuntiabit laudem tuam.

Quoniam si voluisses sacrificium, dedissem utique*: holocaustis non delectaberis.

Sacrificium Deo spiritus contribulatus*: cor contritum et humiliatum, Deus, non despicies.

Benigne fac Domine, in bona voluntate tua Sion*: ut ædificentur muri Jerusalem.

Tunc acceptabis sacrificium justitiæ, oblationes, et holocausta*: tunc imponent super altare tuum vitulos.

Gloria Patri, &c.

℣. Domine, non secundum peccata nostra facias nobis.

℞. Neque secundum iniquitates nostras retribuas nobis.

O Lord, thou wilt open my lips; and my mouth shall declare thy praise.

For if thou hadst desired sacrifice, I would indeed have given it; with burnt-offerings thou wilt not be delighted.

A sacrifice to God is an afflicted spirit: a contrite and humble heart, O God, thou wilt not despise.

Deal favourably, O Lord, in thy good-will with Sion; that the walls of Jerusalem may be built up.

Then shalt thou accept the sacrifice of justice, oblations, and whole burnt-offerings; then shall they lay calves upon thy altar.

Glory, &c.

℣. Deal not with us, O Lord, according to our sins.

℞. Nor reward us according to our iniquities.

**OREMUS.**

Deus, qui culpa offenderis, pœnitentia placaris, preces populi tui supplicantis propitius respice, et flagella tuæ iracundiæ, quæ pro peccatis nostris mereamur averte. Per Christum Dominum nostrum. Amen.

**LET US PRAY.**

O God, who by sin art offended, and by penance pacified; mercifully regard the prayers of thy people who make supplications to thee; and turn away the scourges of thy anger, which we deserve for our sins. Through Christ our Lord. Amen.

### Prayer in any Necessity.

Ne despicias, omnipotens Deus, populum tuum in afflictione clamantem, sed propter gloriam Nominis tui tribulatis succurre placatus. Per Dominum &c.

Turn not away, O Lord, from thy people who cry out to thee in their affliction; but for the glory of thy Name, having compassion on us, assist us in our necessities. Through &c.

## The Manner of Serving at Mass.

The Clerk, kneeling at the left hand of the Priest, shall answer him as follows—

Pr. INTROIBO ad altare Dei.

Cl. Ad Deum, qui lætificat juventutem meam.

Pr. Judica me, Deus, et discerne causam meam de gente non sancta: ab homine iniquo et doloso erue me.

Cl. Quia tu es, Deus, fortitudo mea; quare me repulisti, et quare tristis incedo dum affligit me inimicus?

Pr. Emitte lucem tuam et veritatem tuam: ipsa me deduxerunt, et adduxerunt in montem sanctum tuum et in tabernacula tua.

Cl. Et introibo ad altare Dei: ad Deum qui lætificat juventutem meam.

Pr. Confitebor tibi in cithara, Deus, Deus meus: quare tristis es anima mea, et quare conturbas me.

Cl. Spera in Deo, quoniam adhuc confitebor illi; salutare vultus mei, et Deus meus.

Pr. Gloria Patri, et Filio, et Spiritui Sancto.

Cl. Sicut erat in principio, et nunc, et semper, et in sæcula sæculorum. Amen.

Pr. Introibo ad altare Dei.

Cl. Ad Deum, qui lætificat juventutem meam.

Pr. Adjutorium nostrum in nomine Domini.

Cl. Qui fecit cœlum et terram.

Pr. Confiteor Deo, &c.

Cl. Misereatur tui omnipotens Deus, et dimissis peccatis tuis, perducat te ad vitam æternam.

Pr. Amen.

Cl. Confiteor Deo omnipotenti, beatæ Mariæ semper Virgini, beato Michaeli Archangelo, beato Joanni Baptistæ, sanctis Apostolis Petro et Paulo, omnibus Sanctis, et tibi, pater, quia peccavi nimis cogitatione, verbo et opere [*Here he strikes his breast thrice,*] mea culpa, mea culpa, mea maxima culpa. Ideo precor beatam Mariam semper Virginem, beatum Michaelem Archangelum, beatum Joannem Baptistam, sanctos Apostolos Petrum et Paulum, omnes Sanctos, et te, pater, orare pro me ad Dominum Deum nostrum.

# THE MANNER OF SERVING AT MASS. 137

Pr. Misereatur vestri, &c.
Cl. Amen.
Pr. Indulgentiam, absolutionem, &c.
Cl. Amen.

When a Bishop says Mass, he here takes the Maniple, which the Clerk must be ready to give him.

Pr. Deus, tu conversus, vivificabis nos.
Cl. Et plebs tua lætabitur in te.
Pr. Ostende nobis, Domine, misericordiam tuam.
Cl. Et salutare tuum da nobis.
Pr. Domine, exaudi orationem meam.
Cl. Et clamor meus ad te veniat.
Pr. Dominus vobiscum.
Cl. Et cum spiritu tuo.

Pr. Kyrie eleison. Cl. Kyrie eleison.
Pr. Kyrie eleison. Cl. Christe eleison.
Pr. Christe eleison. Cl. Christe eleison.
Pr. Kyrie eleison. Cl. Kyrie eleison.
Pr. Kyrie eleison.
Pr. Dominus vobiscum, [*a Bishop says* Pax vobis,] *or* Flectamus genua.
Cl. Et cum spiritu tuo, *or* Levate.
Pr. Per omnia sæcula sæculorum.
Cl. Amen.

At the end of the Epistle, say—

Deo gratias.

The Priest's Communion being ended, be ready to give him first wine, and then wine and water. But if there be Communicants, first provide them with a cloth, and say the *Confiteor*. Then remove the book to the left hand of the Altar, take away the cloth from the Communicants, and return to your former place. A Bishop here washes his hands a second time, as at the Offertory.

Pr. Dominus vobiscum.
Cl. Et cum spiritu tuo.
Pr. Ite, Missa est, *or* Benedicamus Domino.
Cl. Deo gratias.

### In Masses for the Dead.

Pr. Requiescant in pace.
Cl. Amen.

Remove the book, if it be left open; kneel and receive the Priest's blessing.

### At a Bishop's Mass.

B. Sit nomen Domini benedictum.
Cl. Ex hoc nunc et usque in sæculum.
B. Adjutorium nostrum in nomine Domini.
Cl. Qui fecit cœlum et terram.
Pr. Pater, et Filius, et Spiritus Sanctus.
Cl. Amen.

At the beginning of the last Gospel.

Pr. Dominus vobiscum.
Cl. Et cum spiritu tuo.
Pr. Initium, *or* Sequentia Sancti Evangelii, &c.
Cl. Gloria tibi, Domine.

At the end say,

Deo gratias.

Put out the candles, and lay all up carefully.

## On the Performance of the Ordinary Actions of the Day.

THE ordinary actions of the day become most valuable if offered to God, and performed for his greater honour and glory. A single action performed without a good intention is no small loss, for the least degree of grace that may be gained by it is of more value than all the treasures of this world. It is a pious and very useful practice to renew this intention of offering up all your actions to God frequently during the day, by some short prayer at the commencement of the more important duties; for the first oblation which is made in the morning is easily forgotten.

the Father, Glory be to the Son, Glory be to the Holy Ghost.

N.B. For reciting every morning, noon and night, thrice the "Gloria Patri" (Glory be to the Father, &c.), in thanksgiving to the Holy Trinity for the graces and privileges bestowed on the Blessed Virgin in her glorious Assumption into Heaven.—(I. 100 days Indulgence for each recital.—II. Plenary Indulgence once a month, on usual conditions. A.)

---

### TO GOD THE FATHER.

(I. 100 days Indulgence once a day.—II. Plenary Indulgence once a year, on usual conditions.—III. Plenary Indulgence, for frequent recital during life, to all who accept death with resignation. A.)

MAY the most just, most high, most adorable will of God be in all things done, and praised, and for ever magnified.

---

(An Indulgence of 100 days each time. A.)

ETERNAL Father! I offer Thee the Precious Blood of Jesus, in satisfaction for my sins, and for the wants of Holy Church.

---

### TO GOD THE SON.

(An Indulgence of 100 days each time.)

My Jesus, mercy!

---

(An Indulgence of 50 days each time. A.)

MY sweetest Jesus, be not thou my Judge, but my Saviour.

(I. 100 days Indulgence once a day.—II. 100 days Indulgence if said at Exposition, Benediction, and the Elevation of both species in the Mass.—III. Plenary Indulgence once a month, on usual conditions, for daily recital. A.)

O Sacrament most holy! O Sacrament divine!
All praise and all thanksgiving be every moment Thine.

---

(I. 100 days Indulgence once a day, if said before a picture of the Sacred Heart.—II. Plenary Indulgence once a month on usual conditions. A.)

My loving Jesus, I (N.N.) give thee my heart; and I consecrate myself wholly to thee out of the grateful love I bear thee, and as a reparation for all my unfaithfulness to grace; and with thine aid I purpose never to sin again.

---

(An Indulgence of 100 days each time.)

May the Sacred Heart of Jesus be everywhere loved.

---

## THE HOLY NAMES.

(I. 25 days Indulgence each time.—II. Plenary Indulgence at the hour of death, if said frequently during life. A.)

Jesus, Mary.

(I. 300 days Indulgence each time for the recital of the following.—II. 100 days for each. A.)

Jesus, Mary, Joseph, I give you my heart and my soul.

Jesus, Mary, Joseph, assist me in my last agony.

Jesus, Mary, Joseph, let my soul send forth her last sigh in peace, with you to aid me.

### TO THE BLESSED VIRGIN.

(I. 300 days Indulgence each time.—II. Plenary Indulgence once a month, on usual conditions, for daily recital. A.)

Sweet Heart of Mary, be my salvation.

(An Indulgence of 100 days for either of the following Ejaculations. A.)

Blessed be the Holy and Immaculate Conception of the Blessed Virgin Mary.

In thy Conception, O Virgin Mary, thou wast Immaculate. Pray for us to the Eternal Father, whose only-begotten Son Jesus thou didst bear, conceived in thy womb by the Holy Ghost.

(An Indulgence of 40 days for the following, if said in time of temptation. A.)

My Queen and my Mother, remember that I belong to thee, preserve and defend me as thy property and possession.

### AN HOURLY EJACULATORY PRAYER.

Jesus, most charitable! Jesus, meek and humble of heart! forgive us our sins; give thy peace to our souls; remember us in thy kingdom. Mary and Joseph, pray for us this hour, and at the hour of our death. Amen.

*As a last Prayer before sleep, add:*

Pray for us this hour and every hour of this night, and at the hour of our death. Amen.

*As a first Prayer in the morning, add:*

Pray for us this hour and every hour of this day, and at the hour of our death. Amen.

### Grace before Meals.

℣. Benedic, Domine, nos et hæc tua dona quæ de tua largitate sumus sumpturi; per Christum Dominum nostrum. ℞. Amen.

℣. Bless us, O Lord, and these thy gifts, which of thy bounty we are about to receive: Through Christ our Lord. ℞. Amen.

### Grace after Meals.

Agimus tibi gratias, omnipotens Deus, pro universis beneficiis tuis; qui vivis et regnas in sæcula sæculorum. Amen.

We give thee thanks, Almighty God, for all thy benefits; who livest and reignest, world without end. Amen.

Retribuere dignare, Domine, omnibus nobis bona facientibus propter nomen tuum, vitam æternam. Amen.

Fidelium animæ, &c.

Vouchsafe, O Lord, to render to all who do us good for thy name's sake, life everlasting. Amen.

May the souls of the faithful, &c.

## Consecration of Study to Mary Immaculate.

Sub patrocinio tuo, Mater dilectissima, et invocato Immaculatæ Conceptionis tuæ mysterio, studia mea laboresque litterarios prosequi volo: quibus me protestor hunc maxime ob finem incumbere, ut melius Divino Honori tuoque cultui propogando lnserviam. Oro te igitur, Mater amantissima, Sedes Sapientiæ, ut sicut hactenus fecisti ita et in posterum laboribus meis benigne faveas: ego vero, quod justum est, pie libenterque promitto, quicquid boni mihi inde successerit, id me tibi totum acceptum relaturum. Amen.

Under thy protection, dearest Mother, and under the invocation of thy Immaculate Conception, do I wish to pursue my studies: and I declare that I study chiefly from this motive, that I may be the better able to assist in spreading God's Glory and thy worship. I beseech thee, therefore, most loving Mother, Seat of Wisdom, that as thou hast hitherto done, so thou wilt continue to assist my progress; and whatever good success I may obtain, I promise on my part, as is but just, to attribute it all to thee. Amen.

## Short Visits to the Blessed Sacrament for Each Day in the Week.

### For Sunday.

**JESUS IN THE BLESSED SACRAMENT: OUR REFUGE.**

Thou remainest, O Jesus! enclosed within our tabernacles, to hear the prayers of those who present themselves before thee: vouchsafe then to hear the prayer offered up to thee by a most ungrateful sinner. Prostrate at thy feet, I ask pardon for all my sins. O my God and my Lord, why have I so basely insulted thee? I desire to love thee for the future, and in all things to do thy most holy will. As I cannot do this unless assisted by thy grace, be pleased to supply for my weakness, and enable me to love thee for the future as much as I have hitherto offended thee. O my Jesus, my God, and my all! I love thee above all things, even more than myself.

SPIRITUAL COMMUNION.—Adorable Jesus, I firmly believe that thou art really present in the Most Blessed Sacrament. I love thee above all things, and desire with all the fervour of my soul to receive thee. But since I cannot now receive thee sacramentally, come at least spiritually into my soul. I unite myself to thee, as if thou wert truly within me. O never suffer me to go away from thee.

(Here also recite the "Anima Christi." Page 52.)

EJACULATORY PRAYER.—"O my Jesus! grant that I may love thee, and for no other reward than that I may love thee more and more." (St. Ignatius.)

### PRAYER TO MARY IMMACULATE.

I BELIEVE in and confess thy Immaculate Conception, O most holy Virgin! By thy virginal purity, by this thy Immaculate Conception, and by thy glorious title of Mother of God, obtain for me of thy dear Son, humility, charity, obedience, a great purity of heart, of body, and of soul, perseverance in good, the gift of prayer, a good life, and a happy death. Amen.

O Mary, conceived without sin, pray for us who have recourse to thee.

---

### For Monday.

**JESUS IN THE BLESSED SACRAMENT: OUR WAY AND OUR LIFE.**

My loving Jesus! thou knowest well how to gain the hearts of men by thy engaging love. Draw then my heart closely to thine, for I desire ardently to love thee, and to live the servant of thy love. Henceforward I place all my hopes, my interests, and my affections in thy loving heart. Be pleased to accept and to dispose of me and mine as thou seest best; I will never more complain of the dispositions of thy Providence; for I know that all thou orderest in my regard will be in thy mercy, and for my greater good. Thy holy will is sufficient for me, and I desire nothing else, either in time or eternity.

SPIRITUAL COMMUNION. (Page 150.)

EJACULATORY PRAYER.—" My Beloved to me, and I to him." (Cant. ii. 16.)

Prayer to Mary Immaculate. (Page 150.)

---

## For Tuesday.

### JESUS IN THE BLESSED EUCHARIST: MODEL OF PATIENCE.

O MY Jesus! thy charity for men has been such that thou wouldst not leave them, but must dwell within the tabernacle patiently waiting for them till they should come to visit thee: why have I lost so many years by spending them without loving thee? O infinite patience of my God! I thank thee for having borne with me during all this time that I have been ungrateful to thee. Never again will I forsake thee, but I will consecrate the remainder of my life to thy service. Thou hast been merciful to me when I went away from thee; thou canst not then refuse to receive me with loving mercy, when I return to thee. O my God, I love thee with all my heart, and my earnest wish is to persevere in thy love and thy service.

SPIRITUAL COMMUNION. (Page 150.)

EJACULATORY PRAYER.—"Indeed the Lord is in this place, and I knew it not." (Gen. xxviii. 16.)

Prayer to Mary Immaculate. (Page 150.)

### For Wednesday.

JESUS IN THE BLESSED EUCHARIST:
MODEL OF OBEDIENCE.

O MOST amiable Jesus! I would gladly give to thee, were it possible for me to do so, as much honour and glory as thou, by thy obedience to man in this Sacrament, givest to thy Eternal Father. Enlighten, O Jesus, all those hearts which know thee not, that they may see and acknowledge the truth of thy divine presence. Take possession of all that is mine, that in all things I may be subject to thee, as thou art to thy Father. Impart to me some portion of thy humility and obedience; and let me live for no other end than to love and to serve thee here, that thus I may reign with thee eternally.

SPIRITUAL COMMUNION. (Page 150.)

EJACULATORY PRAYER.—" O Jesus, thou lovest and art not loved, would that thou wert loved."

Prayer to Mary Immaculate. (Page 150.)

---

### For Thursday.

#### JESUS IN THE BLESSED SACRAMENT: THE LOVER OF US.

O JESUS, God of love! thou hast told us that "thy delight is to be with the children of men," (Prov. viii. 31,) and thou givest to us a proof of this thy love by abiding upon our altars, even though thou art there forgotten and despised; O fill my heart with an ardent love of thee, that I may seek no other comfort but in thy company! The time has been when I felt no satisfaction in thy presence, because I loved thee not; but if thou wilt be pleased to enkindle in my cold breast the flame of divine love, then I shall pass whole days before thy altar without being weary of thy company. Do thou, O Jesus, be my consolation and my love through life, that so, at the hour of my death when thou comest to me to be my Viaticum, thou mayst conduct my soul with thee to Heaven.

SPIRITUAL COMMUNION. (Page 150.)

EJACULATORY PRAYER.—"O my Jesus, by how much the more thou dost humble thyself for me, by so much the dearer art thou to me."

Prayer to Mary Immaculate. (Page 150.)

## For Friday.

### JESUS IN THE BLESSED SACRAMENT: THE GOOD SHEPHERD.

O JESUS, tender Shepherd of souls! thou wast not content in thy infinite love, once to sacrifice thyself upon the cross, but must remain upon our altars, that thou mayst always be ready to knock at the door of our hearts, and seek an entrance there. Why do I profit so little by thy watchful care? Why is not my heart overjoyed, like that of the Spouse in the Canticles, that I may say with her "I sat down under his shadow, whom I desired." (Cant. ii. 3.) O my Jesus, when I see myself so naked and destitute of virtues, I am overwhelmed with shame and confusion, and tremble lest my presence should excite thy indignation. What then shall I do? must I retire from thee? No, dear Lord and loving Shepherd of my soul, I will come before thee, poor as I am, mindful of thy consoling invitation: "Come to me, all ye who labour and are burdened, and I will refresh you." (Matt. xi. 28.)

SPIRITUAL COMMUNION. (Page 150.)

EJACULATORY PRAYER.—"Give me thy love and thy grace, for this is enough for me." (St. Ignatius.)

Prayer to Mary Immaculate. (Page 150.)

## For Saturday.

JESUS IN THE BLESSED SACRAMENT: THE FOOD OF OUR SOULS.

O JESUS, our nourishment and support through life! thou hast made to us magnificent promises, if we will but receive thee: "He that eateth my flesh and drinketh my blood, abideth in me and I in him." (John vi. 57.) Where is there a more thoughtless or more unfaithful creature than I am? Thou knowest my great weakness, and how often I have yielded to my enemies; how often they have taken possession of my soul, and robbed me of my innocence. Strengthen me, that I may no more be so unfortunate as to lose thy grace and friendship. My present wish is never more to be separated from thee. O never suffer me to be so ungrateful!

SPIRITUAL COMMUNION. (Page 150.)

EJACULATORY PRAYER.—" I have found him whom my soul loveth, I have held him, and will not let him go." (Cant. iii. 4.)

Prayer to Mary Immaculate. (Page 150.)

## The Creed of St. Athanasius.

WHOSOEVER will be saved, before all things it is necessary that he hold the Catholic faith.

Which faith, except every one do keep entire and inviolate, without doubt he shall perish everlastingly.

Now the Catholic faith is this; that we worship one God in Trinity, and Trinity in Unity.

Neither confounding the Persons, nor dividing the substance.

For one is the Person of the Father, another of the Son, another of the Holy Ghost.

But the Godhead of the Father, and of the Son, and of the Holy Ghost, is all one; the glory equal, the majesty co-eternal.

Such as the Father is, such is the Son, and such is the Holy Ghost.

The Father is uncreated, the Son is uncreated, the Holy Ghost is uncreated.

The Father is incomprehensible, the Son is incomprehensible, the Holy Ghost is incomprehensible.

The Father is eternal, the Son is eternal, the Holy Ghost is eternal.

And yet they are not three eternals, but one Eternal.

As also they are not three uncreated, nor three Incomprehensibles; but one Uncreated, and one Incomprehensible.

In like manner the Father is almighty, the Son is almighty, and the Holy Ghost is almighty.

And yet they are not three Almighties, but one Almighty.

So the Father is God, the Son is God, and the Holy Ghost is God.

And yet they are not three Gods, but one God.

So likewise the Father is Lord, the Son is Lord, and the Holy Ghost is Lord.

And yet they are not three Lords, but one Lord.

For as we are compelled by the Christian truth to acknowledge every Person by himself to be God and Lord.

So we are forbidden by the Catholic religion to say there are three Gods or three Lords.

The Father is made of none, neither created, nor begotten.

The Son is from the Father alone, not made, nor created, but begotten.

The Holy Ghost is from the Father and the Son, not made, nor created, nor begotten, but proceeding.

So there is one Father, not three Fathers; one Son, not three Sons; one Holy Ghost, not three Holy Ghosts.

And in this Trinity, there is nothing before or after, nothing greater or less; but all the three Persons are co-eternal and co-equal.

So that in all things, as is aforesaid, the Unity is to be worshipped in Trinity and the Trinity in Unity.

He, therefore, that would be saved, must thus think of the Trinity.

Furthermore, it is necessary to everlasting salvation, that he also believe rightly the Incarnation of our Lord Jesus Christ.

Now this is the right faith, that we believe and confess that our Lord Jesus Christ, the Son of God, is both God and man.

He is God of the substance of his Father, begotten before the world; and he is man of the substance of his Mother, born in the world:

Perfect God and perfect man; subsisting of rational soul and human flesh.

Equal to the Father according to his Godhead; and less than the Father according to his manhood.

Who, although he be both God and man, yet he is not two, but one Christ.

One, not by the conversion of the Godhead into flesh, but by the taking of the manhood unto God.

One altogether, not by confusion of substance, but by unity of Person.

For as the rational soul and the flesh is one man, so God and man is one Christ.

Who suffered for our salvation, descended into hell, and rose again the third day from the dead.

He ascended into heaven; he sitteth at the right hand of God the Father Almighty; thence he shall come to judge the living and the dead.

At whose coming all men shall rise again with their bodies, and shall give an account of their own works.

And they that have done good shall go into life everlasting; and they that have done evil, into everlasting fire.

This is the Catholic faith, which except a man believe faithfully and steadfastly, he cannot be saved.

to overcome nature, to correspond with thy grace, to keep thy commandments, and to work out my salvation.

Discover to me, O my God, the nothingness of this world, the greatness of heaven, the shortness of time, and the length of eternity.

Grant that I may prepare for death, that I may fear thy judgments, that I may escape hell, and in the end obtain heaven: Through Jesus Christ. Amen.

---

## Hymn to Jesus, our Saviour.

| | |
|---|---|
| Jesu dulcis memoria, | Jesus, the only thought of thee |
| Dans vera cordi gaudia; | With sweetness fills my breast; |
| Sed super mel et omnia, | But sweeter far it is to see, |
| Ejus dulcis præsentia. | And on thy beauty feast. |
| | |
| Nil canitur suavius, | No sound, nor harmony so gay, |
| Nil auditur jucundius, | Can art or music frame; |
| Nil cogitatur dulcius, | No thoughts can reach, nor words can say, |
| Quam Jesus Dei Filius. | The sweets of thy blest name |

Jesu, spes pœnitentibus,
Quam pius es petentibus!
Quam bonus te quærentibus!
Sed quid invenientibus?

Jesus, our hope, when we repent,
Sweet source of all our grace!
Sole comfort in our banishment!
Oh, what when face to face?

Jesu, dulcedo cordium,
Fons vivus, lumen mentium,
Excedens omne gaudium,
Et omne desiderium!

Jesus! that name inspires my mind
With springs of life and light,
More than I ask in thee I find,
And languish with delight.

Nec lingua valet dicere,
Nec litera exprimere:
Expertus potest credere,
Quid sit Jesum diligere.

No art nor eloquence of man
Can tell the joys of love;
Only the Saints can understand
What they in Jesus prove.

Cum Maria diluculo
Jesum quæram in tumulo,
Clamore cordis querulo,
Mente quæram non oculo.

Before the morning light I'll come
With Magdalen to find,
In sighs and tears, my Jesus' tomb,
And there refresh my mind.

# Litany of the Most Holy Name of Jesus.

AN Indulgence of 300 days was granted by a Rescript, dated April 28, 1864, to the Faithful in England for the devout recitation of the "Litany of the Most Holy Name," by our Most Holy Father Pope Pius IX., who at the same time prohibited any form but that of which the following is a translation, authorized by the Bishops:—

| | |
|---|---|
| **Kyrie** eleison. | Lord have mercy on us. |
| *Christe eleison,* | *Christ have mercy on us.* |
| Kyrie eleison. | Lord have mercy on us. |
| Jesu, audi nos. | Jesus, hear us. |
| *Jesu, exaudi nos.* | *Jesus, graciously hear us.* |
| Pater de cœlis Deus, | God, the Father of heaven, |
| Fili, Redemptor mundi Deus, | God the Son, Redeemer of the world, |
| Spiritus Sancte Deus, | God, the Holy Ghost, |
| Sancta Trinitas, unus Deus, | Holy Trinity, one God, |
| Jesu, Fili Dei vivi. | Jesus, Son of the living God, |
| Jesu, splendor Patris, | Jesus, splendour of the Father, |
| Jesu, candor lucis æternæ, | Jesus, brightness of eternal light, |
| Jesu, Rex gloriæ, | Jesus, King of Glory, |
| Jesu, Sol justitiæ, | Jesus, Sun of justice, |
| Jesu, Fili Mariæ Virginis, | Jesus, Son of the Virgin Mary, |
| Jesu amabilis, | Jesus, most amiable, |
| Jesu admirabilis, | Jesus, most admirable, |
| Jesu, Deus fortis, | Jesus, mighty God, |

*Miserere nobis.* / *Have mercy on us.*

## LITANY OF JESUS. 169

|  |  |
|---|---|
| Jesu, Pater futuri sæculi, | Jesus, Father of the world to come, |
| Jesu, magni consilii Angele, | Jesus, Angel of great counsel, |
| Jesu, potentissime, | Jesus, most powerful, |
| Jesu, patientissime, | Jesus, most patient, |
| Jesu, obedientissime, | Jesus, most obedient, |
| Jesu, mitis et humilis corde, | Jesus, meek and humble of heart, |
| Jesu, amator castitatis, | Jesus, lover of chastity, |
| Jesu, amator noster, | Jesus, lover of us, |
| Jesu, Deus pacis, | Jesus, God of peace, |
| Jesu, auctor vitæ, | Jesus, author of life, |
| Jesu, exemplar virtutum, | Jesus, example of virtues, |
| Jesu, zelator animarum, | Jesus, zealous lover of souls, |
| Jesu, Deus noster, | Jesus, our God, |
| Jesu, refugium nostrum, | Jesus, our refuge, |
| Jesu, Pater pauperum, | Jesus, Father of the poor, |
| Jesu, thesaurus fidelium, | Jesus, treasure of the faithful, |
| Jesu, bone Pastor, | Jesus, Good Shepherd, |
| Jesu, lux vera, | Jesus, true light, |
| Jesu, sapientia æterna, | Jesus, eternal wisdom, |
| Jesu, bonitas infinita, | Jesus, infinite goodness, |
| Jesu, via et vita nostra, | Jesus, our way and our life, |
| Jesu, gaudium Angelorum, | Jesus, joy of Angels, |
| Jesu, Rex Patriarcharum, | Jesus, King of Patriarchs, |
| Jesu, Magister Apostolorum, | Jesus, Master of Apostles, |

*Miserere nobis.* / *Have mercy on us.*

I

Jesu, Doctor Evangelistarum,
Jesu, fortitudo Martyrum,
Jesu, lumen Confessorum,
Jesu, puritas Virginum,
Jesu, corona Sanctorum omnium,
Propitius esto,
*Parce nobis, Jesu.*
Propitius esto,
*Exaudi nos, Jesu.*

Ab omni malo,
Ab omni peccato,
Ab ira tua,
Ab insidiis diaboli,

A spiritu fornicationis,
A morte perpetua,

A neglectu inspirationum tuarum,
Per mysterium sanctæ Incarnationis tuæ,
Per nativitatem tuam,
Per infantiam tuam,
Per divinissimam vitam tuam,
Per labores tuos,
Per agoniam et passionem tuam,

*Miserere nobis.*    *Libera nos, Jesu.*

Jesus, Teacher of Evangelists,
Jesus, strength of Martyrs,
Jesus, light of Confessors,
Jesus, purity of Virgins,
Jesus, crown of all Saints,
Be merciful unto us,
*Spare us, O Jesus.*
Be merciful unto us,
*Graciously hear us, O Jesus.*

From all evil,
From all sin,
From thy wrath,
From the snares of the devil,
From the spirit of uncleanness,
From everlasting death,
From the neglect of thy inspirations,
Through the mystery of thy holy Incarnation,
Through thy nativity,
Through thine infancy,
Through thy most divine life,
Through thy labours,
Through thine agony and passion,

*Have mercy on us.*    *Jesus, deliver us.*

Per crucem et dere- | Through thy Cross
lictionem tuam, | and dereliction,
Per languores tuos, | Through thy faint-
 | ness and weariness,
Per mortem et sepul- | Through thy death
turam tuam, | and burial,
Per resurrectionem | Through thy resur-
tuam, | rection,
Per ascensionem tu- | Through thine ascen-
am, | sion,
Per gaudia tua, | Through thy joys,
Per gloriam tuam, | Through thy glory,

*Libera nos, Jesu.* / *Jesus, deliver us.*

Agnus Dei, qui tollis peccata mundi,

Lamb of God, who takest away the sins of the world,

*Parce nobis, Jesu.*

*Spare us, O Jesus.*

Agnus Dei, qui tollis peccata mundi,

Lamb of God, who takest away the sins of the world,

*Exaudi nos, Jesu.*

*Graciously hear us, O Jesus.*

Agnus Dei, qui tollis peccata mundi,

Lamb of God, who takest away the sins of the world,

*Miserere nobis, Jesu.*

*Have mercy on us, O Jesus.*

Jesu, audi nos. Jesus, hear us.
Jesu, exaudi nos. Jesus, graciously hear us.

OREMUS. | LET US PRAY.

DOMINE, Jesu Christe, qui dixisti: Petite, et accipietis; quærite, et invenietis; pulsate,

O LORD Jesus Christ, who hast said, "Ask, and ye shall receive; seek, and ye shall find;

I 3

et aperietur vobis: quæsumus, da nobis petentibus divinissimi tui amoris affectum, ut te toto corde, ore, et opere diligamus, et a tua nunquam laude cessemus.

Sancti Nominis tui, Domine, timorem pariter et amorem fac nos habere perpetuum, quia nunquam tua gubernatione destituis quos in soliditate tuæ dilectionis instituis. Per Christum Dominum nostrum. Amen.

knock, and it shall be opened unto you," give we beseech thee, to us who ask the grace of thy most divine love, that with all our heart, words, and works, we may love thee, and never cease to praise thee.

Make us, O Lord, to have a perpetual fear and love of thy holy Name, for thou never failest to govern those whom thou dost solidly establish in thy love. Through Christ our Lord. Amen.

## Pontifical Indulgences.

A PLENARY Indulgence on the Feasts of Christmas, Epiphany, Ascension, Pentecost, Trinity Sunday, Corpus Christi; on the Feasts of the Purification, Annunciation, Assumption, and Nativity of the Blessed Virgin Mary; on the Nativity of St. John the Baptist; on the Feasts of each of the Apostles, of St. Joseph, and of All Saints; and at the Hour of Death.

An Indulgence of seven years and two hundred and eighty days, on all the other Feasts of our Lord and of the Blessed Virgin Mary.

An Indulgence of five years and two hundred days, on all Sundays, or any other Feast in the year.

An Indulgence of one hundred days on any other day in the year.

### CONDITIONS.

To obtain the Indulgences above mentioned, it is necessary,—

1°. To have one of the Blessed Medals, Crosses or Beads, which cannot be sold or lent with the intention of communicating Indulgences to another person, without losing its privilege.

2°. To recite once a week the Beads or a third part of the Rosary, or the Office of the B. V. M., or the Office of the Dead, or the Seven Penitential Psalms; or the Gradual Psalms, or to teach the Catechism, or to visit the hospital or prison, or to assist the poor, or to say or hear Mass.

3°. To receive worthily the Sacraments of Penance and the Holy Eucharist.

4°. To pray devoutly to God for the extirpation of heresy and schism, for the propagation of the Catholic Faith, for peace and concord among Christian Princes, and for the other wants of the Roman Catholic Church.

N.B. To obtain the Indulgence at the hour of death, it will be sufficient to be truly peni-

tent, to be prepared to meet death with resignation to God's will, and to pray to Jesus Christ.

An Indulgence of two hundred days for visiting those who are detained in hospitals or prisons, and assisting them in any way, or for giving instructions in the Church, or teaching the Christian Doctrine.

An Indulgence of one hundred days for the recital of the Beads, or the Rosary, or the Office of the B. V. M., or the Office of the Dead, or Vespers, or the Seven Penitential Psalms with the Litanies and Prayers after them, (provided these good works be performed at least once a week). Also, on every Friday, for saying thrice Our Father, &c., and thrice Hail Mary, &c., accompanied with a devout meditation on our Saviour's passion. Likewise, for the evening Examination of Conscience and steadfast purpose of amendment, followed by an Our Father and Hail Mary, repeated three times in honour of the Blessed Trinity, and five times in honour of the Five Wounds of our Lord.

An Indulgence of fifty days for making a devout preparation before Communion, or the recital of the Divine Office, or the Office of the B. V. Mary.

These Indulgences may be applied to the Souls in Purgatory.

# The Rosary of the Most Blessed Virgin Mary.

ST. DOMINIC, the founder of the Order of Friar-Preachers, having recourse to the Blessed Virgin, in order to stem the flood of the Albigensian heresy, which was spreading itself like a plague over many countries but especially over France, instituted, by special revelation from her, in the year 1206, and afterwards effectually promulgated the devotion of the holy Rosary, which has produced the most marvellous results in the Christian world.

The devotion called the Rosary consists of fifteen Pater Nosters and Glorias, and one hundred and fifty Ave Marias, divided into three parts, each containing five "Decades," a Decade consisting of one Pater, ten Aves, and a Gloria. To each of these Decades is assigned one of the principal mysteries of the life of our Saviour, or of his blessed Mother, as matter for meditation.

INDULGENCES.—See Pontifical Indulgences (Page 172.)

Besides these usual Indulgences, there are many others attached to Rosaries, blessed by Dominican Fathers, and to those called Rosaries of St. Bridget.

## INDULGENCES ATTACHED TO ROSARIES BLESSED BY DOMINICAN FATHERS; OR BY PRIESTS WHO MAY HAVE THE PRIVILEGE.

1°. An Indulgence of 100 days for every Pater Noster and every Ave Maria.

2°. A Plenary Indulgence to all who shall say the third part of it once every day for a year, on any one day in the year, after Confession and Communion.

The present Sovereign Pontiff, Pius IX., by a decree of the S. Congr. of Indulgences of May 12, 1851, confirmed these Indulgences, and granted, besides—

3°. An Indulgence of seven years and seven quarantines to every one who, with contrition, shall say a third part of the Rosary in company with others, either in public or private.

4°. A Plenary Indulgence, on the last Sunday in every month, to all who are in the habit of saying with others, at least three times a week, the said third part of the Rosary; and also if on that Sunday they shall, after Confession and Communion, visit a church or public oratory, and pray there, for a time, for his Holiness.

To gain these Indulgences it is requisite that the Rosaries should be blessed by religious of the Order of Friar-Preachers, and that, during the recital of the Rosary, meditation be made on the mysteries of the Birth, Passion, Death, Resurrection, &c., of our Lord Jesus Christ, according to the decree of the S. Congr. of Indulgences of August 12, 1726, approved by Pope Benedict XIII. Note, moreover, that our holy Father declared, in his Constitution *Pretiosus*, of May 16, 1727, Sec. 4, that simple people who cannot meditate may obtain the Indulgence by merely saying the Rosary devoutly.

## The Rosary called St. Bridget's.

THIS Chaplet is recited in honour of the sixty-three years which, it is said, the most holy Mary lived upon this earth; it is composed of six divisions, each division consisting of one Pater Noster, ten Ave Marias, and one Credo. After these, one Pater Noster more is said, and three more Ave Marias: thus in all there will be seven Pater Nosters, to mark the number of her Seven Dolours and Seven Joys; and the three Ave Marias are added to make up the full number of sixty-three years. Moreover, it will be seen in the following summary, that the same Indulgences may be gained by saying the fifteen Decades, or five Decades only, as mentioned in the preceding Rosary.

1°. An Indulgence of 100 days for each Pater, 100 days for each Ave, and 100 days for each Credo, to all the faithful who say the Rosary or Chaplet of St. Bridget.

2°. A Plenary Indulgence to all who shall say at least five Decades daily for a year, on any one day in the year, when, after Confession and Communion, they shall pray for the Holy Church.

3°. A Plenary Indulgence, on the Feast of St. Bridget, to all who say this Rosary of five

Decades at least once a week, and who on this day shall, after Confession and Communion, visit a church, and pray to God there, for the Holy Church.

4°. A Plenary Indulgence to all who, having confessed and communicated, or being at least contrite, shall have been accustomed to say this Rosary as in No. III., when, in "Articulo Mortis," recommending their soul to God, they say the holy name Jesus in their hearts, if unable to do so with their lips.

5°. A Plenary Indulgence, once a month, to all who say this Chaplet daily for a month, on any one day when, after Confession and Communion, they visit a church and pray as above.

6°. An Indulgence of 100 days to all who carry this Rosary, whenever they hear Mass, or assist at a sermon, or accompany the Most Holy Viaticum, or bring back any sinner into the way of salvation, or do any other good work in honour of our Lord Jesus Christ, the Blessed Virgin, or St. Bridget, provided they say also three Pater Nosters and three Ave Marias.

## The Living Rosary.

To enable all to join the more readily in the recitation of the Rosary, an Association has been instituted called the "Living Rosary," the members of which, by reciting daily one Decade, enjoy the privileges accorded as above. It is thus arranged: Fifteen persons associate together, and divide amongst them by lot the fifteen mysteries. Each recites Our Father and ten Hail Marys daily; and by this means the entire Rosary is gone through by the circle every day. The Association was confirmed by a brief of Gregory XVI., January, 1832.

## Indulgences of the Living Rosary.

### PLENARY.

1°. The first Festival after admission.

2°. The Feasts of Christmas, Epiphany, Circumcision, Easter, Ascension, Corpus Christi, Pentecost, Trinity Sunday, on the five greater Feasts of the B. V. Mary, SS. Peter and Paul, All Saints, and the third Sunday of the Month.

### PARTIAL.

1°. Seven years and seven quarantines on all Sundays and Feasts: during the octaves of Christmas, Easter, Corpus Christi, Pentecost, the Assumption B. V. M., her Nativity and Immaculate Conception.

2°. 100 days each time each member recites his Decade of the Rosary.

These Indulgences are applicable to the Souls in Purgatory.

## The Five Joyful Mysteries.

### I. THE ANNUNCIATION.

LET us contemplate, in this mystery, how the Angel Gabriel saluted our Blessed Lady with the title, " Full of grace," and declared unto her the Incarnation of our Lord and Saviour Jesus Christ.

Our Father, &c. once; Hail Mary, &c. ten times; Glory, &c. once.

#### THE PRAYER.

O HOLY Mary, Queen of Virgins, by the most high mystery of the Incarnation of thy beloved Son, our Lord Jesus Christ, by which our salvation was so happily begun; obtain for us, by thy intercession, light to know this great benefit which he hath bestowed upon us, in vouchsafing to become our brother, and making thee, his own most beloved Mother, our Mother also. Amen.

### II. THE VISITATION.

LET us contemplate, in this mystery, how the Blessed Virgin Mary, understanding from the Angel that her cousin, St.

Elizabeth, had conceived, went with haste into the mountains of Judea to visit her, and remained with her three months.

Our Father, &c. as before.

### THE PRAYER.

O HOLY Virgin, most spotless mirror of humility, by that exceeding charity which moved thee to visit thy holy cousin, St. Elizabeth, obtain for us, by thy intercession, that our hearts may be so visited by thy most holy Son, that, being free from all sin, we may praise him and give thanks for ever. Amen.

### III. THE NATIVITY.

LET us contemplate, in this mystery, how the Blessed Virgin Mary, when the time of her delivery was come, brought forth our Redeemer, Christ Jesus, at midnight, and laid him in a manger, because there was no room for him in the inns at Bethlehem.

Our Father, &c.

### THE PRAYER.

O MOST pure Mother of God, by thy virginal and most joyful delivery, by which thou gavest unto the world thy Son our Saviour, we beseech thee obtain for us, by thy intercession, grace to lead so pure and holy a life in this world, that we may worthily sing without ceasing, both by day and night, the mercies of thy Son, and his benefits to us by thee. Amen.

### IV. THE PRESENTATION.

LET us contemplate, in this mystery, how the most Blessed Virgin Mary, on the day of her Purification presented the child Jesus in the Temple, where holy Simeon, giving thanks to God with great devotion, received him into his arms.

Our Father, &c.

### THE PRAYER.

O HOLY Virgin, and admirable mistress and pattern of obedience, who didst present in the Temple, the Lord of the Temple, obtain for us of thy beloved Son, that, with holy Simeon and devout Anna, we may praise and glorify him for ever. Amen.

### V. THE FINDING OF THE CHILD JESUS IN THE TEMPLE.

LET us contemplate, in this mystery, how the Blessed Virgin Mary, having lost her beloved Son in Jerusalem, sought him during three days, and at length found him on the third day in the Temple, in the midst of the doctors, disputing with them, being then but twelve years old.

Our Father, &c.

### THE PRAYER.

MOST Blessed Virgin, more than martyr in thy sufferings, and yet the comfort of such as are afflicted, by that unspeakable joy wherewith thy soul was ravished in finding thy beloved Son in the Temple, in the midst of the doctors, disputing with them, obtain of him for us, so to seek him and to find him in the holy Catholic Church, that we may never be separated from him. Amen.

### THE "SALVE REGINA."

HAIL, holy Queen, Mother of mercy, our life, our sweetness, and our hope: to thee do we cry, poor banished sons of Eve; to thee do we send up our sighs, mourning and weeping in this valley of tears. Turn, then, most gracious Advocate, thine eyes of mercy towards us; and after this our exile, show to us the blessed fruit of thy womb, Jesus; O clement, O pious and sweet Virgin Mary!

℣. Pray for us, O holy Mother of God.

℟. That we may be made worthy of the promises of Christ.

LET US PRAY.

HEAR, O merciful God, the prayers of thy servants, that we, who meet together in the society of the most holy Rosary of the Blessed Virgin Mother of God, may, through her intercession, be delivered by thee from the dangers that continually hang over us. Amen.

O God, whose only begotten Son, by his life, death, and resurrection, hast purchased for us the rewards of eternal life; grant, we beseech thee, that meditating upon those mysteries in the most holy Rosary of the Blessed Virgin Mary, we may imitate what they contain, and obtain what they promise. Through the same Christ our Lord. Amen.

## The Five Sorrowful Mysteries.

**I. THE PRAYER AND SWEAT OF BLOOD OF OUR BLESSED SAVIOUR IN THE GARDEN.**

LET us contemplate, in this mystery, how our Lord Jesus Christ was so afflicted for us in the Garden of Gethsemani, that his body was bathed in a sweat of blood, which ran trickling down in drops to the ground.

Our Father, &c. once; Hail Mary, &c. ten times; Glory, &c. once.

**THE PRAYER.**

MOST Holy Virgin, more than martyr, by that ardent prayer which thy beloved Son poured forth unto his Father in the garden, vouchsafe to intercede for us, that our passions being reduced to the obedience of reason, we may always, and in all things, conform and subject ourselves to the will of God. Amen.

**II. THE SCOURGING OF JESUS AT THE PILLAR.**

LET us contemplate, in this mystery, how our Lord Jesus Christ was most cruelly scourged in Pilate's house; the number of stripes they gave him being above five thousand, as it was revealed to St. Bridget.

Our Father, &c.

### THE PRAYER.

HOLY Mary, Mother of God, since the body of thy beloved Son was for us extended on the cross, so may we be daily more and more devoted to his service, and our hearts wounded with compassion on account of his most bitter sufferings; and thou, O most blessed Virgin, vouchsafe to assist us in the work of our salvation, by thy powerful intercession. Amen.

Hail, holy Queen, &c. as before (p. 183.)

---

## The Five Glorious Mysteries.

### I. THE RESURRECTION.

LET us contemplate, in this mystery, how our Lord Jesus Christ, triumphing gloriously over death, rose again the third day, immortal and impassible.

Our Father, &c.

### THE PRAYER.

O GLORIOUS Virgin Mary, by that unspeakable joy thou receivedst in the Resurrection of thy only-beloved Son, we beseech thee, obtain of him for us, that our hearts may never go astray after the false joys of this world, but may be ever and wholly employed in pursuit of the only true and solid joys of heaven. Amen.

### II. THE ASCENSION.

LET us contemplate, in this mystery, how our Lord Jesus Christ, forty days after his resurrection, ascended into heaven, attended by Angels, in sight of his most holy Mother, and his Apostles and Disciples, to the great admiration of them all.

Our Father, &c.

### THE PRAYER.

O MOTHER of God, comfort of the afflicted, as thy beloved Son, when he ascended into heaven, lifted up his hands and blessed his Apostles, so vouchsafe, most holy Mother, to lift up thy pure hands to him for us, that we may enjoy the benefit of his blessing here on earth, and hereafter in heaven. Amen.

### III. THE DESCENT OF THE HOLY GHOST.

LET us contemplate, in this mystery, how our Lord Jesus Christ, being seated at the right hand of God, sent (as he had promised) the Holy Ghost upon his

## Act of Consecration to the Immaculate Heart of Mary.

O HOLY Mother of God, glorious Queen of heaven and earth, I choose thee this day, for my mother, my queen, and my advocate, at the throne of thy divine Son. Accept the offering which I here make of my heart; may it be irrevocable. It never can be out of danger whilst at my own disposal, never secure but in thy hands.

Ye Choirs of Angels, witnesses of this my oblation, bear me up in the day of judgment; and next to Jesus and Mary, be ye propitious to me should the enemy of my salvation have any claim upon me. Obtain for me at present, the gift of a true repentance, and those graces I may afterwards stand in need of, for the gaining of life everlasting. Amen.

## Little Office of the Immaculate Conception.

THE Latin version of this Office agrees in every respect with that approved of by the Congregation of the Sacred Office in Rome, 1838. At the end of this version the following words are added: *Sanctitas sua concessit tercentum dies Indulgentiæ, quotiescunque recitetur hoc officium, vivæ vocis oraculo.*

### At Matins.

EIA, mea labia, nunc annuntiate, Laudes et præconia Virginis Immaculatæ.

COME, my lips, and wide proclaim, The blessed Virgin's spotless fame.

℣. Domina, in adjutorium meum intende.
℟. Me de manu hostium potenter defende.

℣. O Lady, make speed to befriend me.
℟. From the hands of the enemy powerfully defend me.

℣. Gloria Patri, &c. Alleluia.

℣. Glory be to the Father, &c. Alleluia.

*From Septuagesima to Easter, instead of Alleluia, is said:*

Laus tibi, Domine, Rex æternæ gloriæ.

Praise be to thee, O Lord, King of eternal glory.

K

## HYMN.

Salve, mundi Domina,
Cœlorum Regina:
Salve, Virgo virginum,
Stella matutina.

Salve, plena gratiæ,
Clara luce divina:
Mundi in auxilium,
Domina, festina.

Ab æterno Dominus
Te præordinavit
Matrem Unigeniti
Verbi, quo creavit

Terram, pontum, æthera:
Te pulchram ornavit
Sibi Sponsam, quæ in
Adam non peccavit.

℣. Elegit eam Deus, et præelegit eam.
℟. In tabernaculo suo habitare fecit eam.
℣. Domina, protege orationem meam.
℟. Et clamor meus ad te veniat.

Hail, Queen of the heavens,
Hail, Mistress of earth:
Hail, Virgin most pure,
Of immaculate birth.

Clear star of the morning,
In beauty enshrin'd,
O Lady, make speed
To the help of mankind.

Thee God in the depth
Of eternity chose;
And form'd thee all fair
As his glorious Spouse;

And call'd thee his Word's
Own Mother to be,
By whom he created
The earth, sky, and sea.

℣. God elected her, and pre-elected her.
℟. He made her to dwell in his tabernacle.
℣. O Lady, recommend my prayer.
℟. And let my cry come unto thee.

## IMMACULATE CONCEPTION.

OREMUS.

SANCTA Maria, Regina cœlorum, Mater Domini nostri Jesu Christi, et mundi Domina, quæ nullum relinquis, et nullum despicis; respice me, Domina, clementer oculo tuæ pietatis, et impetra mihi apud tuum dilectum Filium cunctorum veniam peccatorum: ut qui nunc tuam sanctam et immaculatam Conceptionem devoto affectu recolo, æternæ in futurum beatitudinis bravium capiam, ipso, quem virgo peperisti, donante Domino nostro Jesu Christo, qui cum Patre et Sancto Spiritu vivit et regnat in Trinitate perfecta, Deus, in sæcula sæculorum. Amen.

℣. Domina, protege orationem meam.
℞. Et clamor meus ad te veniat.
℣. Benedicamus Domino.

LET US PRAY.

HOLY Mary, Queen of heaven, Mother of our Lord Jesus Christ, and Mistress of the world, who forsakest no one, and despisest none; look upon me, O Lady, with an eye of pity, and obtain for me, of thy beloved Son, the forgiveness of all my sins; that, as I now celebrate with devout affection thy holy and immaculate Conception, so, hereafter, I may receive the prize of eternal blessedness, by the grace of Him whom thou, in virginity, didst bring forth, Jesus Christ our Lord; who with the Father and the Holy Ghost, liveth and reigneth, in perfect Trinity, God, world without end. Amen.

℣. O Lady, recommend my prayer.
℞. And let my cry come unto thee.
℣. Let us bless the Lord.

℟. Deo gratias.

℣. Fidelium animæ per misericordiam Dei requiescant in pace.

℟. Amen.

℟. Thanks be to God.

℣. May the souls of the faithful, through the mercy of God, rest in peace.

℟. Amen.

## At Prime.

℣. Domina, in adjutorium meum intende.

℟. Me de manu hostium potenter defende.

℣. Gloria Patri, &c. Alleluia.

℣. O Lady, make speed to befriend me.

℟. From the hands of the enemy powerfully defend me.

℣. Glory be to the Father, &c. Alleluia.

### HYMN.

SALVE, Virgo sapiens,
Domus Deo dicata,
Columna septemplici
Mensaque exornata.

Ab omni contagio
Mundi præservata,
Ante sancta in utero
Parentis, quam nata.

HAIL, Virgin most wise,
Hail, Deity's shrine,
With seven fair pillars,
And table divine.

Preserv'd from the guilt
Which hath come on us all,
Exempt in the womb,
From the taint of the Fall.

Tu Mater viventium,
Et porta es Sanctorum:
Nova Stella Jacob,
Domina Angelorum.

O new Star of Jacob,
Of Angels the Queen:
O Gate of the Saints,
O mother of men.

Zabulo terribilis
Acies castrorum;
Portus et refugium
Sis Christianorum.

O terrible as
The embattled array;
Be thou of the faithful
The refuge and stay.

℣. Ipse creavit illam in Spiritu Sancto.

℣. The Lord himself created her in the Holy Ghost.

℟. Et exaltavit illam inter omnia opera sua.

℟. And poured her out among all his works.

℣. Domina, protege, &c. (*Pag. 195, cum Oratione et* ℣. *et* ℟. *ut supra.*)

℣. O Lady, recommend, &c. (*with the Prayer and Versicles, as at Page 195.*)

## At Terce.

℣. Domina, in adjutorium meum intende.
℟. Me de manu hostium potenter defende.

℣. O Lady, make speed to befriend me.
℟. From the hands of the enemy powerfully defend me.

℣. Gloria Patri, &c. Alleluia.

℣. Glory be to the Father, &c. Alleluia.

## HYMN.

Salve, Arca fœderis,
Thronus Salomonis,
Arcus pulcher ætheris,
Rubus visionis:

Hail, Solomon's Throne,
Pure Ark of the law,
Fair Rainbow and Bush,
Which the Patriarch saw.

Virga frondens germinis:
Vellus Gedeonis:
Porta clausa Numinis,
Favusque Samsonis.

Hail, Gedeon's Fleece;
Hail, blossoming Rod:
Samson's sweet Honey-comb,
Portal of God.

Decebat tam nobilem
Natum præcavere
Ab originali
Labe matris Evæ,

Well fitting it was,
That a Son so divine
Should preserve from all touch
Of original sin,

Almam, quam elegerat,
Genitricem vere,
Nulli prorsus sinens
Culpæ subjacere.

Nor suffer by smallest
Defect to be stain'd,
That Mother, whom he
For himself had ordain'd.

℣. Ego in altissimis habito.
℞. Et thronus meus in columna nubis.

℣. I dwell in the highest.
℞. And my throne is on the pillar of the clouds.

℣. Domina, protege, &c. (*Pag. 195, cum Oratione, &c. ut supra.*)

℣. O Lady, recommend, &c. (*with the Prayer, &c. as at Page 195.*)

## IMMACULATE CONCEPTION.

## At Sext.

℣. Domina, in adjutorium meum intende.
℟. Me de manu hostium potenter defende.

℣. Gloria Patri. Alleluia.

℣. O Lady, make speed to befriend me.
℟. From the hands of the enemy powerfully defend me.

℣. Glory be to the Father, &c. Alleluia.

### HYMN.

Salve, Virgo puerpera,
Templum Trinitatis,
Angelorum gaudium,
Cella puritatis:

Solamen mœrentium,
Hortus voluptatis,
Palma patientiæ,
Cedrus castitatis.

Terra es benedicta
Et sacerdotalis,
Sancta et immunis
Culpæ originalis.

Civitas Altissimi,
Porta orientalis:
In te est omnis gratia,
Virgo singularis.

Hail, virginal Mother,
Hail, purity's Cell,
Fair Shrine where the Trinity
Loveth to dwell:

Hail, Garden of pleasure,
Celestial balm,
Cedar of chastity,
Martyrdom's palm.

Thou land set apart
From uses profane,
And free from the curse
Which in Adam began.

Thou City of God,
Thou Gate of the east:
In thee is all grace,
O joy of the blest!

℣. Sicut lilium inter spinas.
℟. Sic amica mea inter filias Adæ.
℣. Domina, protege, &c. *(Pag. 195, cum Oratione, &c. ut supra.)*

℣. As the lily among the thorns.
℟. So is my beloved among the daughters of Adam.
℣. O Lady, recommend, &c. *(with the Prayer and Versicles, as at Page 195.)*

## At None.

℣. Domina, in adjutorium meum intende.
℟. Me de manu hostium potenter defende.

℣. Gloria Patri. Alleluia.

℣. O Lady, make speed to befriend me.
℟. From the hands of the enemy powerfully defend me.

℣. Glory be to the Father, &c. Alleluia.

### HYMN.

Salve, urbs refugii,
Turrisque munita
David, propugnaculis
Armisque insignita.

In Conceptione
Charitate ignita,
Draconis potestas
Est a te contrita.

Hail, City of refuge,
Hail, David's high tower,
With battlements crown'd,
And girded with power.

Fill'd at thy Conception
With love and with light,
The dragon by thee
Was shorn of his might.

# IMMACULATE CONCEPTION.

| | |
|---|---|
| O mulier fortis, Et invicta Judith ! Pulchra Abisag Virgo, Verum fovens David. | O Woman most valiant, O Judith thrice blest! As David was nurs'd In fair Abisag's breast, |
| Rachel curatorem Ægypti gestavit : Salvatorem mundi Maria portavit. | As the saviour of Egypt Upon Rachel's knee; So the world's great Redeemer Was cherish'd by thee. |

℣. Tota pulchra es, amica mea.
℟. Et macula originalis numquam fuit in te.

℣. Thou art all fair, my beloved.
℟. And the original stain was never in thee.

℣. Domina, protege, &c. (*Pag. 195, cum Oratione, &c. ut supra.*)

℣. O Lady, recommend, &c. (*with the Prayer, &c. as at Page 195.*)

## At Vespers.

℣. Domina, in adjutorium meum intende.
℟. Me de manu hostium potenter defende.

℣. O Lady, make speed to befriend me.
℟. From the hands of the enemy powerfully defend me.

℣. Gloria Patri. Alleluia.

℣. Glory be to the Father, &c. Alleluia.

## HYMN.

| | |
|---|---|
| Salve, horologium, | Hail, Dial of Achaz, |
| Quo retro gradiatur | On thee the true Sun |
| Sol in decem lineis; | Told backward the course |
| Verbum incarnatur. | Which from old he had run. |
| | |
| Homo ut ab inferis | And that man might be rais'd, |
| Ad summa attollatur, | Submitting to shame, |
| Immensus ab Angelis | A little more low |
| Paulo minoratur. | Than the Angels became. |
| | |
| Solis hujus radiis | Thou, wrapt in the blaze |
| Maria coruscat; | Of his infinite light, |
| Consurgens Aurora | Dost shine as the morn |
| In conceptu micat. | On the confines of night. |
| | |
| Lilium inter spinas, | As the moon on the lost |
| Quæ serpentis conterat | Through obscurity dawns; |
| Caput: pulchra ut luna | The serpent's destroyer; |
| Errantes collustrat. | A lily 'mid thorns. |

℣. Ego feci in cœlis, ut oriretur lumen indeficiens.

℟. Et quasi nebula texi omnem terram.

℣. I made an unfailing light to arise in heaven.

℟. And as a mist, I overspread the whole earth.

℣. Domina protege, &c. (*Pag. 195, cum Oratione, &c. ut supra.*)

℣. O Lady, recommend, &c. (*with the Prayer, &c. Page 195.*)

## At Compline.

℣. Convertat nos, Domina, tuis precibus placatus Jesus Christus Filius tuus.

℟. Et divertat iram suam a nobis.

℣. Domina, in adjutorium meum intende.

℟. Me de manu hostium potenter defende.

℣. Gloria Patri. Alleluia.

℣. May Jesus Christ thy Son, reconciled by thy prayers, O Lady, convert our hearts.

℟. And turn away his anger from us.

℣. O Lady, make speed to befriend me.

℟. From the hands of the enemy powerfully defend me.

℣. Glory be to the Father, &c. Alleluia.

### HYMN.

Salve, Virgo florens,
Mater illibata,
Regina clementiæ,
Stellis coronata.

Hail, Mother most pure;
Hail, Virgin renown'd:
Hail, Queen with the stars
As a diadem crown'd.

Super omnes Angelos
Pura, immaculata,
Atque ad Regis dexteram
Stans veste deaurata.

Above all the Angels
In glory untold,
Standing next to the King
In a vesture of gold.

Per te, Mater gratiæ,
Dulcis spes reorum,
Fulgens stella maris,
Portus naufragorum,

Patens cœli janua,
Salus infirmorum,
Videamus Regem
In aula Sanctorum.

Amen.

℣. Oleum effusum, Maria, nomen tuum.

℟. Servi tui dilexerunt te nimis.

(*Oratio ut supra. Pag.* 195.)

℣. Domina, protege orationem meam.

℟. Et clamor meus ad te veniat.

℣. Benedicamus Domino.

℟. Deo gratias.

℣. Benedicat et custodiat nos omnipotens et misericors Dominus, Pater, et Filius, et Spiritus Sanctus.

℟. Amen.

O Mother of mercy,
O Star of the wave;
O Hope of the guilty,
O Light of the grave!

Through thee may we come,
To the haven of rest;
And see heaven's King
In the courts of the blest!

Amen.

℣. Thy name, O Mary, is as oil poured out.

℟. Thy servants have loved thee exceedingly.

(*Prayer as at Page* 195.)

℣. O Lady, recommend my prayer.

℟. And let my cry come unto thee.

℣. Let us bless the Lord.

℟. Thanks be to God.

℣. May the almighty and merciful Lord, Father, Son, and Holy Ghost, bless and keep us.

℟. Amen.

## The Commendation.

| | |
|---|---|
| SUPPLICES offerimus Tibi, Virgo pia, Hæc laudum præconia; Fac nos ut in via | THESE praises and prayers I lay at thy feet, O Virgin of Virgins, O Mary most sweet! |
| Ducas cursu prospero; Et in agonia Tu nobis assiste, O dulcis Maria. | Be thou my true Guide Through this pilgrimage here; And stand by my side, When death draweth near. |
| ℣. Deo gratias. *Ant.* Hæc est Virga in qua nec nodus originalis nec cortex actualis culpæ fuit. | ℣. Thanks be to God. *Ant.* This is the rod, in which neither the knot of original, nor bark of actual sin was found. |

### PRAYER.

| | |
|---|---|
| DEUS, qui per Immaculatam Virginis Conceptionem dignum Filio tuo habitaculum præparasti, ejus nobis intercessione concede, ut cor et corpus nostrum immaculatum tibi, qui eam ab omni labe præservasti fideliter, custodiamus. Per eumdem Dominum nostrum Jesum Christum Filium tuum, qui tecum, &c. | O GOD, who by the Immaculate Conception of the Virgin, didst prepare a fit dwelling place for thy Son, grant through her intercession, that we may faithfully keep our body and soul free from sin for thee, who preserved her from all stain: Through the same Jesus Christ, &c. |

# The Litany of St. Joseph.

Lord, have mercy on us.
*Lord, have mercy on us.*
Christ, have mercy on us.
*Christ, have mercy on us.*
Lord, have mercy on us.
*Lord, have mercy on us.*
Jesus, receive our prayers.
*Lord Jesus, grant our petition.*

God the Father, Creator of the world,
God the Son, Redeemer of mankind,
God the Holy Ghost,
Holy Trinity, one God,
} *Have mercy on us.*

Holy Mary, Spouse of St. Joseph,
St. Joseph, advocate of the humble,
St. Joseph, blessed amongst men,
St. Joseph, defender of the meek,
St. Joseph, exiled with Christ into Egypt,
St. Joseph, favourite of the King of Heaven,
St. Joseph, guardian of the Word Incarnate,
St. Joseph, honoured amongst men,
St. Joseph, pattern of humility and obedience,
} *Pray for us.*

# LITANY OF ST. JOSEPH.

St. Joseph, kind intercessor for the afflicted,
St. Joseph, lily of chastity and temperance,
St. Joseph, example of silence and resignation,
St. Joseph, nursing father to the Son of God,
St. Joseph, the just and perfect man,
St. Joseph, pattern of the industrious and innocent,
St. Joseph, endowed with all virtue,
St. Joseph, ruler of the family of Jesus,
St. Joseph, spouse of the ever blessed Virgin,
St. Joseph, possessed of all glorious privileges,
St. Joseph, union of all Christian perfections,
St. Joseph, protector of the dying,
St. Joseph, our dear patron and defender,

} *Pray for us.*

Lamb of God, who takest away the sins of the world. *Spare us, O Lord.*

Lamb of God, who takest away the sins of the world. *Graciously hear us, O Lord.*

Lamb of God, who takest away the sins of the world. *Have mercy on us.*

℣. Pray for us, O holy St. Joseph.

℟. That we may be made worthy of the promises of Christ.

LET US PRAY.

O GOD, who didst make choice of holy St. Joseph to be the spouse of the blessed Virgin Mary, the nurse and guardian of thy beloved Son Jesus, we humbly beseech thee to grant us, through his intercession, purity both of soul and body, that being free from all sin, and adorned with the wedding garment, we may be admitted to the nuptials of the Lamb in eternal glory, through the same Lord Jesus Christ thy Son, who liveth and reigneth with thee, in the unity of the Holy Ghost, world without end. Amen.

---

"I choose the glorious St. Joseph for my patron," writes St. Teresa in the sixth chapter of her life, "and I commend myself in all things particularly to his intercession. I do not remember ever to have asked of God anything through his prayers which I did not obtain. I never knew any one who, invoking him, did not advance much in virtue."

## The Seben Penitential Psalms.

**ANTHEM.**

REMEMBER not, O Lord, our offences, nor those of our parents, and take not revenge on our sins.

Psalm vi. *Domine ne in furore.*

O LORD, rebuke me not in thy indignation, nor chastise me in thy wrath.

Have mercy on me, O Lord, for I am weak: heal me, O Lord, for my bones are troubled.

And my soul is troubled exceedingly: but thou, O Lord, how long?

Turn to me, O Lord, and deliver my soul: O save me for thy mercy's sake.

For there is no one in death, that is mindful of thee, and who shall confess to thee in hell?

I have laboured in my groanings, every night I will wash my bed, I will water my couch with my tears.

My eye is troubled through indignation: I have grown old amongst all my enemies.

Depart from me, all ye workers of iniquity, for the Lord hath heard the voice of my weeping.

My sores are putrified and corrupted, because of my foolishness.

I am become miserable, and am bowed down even to the end; I walked sorrowful all the day long.

For my loins are filled with illusions; and there is no health in my flesh.

I am afflicted, and humbled exceedingly: I roared with the groaning of my heart.

Lord, all my desire is before thee; and my groaning is not hidden from thee.

My heart is troubled, my strength hath left me; and the light of my eyes itself is not with me.

My friends and my neighbours have drawn near, and stood against me.

And they that were near me stood afar off; and they that sought my soul used violence.

And they that sought evils to me spoke vain things, and studied deceits all the day long.

But I, as a deaf man, heard not; and as a dumb man not opening his mouth.

And I became as a man that heareth not; and that hath no reproofs in his mouth.

For in thee, O Lord, have I hoped: thou wilt hear me, O Lord my God.

For I said: lest at any time my enemies rejoice over me : and whilst my feet are moved, they speak great things against me.

For I am ready for scourges; and my sorrow is continually before me.

For I will declare my iniquity, and I will think for my sin.

But my enemies live, and are stronger than I : and they that hate me wrongfully are multiplied.

They that render evil for good, have detracted me, because I followed goodness.

Forsake me not, O Lord my God; do not thou depart from me.

Attend unto my help, O Lord, the God of my salvation.

Glory be to the Father, &c.

Psalm l. *Miserere mei Deus.* (Page 131.)

Psalm ci. *Domine exaudi.*

HEAR, O Lord, my prayer, and let my cry come to thee.

Turn not away thy face from me ; in the day when I am in trouble, incline thy ear to me.

In what day soever I shall call upon thee, hear me speedily.

In the beginning, O Lord, thou foundedst the earth; and the heavens are the works of thy hands.

They shall perish, but thou remainest; and all of them shall grow old like a garment.

And as a vesture thou shalt change them, and they shall be changed: but thou art always the self-same, and thy years shall not fail.

The children of thy servants shall continue, and their seed shall be directed for ever.

Glory be to the Father, &c.

### Psalm cxxix. *De profundis.*

Out of the depths I have cried to thee, O Lord; Lord, hear my voice.

Let thine ears be attentive to the voice of my supplication.

If thou, O Lord, wilt mark iniquities, Lord, who shall stand it?

For with thee there is merciful forgiveness: and by reason of thy law, I have waited for thee, O Lord.

My soul hath relied on his word; my soul hath hoped in the Lord.

From the morning watch even until night, let Israel hope in the Lord.

Because with the Lord there is mercy; and with him plentiful redemption.

And he shall redeem Israel from all his iniquities.

Glory be to the Father, &c.

Psalm cxlii. *Domine exaudi.*

HEAR, O Lord, my prayer: give ear to my supplication in thy truth; hear me in thy justice.

And enter not into judgment with thy servant; for in thy sight no man living shall be justified.

For the enemy hath persecuted my soul; he hath brought down my life to the earth.

He hath made me to dwell in darkness as those that have been dead of old, and my spirit is in anguish within me: my heart within me is troubled.

I remember the days of old, I meditated on all thy works; I meditated upon the works of thy hands.

I stretched forth my hands to thee: my soul is as earth without water unto thee.

Hear me speedily, O Lord; my spirit hath fainted away.

Turn not away thy face from me, lest I be like unto them that go down into the pit.

Cause me to hear thy mercy in the morning; for in thee have I hoped.

Make the way known to me wherein I should walk; for I have lifted up my soul to thee.

Deliver me from my enemies, O Lord, to thee have I fled: teach me to do thy will, for thou art my God.

Thy good spirit shall lead me into the right land: for thy name's sake, O Lord, thou wilt quicken me in thy justice.

Thou wilt bring my soul out of trouble; and in thy mercy, thou wilt destroy my enemies.

And thou wilt cut off all of them that afflict my soul: for I am thy servant.

Glory be to the Father, &c.

## Litany of the Saints.

| | |
|---|---|
| Ne reminiscaris, Domine, delicta nostra, vel parentum nostrorum; neque vindictam sumas de peccatis nostris. | REMEMBER not, O Lord, our offences, nor those of our parents; neither take thou vengeance of our sins. |
| Kyrie eleison. | Lord have mercy on us. |
| *Christe eleison.* | *Christ have mercy on us.* |
| Kyrie eleison. | Lord have mercy on us. |
| *Kyrie eleison.* | *Lord have mercy on us.* |

# LITANY OF THE SAINTS.

Christe audi nos. — Christ hear us.
*Christe exaudi nos.* — *Christ graciously hear us.*

Pater de cœlis Deus, — God, the Father of heaven,
Fili, Redemptor mundi Deus, — God the Son, Redeemer of the world,
Spiritus Sancte Deus, — God, the Holy Ghost,
Sancta Trinitas, unus Deus, — Holy Trinity, one God,

*Miserere nobis.* — *Have mercy on us.*

Sancta Maria, — Holy Mary,
Sancta Dei Genitrix, — Holy Mother of God,
Sancta Virgo virginum, — Holy Virgin of virgins,
Sancte Michael, — St. Michael,
Sancte Gabriel, — St. Gabriel,
Sancte Raphael, — St. Raphael,
Omnes sancti Angeli et Archangeli, *Orate pro nobis.* — All ye holy Angels and Archangels,
Omnes sancti beatorum Spirituum ordines, *Orate, &c.* — All ye holy orders of blessed Spirits,
Sancte Joannes Baptista, *Ora, &c.* — St. John Baptist,
Sancte Joseph, *Ora, &c.* — St. Joseph,
Omnes sancti Patriarchæ et Prophetæ, *Orate, &c.* — All ye holy Patriarchs and Prophets,
Sancte Petre, — St. Peter,
Sancte Paule, — St. Paul,
Sancte Andrea, — St. Andrew,
Sancte Jacobe, — St. James,
Sancte Joannes, — St. John,
Sancte Thoma, — St. Thomas,

*Ora pro nobis.* — *Pray for us.*

| | |
|---|---|
| Sancte Jacobe, | St. James, |
| Sancte Philippe, | St. Philip, |
| Sancte Bartholomæe, | St. Bartholomew, |
| Sancte Matthæe, | St. Matthew, |
| Sancte Simon, | St. Simon, |
| Sancte Thaddæe, | St. Thaddeus, |
| Sancte Matthia, | St. Matthias, |
| Sancte Barnaba, | St. Barnabas, |
| Sancte Luca, | St. Luke, |
| Sancte Marce, | St. Mark, |
| Omnes sancti Apostoli et Evangelistæ, *Orate, &c.* | All ye holy Apostles and Evangelists, |
| Omnes sancti Discipuli Domini, *Orate, &c.* | All ye holy Disciples of our Lord, |
| Omnes sancti Innocentes, *Orate, &c.* | All ye holy Innocents, |
| Sancte Stephane, *Ora, &c.* | St. Stephen, |
| Sancte Laurenti, *Ora, &c.* | St. Lawrence, |
| Sancte Vincenti, *Ora, &c.* | St. Vincent, |
| Sancti Fabiane et Sebastiane, | SS. Fabian and Sebastian, |
| Sancti Joannes et Paule, | SS. John and Paul, |
| Sancti Cosma et Damiane, | SS. Cosmas and Damian, |
| Sancti Gervasi et Protasi, | SS. Gervase and Protase, |
| Omnes sancti Martyres, | All ye holy Martyrs, |
| Sancte Sylvester, | St. Sylvester, |
| Sancte Gregori, | St. Gregory, |
| Sancte Ambrosi, | St. Ambrose, |

# LITANY OF THE SAINTS.

| | |
|---|---|
| Sancte Augustine, | St. Augustine, |
| Sancte Hieronyme, | St. Jerome, |
| Sancte Martine, | St. Martin, |
| Sancte Nicolae, | St. Nicholas, |
| Omnes sancti Pontifices et Confessores, *Orate, &c.* | All ye holy Bishops and Confessors, |
| Omnes sancti Doctores, *Orate, &c.* | All ye holy Doctors, |
| Sancte Antoni, | St. Anthony, |
| Sancte Benedicte, | St. Benedict, |
| Sancte Bernarde, | St. Bernard, |
| Sancte Dominice, | St. Dominic, |
| Sancte Francisce, | St. Francis, |
| Omnes sancti Sacerdotes et Levitæ, *Orate, &c.* | All ye holy Priests and Levites, |
| Omnes sancti Monachi et Eremitæ, *Orate, &c.* | All ye holy Monks and Hermits, |
| Sancta Maria Magdalena, | St. Mary Magdalen, |
| Sancta Agatha, | St. Agatha, |
| Sancta Lucia, | St. Lucy, |
| Sancta Agnes, | St. Agnes, |
| Sancta Cæcilia, | St. Cecily, |
| Sancta Catharina, | St. Catharine, |
| Sancta Anastasia, | St. Anastasia, |
| Omnes sanctæ Virgines et Viduæ, *Orate, &c.* | All ye holy Virgins and Widows, |
| Omnes Sancti et Sanctæ Dei, *Intercedite pro nobis.* | All ye holy men and women, Saints of God, *Make intercession for us.* |
| Propitius esto, *Parce nobis, Domine.* | Be merciful unto us, *Spare us, O Lord.* |

*Ora, &c.* / *Ora pro nobis.* / *Pray for us.*

Propitius esto,
Exaudi nos, Domine.

Ab omni malo,
Ab omni peccato,
Ab ira tua,
A subitanea et improvisa morte,
Ab insidiis diaboli,

Ab ira et odio, et omni mala voluntate,
A spiritu fornicationis,
A fulgure et tempestate,
A flagello terræmotus,
A peste, fame et bello,
A morte perpetua,

Per mysterium sanctæ Incarnationis tuæ,

Per Adventum tuum,
Per Nativitatem tuam

Per Baptismum et sanctum jejunium tuum,
Per Crucem et Passionem tuam,
Per Mortem et Sepulturam tuam,
Per sanctam Resurrectionem tuam,

Be merciful unto us,
Graciously hear us, O Lord.

From all evil,
From all sin,
From thy wrath,
From a sudden and unprovided death,
From the snares of the devil,

From anger and hatred, and all ill will,
From the spirit of fornication,
From lightning and tempest,
From the scourge of earthquake,
From pestilence, famine and war,
From everlasting death,

Through the mystery of thy holy Incarnation,

Through thy Coming,
Through thy Nativity,

Through thy Baptism and holy Fasting,

Through thy Cross and Passion,
Through thy Death and Burial,
Through thy holy Resurrection,

*Libera nos, Domine.*

*O Lord, deliver us.*

# LITANY OF THE SAINTS.

| Per admirabilem Ascensionem tuam, | Through thy admirable Ascension, |
| Per adventum Spiritus Sancti Paracliti, | Through the coming of the Holy Ghost the Paraclete, |
| In die judicii, | In the day of judgment, |

*Libera, &c.* / *O Lord, &c.*

Peccatores,
We sinners,
*Te rogamus, audi nos.*
*Beseech thee, hear us.*

Ut nobis parcas,
That thou wouldst spare us,

Ut nobis indulgeas,
That thou wouldst pardon us,

Ut ad veram pœnitentiam nos perducere digneris,
That thou wouldst bring us to true penance,

Ut Ecclesiam tuam sanctam regere et conservare digneris,
That thou wouldst vouchsafe to govern and preserve thy holy Church,

Ut Domnum Apostolicum, et omnes ecclesiasticos ordines in sancta religione conservare digneris,
That thou wouldst vouchsafe to preserve our Apostolic Prelate, and all orders of the Church in holy religion,

Ut inimicos sanctæ Ecclesiæ humiliare digneris,
That thou wouldst vouchsafe to humble the enemies of holy Church,

Ut Regibus et Principibus Christianis pacem et veram concordiam donare digneris,
That thou wouldst vouchsafe to give peace and true concord to Christian Kings and Princes,

*Te rogamus, audi nos.* / *We beseech thee, hear us.*

| | |
|---|---|
| Ut cuncto populo Christiano pacem et unitatem largiri digneris, | That thou wouldst vouchsafe to grant peace and unity to all Christian people, |
| Ut nosmetipsos in tuo sancto servitio confortare et conservare digneris, | That thou wouldst vouchsafe to confirm and preserve us in thy holy service, |
| Ut mentes nostras ad cœlestia desideria erigas, | That thou wouldst lift up our minds to heavenly desires, |
| Ut omnibus benefactoribus nostris sempiterna bona retribuas, | That thou wouldst render eternal good things to all our benefactors, |
| Ut animas nostras, fratrum, propinquorum, et benefactorum nostrorum, ab æterna damnatione eripias, | That thou wouldst deliver our souls, and the souls of our brethren, relations, and benefactors, from eternal damnation, |
| Ut fructus terræ dare et conservare digneris, | That thou wouldst vouchsafe to give and preserve the fruits of the earth, |
| Ut omnibus fidelibus defunctis requiem æternam donare digneris, | That thou wouldst vouchsafe to grant eternal rest to all the faithful departed, |
| Ut nos exaudire digneris, | That thou wouldst vouchsafe graciously to hear us, |
| Fili Dei, | Son of God, |

*Te rogamus, audi nos.* — *We beseech thee, hear us.*

## LITANY OF THE SAINTS.

Agnus Dei, qui tollis peccata mundi,

Lamb of God, who takest away the sins of the world,

Parce nobis, Domine.

Spare us, O Lord.

Agnus Dei, qui tollis peccata mundi,

Lamb of God, who takest away the sins of the world,

Exaudi nos, Domine.

Graciously hear us, O Lord.

Agnus Dei, qui tollis peccata mundi,

Lamb of God, who takest away the sins of the world,

Miserere nobis.
Christe audi nos.
Christe exaudi nos.

Have mercy on us.
Christ hear us.
Christ graciously hear us.

Kyrie eleison.

Lord have mercy on us.

Christe eleison.

Christ have mercy on us.

Kyrie eleison.

Lord have mercy on us.

Pater noster (secreto).

Our Father (in secret).

℣. Et ne nos inducas in tentationem.

℣. And lead us not into temptation.

℟. Sed libera nos a malo.

℟. But deliver us from evil.

Psalm lxix. *Deus in adjutorium.*

DEUS in adjutorium meum intende:* Domine ad adjuvandum me festina.

O God, come to my assistance: O Lord, make haste to help me.

Confundantur et revereantur,\* qui quærunt animam meam.

Avertantur retrorsum, et erubescant,\* qui volunt mihi mala.

Avertantur statim erubescentes,\* qui dicunt mihi, Euge, euge.

Exultent et lætentur in te omnes qui quærunt te,\* et dicant semper: Magnificetur Dominus, qui diligunt salutare tuum.

Ego vero egenus et pauper sum:\* Deus, adjuva me.

Adjutor meus et liberator meus es tu:\* Domine, ne moreris.

Gloria Patri, &c.

℣. Salvos fac servos tuos,

℟. Deus meus, sperantes in te.

℣. Esto nobis, Domine, turris fortitudinis,

℟. A facie inimici.

Let them be confounded and ashamed that seek my soul.

Let them be turned backward, and blush for shame, that desire evils to me.

Let them presently be turned away blushing for shame, that say to me: 'Tis well, 'tis well.

Let all that seek thee rejoice and be glad in thee; and let such as love thy salvation say always: The Lord be magnified.

But I am needy and poor: O God, help me.

Thou art my helper and my deliverer: O Lord, make no long delay.

Glory be, &c.

℣. Save thy servants,

℟. Who hope in thee, O my God.

℣. Be unto us, O Lord, a tower of strength,

℟. From the face of the enemy.

℣. Nihil proficiat inimicus in nobis.

℟. Et filius iniquitatis non apponat nocere nobis.

℣. Domine, non secundum peccata nostra facias nobis.

℟. Neque secundum iniquitates nostras retribuas nobis.

℣. Oremus pro Pontifice nostro, N.

℟. Dominus conservet eum, et vivificet eum, et beatum faciat eum in terra; et non tradat eum in animam inimicorum ejus.

℣. Oremus pro benefactoribus nostris.

℟. Retribuere dignare, Domine, omnibus nobis bona facientibus, propter nomen tuum, vitam æternam. Amen.

℣. Oremus pro fidelibus defunctis.

℟. Requiem æternam dona eis, Domine; et lux perpetua luceat eis.

℣. Let not the enemy prevail against us.

℟. Nor the son of iniquity have power to hurt us.

℣. O Lord, deal not with us according to our sins.

℟. Neither requite us according to our iniquities.

℣. Let us pray for our Sovereign Pontiff, N.

℟. The Lord preserve him and give life, and make him blessed upon earth, and deliver him not up to the will of his enemies.

℣. Let us pray for our benefactors.

℟. Vouchsafe, O Lord, for thy name's sake, to reward with eternal life all those who do good to us. Amen.

℣. Let us pray for the faithful departed.

℟. Eternal rest give unto them, O Lord; and let perpetual light shine upon them.

℣. Requiescant in pace.

℟. Amen.

℣. Pro fratribus nostris absentibus.

℟. Salvos fac servos tuos, Deus meus, sperantes in te.

℣. Mitte eis, Domine, auxilium de sancto.

℟. Et de Sion tuere eos.

℣. Domine, exaudi orationem meam.

℟. Et clamor meus ad te veniat.

℣. May they rest in peace.

℟. Amen.

℣. For our absent brethren.

℟. Save thy servants, who hope in thee, O my God.

℣. Send them help, O Lord, from thy holy place.

℟. And defend them out of Sion.

℣. O Lord, hear my prayer.

℟. And let my cry come unto thee.

OREMUS.

DEUS, cui proprium est misereri semper, et parcere: suscipe deprecationem nostram; ut nos, et omnes famulos tuos, quos delictorum catena constringit, miseratio tuæ pietatis clementer absolvat.

Exaudi, quæsumus Domine, supplicum preces, et confitentium tibi parce peccatis: ut pariter nobis indulgenti-

LET US PRAY.

O GOD, whose property is always to have mercy and to spare, receive our petition; that we, and all thy servants who are bound by the chain of sin, may, by the compassion of thy goodness, mercifully be absolved.

Graciously hear, we beseech thee, O Lord, the prayers of thy suppliants, and forgive the sins of those who

# LITANY OF THE SAINTS.

am tribuas benignus et pacem.

Ineffabilem nobis, Domine, misericordiam tuam clementer ostende; ut simul nos et a peccatis omnibus exuas, et a pœnis, quas pro his meremur, eripias.

Deus, qui culpa offenderis, pœnitentia placaris, preces populi tui supplicantis propitius respice; et flagella tuæ iracundiæ, quæ pro peccatis nostris meremur, averte.

Omnipotens sempiterne Deus, miserere famulo tuo Pontifici nostro N. et dirige eum secundum tuam clementiam in viam salutis æternæ; ut te donante, tibi placita cupiat, et tota virtute perficiat.

confess to thee; that, in thy bounty, thou mayest grant us pardon and peace.

In thy clemency, O Lord, show thy unspeakable mercy to us; that thou mayest both loose us from all our sins, and deliver us from the punishments which we deserve for them.

O God, who by sin art offended, and by penance pacified, mercifully regard the prayers of thy people making supplication to thee, and turn away the scourges of thine anger, which we deserve for our sins.

Almighty and everlasting God, have mercy upon thy servant N., our Sovereign Pontiff, and direct him, according to thy clemency, in the way of everlasting salvation; that by thy grace he may both desire those things that are pleasing to thee, and perform them with all his strength.

℣. Dominus vobiscum.
℟. Et cum spiritu tuo.

℣. Exaudiat nos omnipotens et misericors Dominus.
℟. Amen.

℣. Et fidelium animæ per misericordiam Dei requiescant in pace.
℟. Amen.

℣. The Lord be with you.
℟. And with thy spirit.

℣. May the almighty and merciful Lord graciously hear us.
℟. Amen.

℣. And may the souls of the faithful, through the mercy of God, rest in peace.
℟. Amen.

---

## Night Prayers.

### LITANY OF THE BLESSED VIRGIN MARY.

Sub tuum præsidium confugimus sancta Dei Genitrix, nostras deprecationes ne despicias in necessitatibus nostris, sed a periculis cunctis libera nos, semper Virgo gloriosa et benedicta.

Kyrie eleison.
*Christe eleison.*
Kyrie eleison.
Christe audi nos.
*Christe exaudi nos.*

We fly to thy patronage, O holy Mother of God, despise not our petitions in our necessities, but deliver us from all dangers, O ever glorious and blessed Virgin.

Lord have mercy on us.
*Christ have mercy on us.*
Lord have mercy on us.
Christ hear us.
*Christ graciously hear us.*

|  |  |
|---|---|
| Pater de cœlis Deus, *miserere nobis.* | God, the Father of heaven, *have mercy on us.* |
| Fili, Redemptor mundi Deus, *miserere nobis.* | God the Son, Redeemer of the world, *have mercy on us.* |
| Spiritus Sancte Deus, *miserere nobis.* | God, the Holy Ghost, *have mercy on us.* |
| Sancta Trinitas, unus Deus, *miserere nobis.* | Holy Trinity, one God, *have mercy on us.* |
| Sancta Maria, | Holy Mary, |
| Sancta Dei Genitrix, | Holy Mother of God, |
| Sancta Virgo virginum, | Holy Virgin of virgins, |
| Mater Christi, | Mother of Christ, |
| Mater divinæ gratiæ, | Mother of divine grace, |
| Mater purissima, | Mother most pure, |
| Mater castissima, | Mother most chaste, |
| Mater inviolata, | Mother inviolate, |
| Mater intemerata, | Mother undefiled, |
| Mater amabilis, | Amiable Mother, |
| Mater admirabilis, | Admirable Mother, |
| Mater Creatoris, | Mother of our Creator, |
| Mater Salvatoris, | Mother of our Redeemer, |
| Virgo prudentissima, | Virgin most prudent, |
| Virgo veneranda, | Venerable Virgin, |
| Virgo prædicanda, | Renowned Virgin, |
| Virgo potens, | Powerful Virgin, |
| Virgo clemens, | Merciful Virgin, |
| Virgo fidelis, | Faithful Virgin, |
| Speculum justitiæ, | Mirror of justice, |
| Sedes sapientiæ, | Seat of wisdom, |
| Causa nostræ lætitiæ, | Cause of our joy, |
| Vas spirituale, | Spiritual vessel, |
| Vas honorabile, | Honourable vessel, |

*Ora pro nobis.* / *Pray for us.*

| | |
|---|---|
| Monstra te esse Matrem. | Exert for us a mother's care, |
| Sumat per te preces, | And us thy children own, |
| Qui pro nobis natus, | Prevail with him to hear our prayer, |
| Tulit esse tuus. | Who chose to be thy Son. |
| Virgo singularis, | O spotless maid! whose virtues shine |
| Inter omnes mitis, | With brightest purity, |
| Nos culpis solutos, | Each action of our lives refine, |
| Mites fac et castos. | And make us pure like thee; |
| Vitam præsta puram, | Preserve our lives unstained with ill, |
| Iter para tutum, | In this infectious way, |
| Ut videntes Jesum, | That heaven alone our souls may fill |
| Semper collætemur. | With joys that ne'er decay. |
| Sit laus Deo Patri, | To God the Father endless praise, |
| Summo Christo decus, | To God the Son the same, |
| Spiritui Sancto, | And Holy Ghost, whose equal rays, |
| Tribus honor unus. Amen. | One equal glory claim. Amen. |

SUB tuum præsidium confugimus sancta Dei Genitrix, nostras deprecationes ne despicias in necessitatibus nostris, sed a periculis cunctis libera nos, semper Virgo gloriosa et benedicta.

℣. Ora pro nobis, sancta Dei Genitrix.
℟. Ut digni efficiamur promissionibus Christi.

WE fly to thy patronage, O holy Mother of God, despise not our petitions in our necessities, but deliver us from all dangers, O ever glorious and blessed Virgin.

℣. Pray for us, O holy Mother of God.
℟. That we may be made worthy of the promises of Christ.

OREMUS.

DEFENDE, quæsumus, Domine, beata Maria semper virgine intercedente, istam ab omni adversitate familiam : et toto corde tibi prostratam, ab hostium propitius tuere clementer insidiis. Per Christum Dominum nostrum. Amen.

Sanctissimæ Genitricis tuæ Sponsi, quæsumus Domine, meritis adjuvemur, ut quod possibilitas nostra non

LET US PRAY.

DEFEND, we beseech thee, O Lord, by the intercession of blessed Mary ever virgin, this thy family from all adversity; and being prostrate before thee with all our hearts, mercifully protect us from the snares of the enemy. Through Christ our Lord. Amen.

Assist us, O Lord, we beseech thee, by the merits of the Spouse of thy most holy Mother, that what

| | |
|---|---|
| umque tuarum remissionem cunctorum tribue peccatorum; ut indulgentiam, quam semper optaverunt, piis supplicationibus consequantur. Qui vivis et regnas, &c. | vants departed the remission of all their sins; that, through pious supplications, they may obtain the pardon which they have always desired. Who livest and reignest, &c. |
| Et fidelium animæ per misericordiam Dei requiescant in pace. Amen. | And may the souls of the faithful, through the mercy of God, rest in peace. Amen. |

## Examination of Conscience.

IN the name of the Father, and of the Son, and of the Holy Ghost. Amen.

Blessed be the holy and undivided Trinity, now and for ever. Amen.

Our Father, &c. Hail Mary, &c. I believe in God, &c. (Page 2.)

*Invoke the assistance of the Holy Ghost, saying,*

COME, O Holy Spirit! fill the hearts of thy faithful, and kindle in them the fire of thy love.

℣. Send forth thy Spirit, and our hearts shall be regenerated.

℟. And thou shalt renew the face of the earth.

Place yourselves in the presence of God, and give him thanks for all the benefits you have received from him, particularly this day.

O MY God, I firmly believe thou art here, and perfectly seest me, and that thou observest all my actions, . all my thoughts, and the most secret motions of my heart. Thou watchest over me with incomparable love, every moment bestowing favours, and preserving me from evil. Blessed be thy holy name, and may all creatures bless thy goodness, for the benefits I have ever received from thee, and particularly this day. May the Saints and Angels supply my defect in rendering thee due thanks. Never permit me to be so base and wicked as to repay thy bounties with ingratitude, and thy blessings with offences and injuries.

Ask our Lord Jesus Christ grace to discover the sins you have committed this day; and beg of him a true sorrow for them.

O MY Lord Jesus Christ, judge of the living and the dead, before whom I must appear one day to give an exact account of my whole life; enlighten me, I beseech thee, and give me a humble and contrite heart, that I may see wherein I have offended thine infinite Majesty; and judge myself now with such a just severity, that then thou mayest judge me with mercy and clemency.

Here examine what sins you have committed this day, by thought, word, deed, or omission. But if nothing occur to your mind wherein you have offended, reflect again on the chief sins of your life past. Then conceive a great sorrow for having offended God, and say,

O MY God, I detest these and all other sins which I have committed against thy divine Majesty. I am extremely sorry that I have offended thee, because thou art infinitely good, and sin displeases thee. I love thee with my whole heart, and firmly purpose, by the help of thy grace, never more to offend thee. I resolve to avoid the occasions of sin; I will confess my sins, and will endeavour to make satisfaction for them. Have mercy on me, O God, have mercy and pardon me, a wretched sinner. In the name of thy beloved Son, Jesus, I humbly beg of thee so to wash me with his precious blood, that my sins may be entirely remitted.

Endeavour as much as possible to put yourselves in the condition you desire to be found in at the hour of death.

O my God, I accept of death as an act of homage and adoration which I owe to thy divine Majesty, as a punishment justly due to my sins, in union with the death of my dear Redeemer, and as the only means of coming to thee, my beginning and my last end.

I firmly believe all the sacred truths the Catholic Church believes and teaches, because thou hast revealed them; and by the assistance of thy holy grace, I am resolved to live and die in the communion of this thy Church.

Relying upon thy goodness, power, and promises, I hope to obtain pardon of my sins, and life everlasting, through the merits of thy Son Jesus Christ, my only Redeemer, and by the intercession of his blessed Mother, and of all the Saints.

I love thee with all my heart and soul, and desire to love thee as the blessed do in heaven. I adore all the designs of thy divine providence, resigning myself entirely to thy will.

I also love my neighbour for thy sake, as I love myself; I sincerely forgive all who have injured me, and ask pardon of all whom I have injured.

I renounce the devil, with all his works; the world, with all its pomps; the flesh, with all its temptations.

I desire to be dissolved, and to be with Christ. Father, into thy hands, I commend my Spirit; Lord Jesus receive my soul.

May the blessed Virgin Mary, St. Joseph, and all the Saints, pray for us to our Lord, that we may be preserved this night from all sin and evil.

Blessed St. Michael, defend us in the day of battle, that we may not be lost at the dreadful judgment.

O my good Angel, whom God, in his divine mercy, has appointed to be my guardian, enlighten and protect me, direct and govern me this night. Amen.

Almighty God, have mercy on us, and, our sins being forgiven, bring us to life everlasting. Amen.

May the almighty and merciful Lord grant us pardon, absolution, and remission of our sins. Amen.

℣. Vouchsafe, O Lord, this night,
℟. To keep us without sin.

℣. Have mercy on us, O Lord.
℟. Have mercy on us.
℣. Let thy mercy, O Lord, be upon us.
℟. As we have hoped in thee.
℣. O Lord, hear our prayer.
℟. And let our cry come to thee.

### LET US PRAY.

VISIT, we beseech thee, O Lord, this house and family, and drive far from it all the snares of our enemy: let thy Angels dwell herein, who may keep us in peace; and may thy blessing be always upon us: through our Lord Jesus Christ. Amen.

May our Lord bless us, and preserve us from all evil, and bring us to life everlasting.

And may the souls of the faithful, through the mercy of God, rest in peace. Amen.

## Short Meditations on Death.

### ON SUNDAY.

WE must all die, and quit all in which we now take content.

Our best friends will abandon us, and leave us nothing but a winding-sheet.

Therefore quit all affection to creatures, before they quit you.

### ON MONDAY.

DEATH is certain : the time and manner are uncertain: whether by a long disease, or by some unexpected accident.

The Son of man will come at an hour when we little expect him.

Be therefore ready every moment, seeing you may die at any moment.

### ON TUESDAY.

You can only die once ; and if you die ill, the loss is irreparable.

If any one from hell could return to life, how would he prepare for death ?

Let the misery of others be an instruction to you.

### ON WEDNESDAY.

CONSIDER what will most alarm you at the hour of death : the sins you have committed, the doubtful state of your soul, and the thought of eternity.

O death ! how bitter is thy remembrance to a man who has peace in his sins.

Quit, therefore, all affection to temporal felicity.

### ON THURSDAY.

LEARN every day the art of dying well.

Defer not doing penance till the hour of death.

At that time the pains of your body, and the anguish of your mind will take up all your thoughts.

### ON FRIDAY.

LIVE as you intend to die, for you will die as you live.

If you forget God in your life-time, you will be forgotten at the hour of death.

The death of the wicked is miserable; the death of the just is precious in the sight of God.

### ON SATURDAY.

DEATH is often nearer than you imagine; and many who have promised themselves a long life, have been cut off suddenly in their sins.

Are you so ready, that if death should come to-night, you would not be surprised?

Do not live in a state in which you dare not die.

## On the Choice of a State of Life.

ALMIGHTY God, in his Providence, has established a diversity of states and employments for mankind, distributing them in his wisdom, as the father of a family divides among his servants the offices of his house. Hence he bestows upon men various inclinations and natural abilities, and dispenses his graces according to the wants of the respective states to which he calls them.

It follows manifestly, that it is of the greatest consequence that each one should make a right choice of a state of life. This choice is of such moment, that on it depends the special blessing of God in this life, and, if not our eternal happiness, at least our degree of glory in the next.

To ensure success in this important choice,

Beg fervently and confidently the special assistance of God, through the intercession of Mary, of your Patron Saints, and of your Guardian Angel.

Consider well, and answer sincerely, the following questions:—1°. Of those states of life within your reach, which is the one that presents to you the most powerful helps to enable you to arrive at your last end, the love and service of God in this world, and after death, eternal happiness?

2°. If some other person, whose salvation or perfection was of great interest to you, found himself in the same position as yourself, and in his uncertainty consulted you, what advice would you give him for the greater glory of God, and the good of his own soul? The counsel that you would give him is that which you ought to follow yourself.

3°. At the moment of death, how would you wish you had conducted yourself in this deliberation? Make the same choice now, for it is the one that will give you the most confidence at that important hour.

Your resolution being fixed, offer it to God in humble prayer, and beg of him to accept and bless it.

PRAYER TO SECURE THE BLESSING OF GOD IN
THE CHOICE OF A STATE OF LIFE.

O JESUS, Eternal Wisdom and most charitable Counsellor of all who apply to thee, I come to consult thee, and to ask thee for light and direction. Let me see, I beseech thee, how I am to act, and what is most agreeable to thy will. Let me see, by means best known to thyself, what it is that thou requirest of me. Teach me in what manner I am to conduct myself, and the means I am to make use of, that all I do may succeed to thy glory, and the welfare of my soul. I offer thee a heart prepared to follow thy divine directions, and to execute thy orders; because it is in thee that I place all my hopes, and I desire nothing more than the accomplishment of thy will. Let, therefore, thy divine light shine upon me, and do not abandon me to my own darkness. Amen.

Say the Our Father and Hail Mary, or the Memorare, and some Prayer to your Patron Saint, and Guardian Angel.

# The Sacraments.

## Instructions and Devotions for Confession.

PENANCE is a Sacrament instituted by Christ, in which, by the ministry of the Priest, actual sins are forgiven, the eternal punishment due to mortal sin is remitted, and part or the whole of the temporal punishment, according to the dispositions of the penitent.

Although confession of sin may seem at first sight to be both bitter and painful, yet the consequences of neglect in approaching to this Sacrament are so terrible, that no Catholic who is conscious that he has fallen into mortal sin, ought to defer having recourse to this fountain of divine mercy. For (1°) The longer the time granted to the sinner for conversion, the greater is his ingratitude in resisting God's goodness. (2°) The commission of one mortal sin makes a second easier, and a second offence disposes the soul for many others. (3°) Whilst he remains in the state of mortal sin, a sinner loses the merit of all the good works he performs. Lastly, as the longer a stain remains upon a garment, the more difficult it is to remove it, and the more we neglect to cleanse our chambers or our persons, the more defiled they become, so too, the longer the soul neglects to purge herself by Confession, the more difficult the work will be, and hence the greater danger of its being left undone.

THE PARTS OF PENANCE.—They are three: Contrition, Confession, and Satisfaction; these are necessary for the perfection of the Sacrament.

CONTRITION consists in a hearty sorrow and detestation of our sins, because by them we have offended God, whom we ought to love above all things; to this sorrow must be joined a firm purpose of amendment of life. Contrition for sin should be—(1°) *Internal:* that is, it should spring from, and reside in the heart, and hence mere external signs or expressions of sorrow are not sufficient. (2°) *Supernatural:* that is, it should arise from motives derived from Faith, and excited in us by the Holy Ghost; such for instance, as the loss of God's favour, or of heaven, the anger of God, or his goodness, &c. The motives should not be merely natural ones, as disgrace in the eyes of men, temporal losses, &c. (3°) *Universal:* that is, it must extend to all our mortal sins, without any exception. (4°) *Predominant:* that is, we must prefer to suffer anything rather than offend God by committing a mortal sin; for sin is the greatest of all evils, indeed, strictly speaking, it is the only evil in this world.

CONFESSION is the accusing ourselves of our sins to a Priest. This accusation must be—(1°) *Entire:* that is, all mortal sins, both as regards their number, as also any circumstance that may change the nature of them, must be fully and distinctly confessed. (2°) *Humble:* that is, we should confess our sins in the spirit of true penitents, covered with shame and confusion. (3°) *Simple:* that is, we should confine ourselves to the declaration of our sins, or what concerns our own conscience, without entering into useless details which take off from the attention that should accompany so holy a duty. We should avoid all excesses, and not mention unnecessarily the sins of others, or name a third person.

SATISFACTION is the performance of the penance enjoined by the Priest in Confession. This is called Sacramental Satisfaction. But besides this, there is a Voluntary Satisfaction that we impose on ourselves, such as penitential works that we may do in atonement for sins committed. These works are of three kinds, Prayer, Almsgiving, and Fasting, or other corporal austerities.

CAUSES WHICH RENDER CONFESSION INVALID.—(1°) When any mortal sin is omitted wilfully, through shame or any other sinful motive. (2°) When any grievous falsehood is told in Confession. (3°) When any mortal sin is forgotten, which might have been remembered had there not been gross negligence in the examination of conscience. (4°) When there is not a full purpose of abandoning mortal sin, and of avoiding the dangerous and unnecessary occasions of it.

### PREPARATORY PRAYER.

O GOD, Creator of heaven and earth, and King of kings, who hast made me out of nothing unto thine own image and likeness, and hast redeemed me by thine own most precious blood, whom I, a wretched sinner, am not worthy to name or invoke, or even think of, I suppliantly beseech thee to look down with pity on thine unworthy servant. Have mercy on me, O God, who hadst mercy on the Cananean woman and on Mary Magdalen, who forgavest the publican and the thief hanging on the cross. To thee, most loving Father, I confess my sins. Forgive me, dear Lord, for I have grievously offended thee in thought, word and deed. Thou didst come down from heaven for my salvation. Thou art my Creator and my Redeemer, my Lord and my Saviour, my King and my God. Thou art my hope and my trust, my guide and my support, my comfort and my strength, my defence and my deliverance, my life, my salvation and my resurrection, my light and my desire, my help and my protection. I beg and beseech thee to assist me, and I shall be saved; direct me and defend me. Raise me from death, for I am the work of thy hands. Do not despise me, O Lord, for I am thy servant and slave, however wicked, sinful and unworthy. If I am blind thou canst enlighten me; if I am dead thou canst raise me to life again; because thy mercy is greater than my iniquity; thy loving forgiveness greater than my sinfulness. I beseech thee, O most merciful Father, by thy great mercy, I entreat and implore thee to lead me to a true sorrow, a sincere confession, and an entire satisfaction for all my sins. Amen.

### A PRAYER TO OBTAIN A FULL KNOWLEDGE OF, AND A TRUE SORROW FOR OUR SINS.

O ETERNAL Father, Father of mercies, and God of all consolation, now that I am about to examine all my actions, I am filled with fear and alarm: for thou layest open what is hidden, unlockest what is closed, and searchest the depths of the human heart. Wherefore, I humbly ask of thee to grant me that I may be able, by thy holy grace, to remember all the sins by which I have most shamefully enslaved my soul, and to weep over them. Excite in me so deep a feeling of grief and sorrow, that I may thus deserve to obtain thy pardon in the Sacrament of Penance.

(You would here do well to have recourse to our Blessed Lady and to your Angel Guardian by means of some short prayer, that they may assist you to prepare for this holy Sacrament worthily.)

# Examination of Conscience.

### FIRST COMMANDMENT.

Have I made sacrilegious confessions by concealing any mortal sin in confession, or through want of the necessary sorrow and purpose of amendment?

Have I approached Holy Communion when I had broken my fast, or received this or any other Sacrament after a sacrilegious confession, or in the state of mortal sin?

Have I, through neglect, omitted my penance after confession?

Have I voluntarily entertained doubts against any Article of Faith?

Have I spoken against the Catholic Religion, or its holy practices, have I turned them to ridicule? if so, what motive had I for so doing? Have I ever induced others to do so?

Have I wilfully exposed myself to temptations against Faith, by dangerous conversations, or by reading books written against Religion?

Have I lent such books to others?

Have I neglected my prayers for any length of time? for how long? When at prayer have I been wilfully distracted?

Have I dishonoured God by superstitious practices? have I really believed in them? have I taught such things to others, if so, what was my motive?

Have I ever boasted of my sins? In this spirit, have I ever pretended that I had committed sins which I never did commit? What was my motive in so doing?

Have I gone on in my sins, trusting to the mercy of God, and to a death-bed repentance?

Have I despaired of the mercy of God?

Have I tempted God in any way?

### SECOND COMMANDMENT.

Have I used the name of God, or that of his Saints and Angels in a disrespectful manner?

Have I cursed: that is, wished that God would inflict any evil on others? Did I really wish the evil? Did I express such a wish in words?

·Have I sworn: that is, called God to bear witness to anything, without sufficient reason? Was the assertion false, or did I doubt the truth of it?

Have I blasphemed: that is, spoken in an insulting manner of God or of Holy Things?

Have I taught such words to others, or listened to them with pleasure, when uttered by others? Have I put a stop to such conversations, when in my power to do so?

Have I made rash or unlawful vows or promises to God? have I broken lawful vows or promises?

### THIRD COMMANDMENT.

Have I neglected Mass, or any considerable portion of it, upon Sundays or Holydays? how much have I lost? was it through my own fault?

Have I wilfully entertained distracting

thoughts during Mass, was it throughout the Mass, or only during a small portion of it?

Have I been the guilty occasion of others missing Mass, or a part of it, on Sundays or Holydays?

Have I been the cause of others hearing Mass in a distracted manner?

Have I done unnecessary servile work on Sundays or Holydays, or caused others to do so, and for how long a time?

Have I neglected to sanctify the Sundays and Holydays, and made a habit of neglecting Sermons and Evening Devotions? What was my motive for so doing?

### FOURTH COMMANDMENT.

Have I loved, respected, and obeyed my Parents and lawful Superiors?

Have I acted against their just commands or good advice? Was it in matters of consequence?

Have I ever used insulting or disrespectful language towards them, or induced others to do so, or listened with pleasure to such language?

Have I wished them ill, despised them or really wished death or any serious injury to them?

Have I struck them or wished to do so?

Have I ever cursed them?

Have I idled away my time and thus neglected study, or other duties of my state of life?

### FIFTH COMMANDMENT.

Have I done any serious injury to anyone, or wished to do so?

Have I borne hatred towards anyone, or refused to speak to or be reconciled to him? For how long a time?

Have I ever seriously wished the death of anyone? of whom?

Have I given way to anger or violent passion?

Have I revenged myself on anyone, by word or action? Have I wished to do so?

Have I challenged or provoked others to fight or quarrel, or encouraged others to do these things?

Have I committed excesses in eating or drinking? have I thus, or in any other way injured my health? have I been the occasion of others giving way to these excesses?

Have I ever tried to draw others into sin by scandal or bad example? into what sin, and how many souls have I thus wounded? have I taught another to commit sin?

N.B.—Since the sin of scandal includes two sins, one against the Fifth Commandment, on account of the breach of charity in thus wounding the soul of your neighbour, and the other against the Commandment that is violated, it is necessary that the penitent should state distinctly, in Confession, how he has given scandal, whenever he has caused another to commit a grievous sin.

### SIXTH AND NINTH COMMANDMENTS.

(The Ninth Commandment forbids in thought and desire whatever the Sixth forbids in action. In no other Commandment is the danger of mortal sin so great as in these, whenever there is any wilful transgression.)

# EXAMINATION OF CONSCIENCE.

Have I willingly consented to immodest thoughts or imaginations?

Did I wish to do anything immodest, had I the opportunity: and if so, what did I wish to do, and with whom?

Have I wilfully and with pleasure looked at objects that would fill my mind with bad and dangerous thoughts?

Have I joined in immodest and dangerous conversation and taken pleasure in it? with how many have I held such conversations?

Have I read immodest books, or sung bad songs, or drawn immodest objects? have I shown or taught these things to others? to how many?

Have I acted immodestly with myself or others from bad motives, or have I allowed others to take improper liberties with me, and so been the occasion of their sin as well as my own? what sort of persons were they?

Have I presumed too much on my own strength, and thus not avoided what I knew in my conscience would lead me into sin?

Have I taught or induced others to commit any sins against these Commandments?

(N.B.—Whenever you doubt whether what you have done or allowed others to do to you, be sinful or not, lay open your difficulty to your Confessor, and abide by his decision.)

## SEVENTH AND TENTH COMMANDMENTS.

(The Tenth Commandment forbids in thought and desire, what the Seventh Commandment forbids in action.)

Have I stolen? from whom? how much?

Have I cheated in buying, or selling, or in dealing with others? how much?

Have I wantonly injured the property of others? to what extent?

Have I neglected to pay my debts? to what extent have I thus injured my creditors?

Have I made restitution, as far as I was able, to those whom I have injured?

Have I caused others to steal, or in any other way to injure their neighbour? how many have I thus led into sin?

Have I unjustly coveted or sought the goods of others?

### EIGHTH COMMANDMENT.

Have I borne false witness against my neighbour in a court, or before anyone in office?

Have I been guilty of calumny, by telling lies of anyone, or saying what I did not know to be true? before how many?

Have I been guilty of detraction by disclosing the secret sins of my neighbour, or injured his character by speaking of things which, though true, I had no right to mention to others? Before how many have I so spoken?

Have I told lies? Were they in matters of consequence or injurious to others?

Have I restored the good name of my neighbour, as far as I was able, when I have deprived him of it?

Have I entertained a bad opinion of my neighbour, without just grounds, or judged rashly of his actions or intentions?

Have I willingly listened to calumny or detraction, or in any way encouraged such conversations?

EXAMINATION OF CONSCIENCE. 261

Have I created jealousies and quarrels by talebearing, or have I disclosed secrets entrusted to me? Were they in matters of consequence?

COMMANDMENTS OF THE CHURCH.

Have I neglected the days of fasting and of abstinence without sufficient reason? What was my motive?

Have I received Holy Communion worthily at Easter?

Have I, by my advice, or in any other way, caused others to violate the Commandments of the Church?

---

HELPS TO EXCITE IN OURSELVES TRUE CONTRITION.—(1°) Place before your eyes as clearly as you can all the sins which you are going to confess. (2°) Read over attentively the Meditation on the Grievousness of Mortal Sin (page 28): that on Hell (page 29), and, if time allows, some of those that follow immediately after. Meditate too upon the goodness of God as shown to us in the Parable of the Prodigal Son (page 41), as also in the bitter sufferings of Jesus Christ (page 58.) Consider also the great recompense held out to you if you are faithful to the end in the service of God (page 66), and even extend your desires still further, and strive to enter into the spirit of those purer and more perfect dispositions brought before you in the Meditation on the Love of God (page 67.)

### PRAYER TO OBTAIN CONTRITION.

I HAVE now before me, O Lord, a sad prospect of the many offences, by which I have displeased thy divine Majesty; and which I am assured will appear in judgment against me, if I repent not, and my soul be not disposed by a hearty sorrow to receive thy pardon. But this sorrow, O Lord, this repentance, must be thy free gift; and if it come not from the hand of thy mercy, all my endeavours will be in vain, and I shall be for ever miserable. Have mercy, therefore, on me, O Father of Mercies, and pour forth into my heart thy grace, whereby I may sincerely repent of all my sins. Give me a true contrition that I may bewail my past misery and ingratitude, and grieve from my heart for having offended thee, so good a God. Permit me not to be deluded with a false sorrow, as, I fear, I have been too often, through my own weakness or neglect; but let it be now thy gift descending from thee, the Father of lights, that so my repentance may be accompanied with amendment and a change of life, and I may be fully acquitted from the guilt of all my sins, and once more received into the number of thy servants. Through Jesus Christ our Lord. Amen.

## ACTS OF CONTRITION.

O MY God, I hate and detest these and all other sins which I have committed against thy divine Majesty. I am extremely sorry that I have offended thee, because thou art infinitely good, and sin displeases thee. I love thee with my whole heart; and firmly purpose, by the help of thy grace, never more to offend thee. I resolve to avoid the occasions of sin; I will confess my sins, and will endeavour to make satisfaction for them. Have mercy on me, O God, have mercy and pardon me, a wretched sinner. In the name of thy beloved Son Jesus, I humbly beg of thee so to wash me with his precious blood, that my sins may be entirely remitted.

O Lord Jesus Christ, most ardent lover of our souls, who through boundless love willest not the death of a sinner, but rather that he be converted and live: I am grieved from the bottom of my heart for having offended thee, my God, my most loving Father and most bountiful Saviour, to whom all sin is infinitely displeasing, and who hast loved me, a vile and miserable slave, so far, as to shed thy most precious blood and to undergo a most bitter death for my sake. O infinite Goodness! O my God! Would that I had never offended thee, who art infinitely good, and so deserving of all love! Pardon me, good Jesus, pardon me most humbly imploring thy mercy: have pity on me a sinner, in whose behalf thy blood pleads in the sight of thy eternal Father. For the love of thee, my most gracious Lord, I forgive all who have ever offended me, and I firmly purpose to shun all sin, and to avoid all dangerous occasions that may lead me into it, to confess in the bitterness of my soul those sins of which I have been guilty, and to love thee my God, above all things, now and for ever. O sweet Jesus, give me thy grace, that thus I may be enabled to fulfil these my good resolutions.

My Lord and my all! I am confounded at the multitude and enormity of my offences against so good a God; I dare not presume even to lift up mine eyes to heaven, much less to come near thy altar, after so many treasons against thee. Alas! what shall I now do, O Lord? What shall I say? But with the humble publican, strike my breast, and cry out to thee, O God, be merciful to me a sinner!

My sins exceed in number the hairs of my head, and the sands of the sea: but thy mercy is greater than mine iniquity. O God of mercy, have compassion on a poor miserable sinner, and make me now at least a true penitent. Father, I have sinned against heaven, and in thy sight, and am not worthy to be called thy child: receive me now as one of the least of thy servants, and never suffer me to go astray from thee any more. It grieves me, O my good God, that I have offended thee: I am heartily sorry for all the sins which I have committed against thine infinite goodness. Oh, that I could worthily lament them, even with tears of blood. Who will give water to my head, and a fountain of tears to mine eyes, that night and day I may weep for my sins and ingratitude? Would that I had never offended my God, that I had never sinned! Happy those souls who have never lost their baptismal innocence. O sweet Jesus, that I had been so happy! Have mercy on me, O God, according to thy great mercy; and according to the multitude of thy tender mercies blot out mine iniquity. Wash me yet more from mine iniquity, and cleanse me from my sin; for I know mine iniquity, and my sin is always before me. Oh, that I could now, like Magdalen, present myself at the feet of my dear Saviour! that I could wash them with my tears! Suffer me dear Lord, to lay down all my sins at thy feet, to be cancelled by thy most precious blood. Lord, thou hast said, there is joy in heaven upon one sinner doing penance, more than upon ninety-nine just: give me now the grace to be a true penitent indeed, so that heaven may rejoice at my conversion. I am resolved, by thy grace, never more to return to my sins; rather let me die than offend thee wilfully any more. I am resolved to fly all evil company, and dangerous occasions, and to take proper measures for a thorough amendment of my life for the future. All this I resolve; but thou knowest my frailty, O my God; and if thou assist me not by thy grace, all my resolutions will prove ineffectual, and I shall be for ever miserable: look to me, O Lord, that I may never betray thee any more.

Here the Penitent may recite the Miserere (Page 131), or any other of the Penitential Psalms (Page 209.)

## DIRECTIONS FOR CONFESSION.

APPROACH the Confessional with sentiments of humility and contrition, and kneeling down beside your Confessor, make the sign of the Cross, and say: "Father, give me your blessing, for I have sinned." When you have received the blessing of the Priest, say the "Confiteor" as far as "through my fault, &c." Then confess your sins with great truthfulness and profound humility, attending to the instructions given above (Page 251).

Conclude by some general clause to the following effect. "For these and all my sins which I have at any time committed I am heartily sorry : I purpose amendment, and ask pardon of God, and penance and absolution from you, my spiritual Father." Then say the second part of the "Confiteor," "Therefore I beseech, &c."

N.B.—If you go frequently to Confession, and find that you have no grievous sin to confess, you would do well to mention some one sin of your past lifetime, for which you are truly sorry, that thus you may not run the risk of losing the grace of the Sacrament through a want of proper contrition for sins confessed. Listen respectfully and attentively to whatever your Confessor, either by way of advice or exhortation, may say to you : and having received a penance together with absolution, depart with a firm determination to carry out whatever your Confessor shall have enjoined you, whether it be to make restitution or reparation, to be reconciled to your enemies, to avoid proximate occasions of sin, &c.

## AFTER CONFESSION.

AFTER Confession recollect yourself, and observe three things:

1°. Perform the Penance which was enjoined as soon as you can do so conveniently; renew your firm purpose of avoiding, with God's grace, all the sins which you have confessed, and, as far as possible, the occasions of them. You may then have a perfect confidence that, through God's goodness, and the efficacy of the Sacrament, all your sins are forgiven.

2°. Consider how you can amend your life. This will best be done by fixing your attention on one or two of your more prominent defects. and directing your chief efforts to overcome them by such means as the following. (1°.) Conceive a strong desire to overcome these faults, frequently renew your resolution, and examine yourself particularly upon them. (2.) When you commit them, punish yourself in some way. (3°.) Address some short prayers to Jesus Christ, or to Our Blessed Lady, when you are tempted, or in the occasion of sin.

3°. Endeavour to dispose yourself gradually for an increase of divine grace, and have an earnest desire to make amends in future by true piety and devotion for all the errors of your past life, and by calling to mind your sins, strive to become daily more humble, and more fervent in the pursuit of virtue.

### PRAYER AFTER CONFESSION.

"Behold thou art made whole: sin no more, lest some worse thing happen to thee." (John v. 14.)

O MOST merciful Redeemer, most loving Physician of the human race, thou hast made me whole by the outpouring of thy most precious blood. Thou hast not refused to pour into my wounds the sweetest balm drawn from the hallowed fountain of thy Sacred Heart. O most bountiful Samaritan, I acknowledge thy love, I embrace thine infinite mercy. Thou hast rescued me from death; thou hast made me thy son, and thou hast appointed by thy will, that the inheritance of eternal life shall come to me. What have I found in thee, O Sovereign Goodness, O Lord my God, that I should keep my mind estranged from thee? And what have I discovered in myself that I have deemed worthy of so much love? How often, O Lord, can I assert that I have been snatched from the jaws of death by thy goodness? And how often have I not proved myself my worst enemy? Oh that thou wouldst this once open the eyes of my understanding, that I may know thee and know myself! myself, that I may fly from myself as from a mass of corruption, but Thee, that I may ever follow thee. Let this my confession, I beseech thee, O Lord, be pleasing and acceptable to thee through the merits of the ever blessed Virgin Mary, thy Mother and mine, and through those of all the Saints ; and whatever defect there has been now, and at other times in the sufficiency of my contrition, and in the purity and integrity of my confession may it be supplied by thy goodness and mercy, according to which I beg thee to hold me fully and perfectly absolved in heaven. Who livest and reignest for ever and ever. Amen.

### CONSIDERATIONS AFTER CONFESSION.

1°. CONTEMPLATE Almighty God: fix your eyes on him who ought above all things to be feared and loved; who created, who preserves and governs the universe; who is everywhere present and sees all things ; at whose nod the pillars of heaven tremble ; whose eyes are brighter than the sun, and penetrate the inmost recesses of the human heart. Ought not then every one always and everywhere to have Him before his eyes, who is at once the witness and judge of all his actions ? Let that golden sentence of St. Augustine be deeply engraven on your heart: "We, who do our actions in the presence of a Judge who sees all things, are under a great necessity of living holily and righteously."

2°. Ponder also with St. Gregory the Great : "That which delights is momentary, but that which torments is eternal." Oh what a miserable exchange ! for the sake of a trifling and short satisfaction, to be despoiled of everlasting bliss, and by yielding to the allurements of some earthly pleasure, to entail on oneself continual and never-ending pains! And what, I ask, is there desirable in the pleasures of the world? They weary and fatigue us when we run after them, infatuate us when we have acquired them, torment us when we have lost them.

3°. In order to secure yourself also more and more against all kinds of sins and imperfections, it will be a great help ever to bear in mind the presence, not only of God the witness of all your actions; but also of your Angel Guardian.

4°. Lastly, it will be found useful to meditate on the beauty and nobleness of virtue, the shortness of pleasure, the foulness of sin, the precariousness of life, the uncertainty of the hour of death, the peace of a good conscience, the dignity of man, the benefits of Almighty God, and above all, the life, death and cross of Christ. Love Christ, therefore, and keep his commandments, and doubt not but that he will give you a share in his joys who deigned to take upon himself your sorrows. The labour is certainly great, but the reward is inestimable, namely, to be what the Martyrs are, to be what the Apostles are, to be like unto Christ himself.

### AN ADMONITION TO THE SINNER.

"Go, and now sin no more." (John viii. 11.)

AND what is it to sin? What else but, as it were, to revile Almighty God, and say to him: " Thou forbiddest me to do this, yet I will do it, even to thy dishonour and in thy sight. Thou wilt in consequence become mine enemy, and wilt hold me in abomination as guilty of treason to thy divine Majesty, as thy foe, yet I will sin. I shall trample under foot the blood of Jesus Christ, yet I will sin. I shall lose the everlasting joys of heaven, yet I will sin. I shall let loose upon myself the powers of hell, yet I will sin."

Tremble, poor sinner, and fear lest those words be spoken to you by Almighty God in his wrath: "Depart from me, you cursed, into everlasting fire, which has been prepared for the devil and his angels." (Matt. xxv. 41.)

You must beware, as far as possible, of venial sins, because they entail punishment in this world, and in the next; lessen the fire of charity, defile the soul, and weaken her in the exercise of good works, defer the joys of eternal life, and dispose to mortal sin, according to those words, "He that contemneth small things will fall by little and little." (Eccles. xix. 1.) You must refrain from them, considering as St. Jerome says, not that they are small in themselves, but that God whom they displease is great. You should not commit even the smallest sin, were it to obtain all the advantages this world can afford.

"Although we do not believe that the soul is death-stricken by our small daily sins, yet they render her so deformed by covering her, as it were, with certain ulcers and disgusting sores that they scarcely, or at least with great difficulty, allow her to approach to the embraces of her Divine Spouse." (St. Augustine.)

# The Sacrament of the Holy Eucharist.

### INSTRUCTIONS AND DEVOTIONS FOR COMMUNION.

THE holy Eucharist is the body and blood of Jesus Christ, true God, and true man, under the appearances of bread and wine. *The bread, says Jesus Christ, that I will give, is my flesh, for the life of the world.* (St. John vi. 52.) And at his last supper, *he took bread, and blessed and broke, and gave to his disciples, and said, Take ye, and eat, this is my body. And taking the chalice he gave thanks and gave to them, saying, Drink ye all of this; for this is my blood of the New Testament, which shall be shed for many unto the remission of sins.* (St. Matt. xxvi. 26, &c.)

Our blessed Redeemer, having thus instituted this adorable Sacrament, ordained his Apostles priests of the new law, and gave to them and their lawful successors power and authority to do what he had done, that is, to change bread and wine into his sacred body and blood. This change, which is called Transubstantiation, is effected by those divine words of our Redeemer, which the Priest in the Mass, at the consecration, pronounces in the name and person of Jesus Christ. It is God himself who works this wonderful change by the ministry of his Priest.

*Let a man prove himself,* says St. Paul (1 Cor. xi. 28), *and so let him eat of that bread, &c.* This proving or trying yourself is the first and most necessary preparation for holy Communion, and consists in looking diligently into the state of your soul, in order to discover what sins may lie there concealed, and in applying a proper remedy to them by sincere repentance and confession; lest otherwise approaching the Holy of Holies with a soul defiled with the guilt of mortal sin, you become "*guilty of the body and blood of the Lord, and receive judgment to yourself not discerning the body of the Lord.*" (1 Cor. xi.)

The person who receives the blessed Sacrament must have been fasting from midnight, by the command of the Church, and by a most ancient and apostolical tradition, ordaining, that this act of respect should be paid to the Body of Christ, by all who wish to receive it. Hence, if through inadvertence, or otherwise, you have taken anything, though ever so little, after twelve o'clock at night, you must by no means receive that day, except in the case of danger of approaching death, when the blessed Sacrament is received by way of Viaticum.

ACTS OF DEVOTION BEFORE COMMUNION.

I. *Direct your Intention.*

O LORD Jesus Christ, behold I desire to come to thee this day, and to receive thy body and blood in this adorable Sacrament, for thy honour and glory, and for the good of my soul: I desire to receive thee, because it is thy wish, and thou hast so ordained; blessed be thy Name for ever. I desire to come to thee like Magdalen, that I may be delivered from all my evils, and embrace thee my only good. I desire to come to thee, that I may be happily united to thee, that I may henceforth abide in thee, and thou in me, and that nothing in life or death may ever separate me from thee.

II. *Commemorate the Passion of Christ.*

I DESIRE, in these holy mysteries, to commemorate, as thou hast commanded, all thy sufferings, thine agony and bloody sweat; thy being betrayed and apprehended; all the reproaches and calumnies, all the blows and buffets which thou hast endured for me; thy having been scourged, crowned with thorns, and loaded with a heavy cross for my sins, and for those of the whole world; thy crucifixion and death, together with thy glorious resurrection and triumphant ascension. I adore thee, and give thee thanks for all thou hast done and suffered for me; and for giving me, in this blessed Sacrament, this pledge of my redemption, this victim of my ransom, this body and blood which were offered for me.

### III. *Make an Act of Faith.*

I MOST firmly believe that in this holy Sacrament thou art truly present; that here are thy body and blood, thy soul and thy divinity. I believe that thou my Saviour, true God and true man, art really here with all thy treasures; that here thou communicatest thyself to me, makest me partaker of the fruit of thy passion, and givest me a pledge of eternal life. I believe that there cannot be a greater happiness than to receive thee worthily, nor a greater misery than to receive thee unworthily. All this I most steadfastly believe, because it is what thou hast taught me by thy word, and by thy Church.

### IV. *Conceive a great fear, and humble yourself.*

BUT, O my God, how shall I dare approach to thee, so wretched a worm to such infinite Majesty? so filthy a sinner to such purity and sanctity? Alas! my soul is covered with an universal leprosy, and how shall I presume to embrace thee? my whole life has been nothing but misery and sin, and it is only through thy mercy that I have not been long since in hell, which I have deserved so often; and how shall I venture to lift up mine eyes to thee, or receive thee within my breast? I tremble at the sentence of thy Apostle, that "*he that eateth and drinketh unworthily, eateth and drinketh judgment to himself*" (1 Cor. xi. 29); for I cannot but acknowledge myself most unworthy: nor should I dare ever to come to thee, were I not incited by thy most loving and pressing invitation, and encouraged by thine infinite goodness and mercy. It is in this mercy, which is above all thy works, I put my whole trust; and it is in this confidence alone that I presume to approach to thee. O grant that it may be with a contrite and humble heart; for this I know, thou wilt not despise.

V. *Make an Act of Contrition.*

O LORD, I detest with my whole heart, all the sins by which I have ever offended thy divine Majesty, from the first moment that I was capable of committing sin to this hour. I desire to lay them all at thy feet, to be cancelled by thy precious blood. What can I do for them, but humbly confess and lament them all my life: and this I heartily desire to do, and from this moment continually to cry to thee for mercy.

the sake of this same precious blood, which thou hast shed for me, deliver me from so great an evil : rather let me die than thus presume to crucify thee again.

VIII. *Implore the Prayers of the Blessed Virgin and of the Saints.*

O ALL ye holy Angels and Saints of God, who see Him face to face, whom I here receive under these humble veils, thou most especially, ever blessed Virgin, Mother of this same God and Saviour, assist me by your prayers and intercession, that I may in such manner receive him here, in this place of banishment, as to be brought one day to enjoy him with you in our true country, there to praise him and love him for ever.

PRAYER OF ST. THOMAS OF AQUIN.

ALMIGHTY and eternal God, behold I approach this Sacrament of thine only begotten Son, Jesus Christ our Lord: I approach as one who is sick to the Physician of life, as one unclean to the Fountain of mercy, as one blind to the Light of eternal brightness, as one poor and needy to the Lord of heaven and earth. Wherefore, I beseech thine infinite goodness that thou wouldst deign to heal mine infirmities, to wash away my filth, to enlighten my blindness, to enrich my poverty, and clothe my nakedness; that I may receive the Bread of Angels, the King of Kings and Lord of Lords, with such reverence and humility, such contrition and devotion, such faith and purity, and with such good resolutions as may conduce to the salvation of my soul.

Grant, I beseech thee, O Lord, that I may receive, not only the Sacrament of thy body and blood, but also the fruit and virtue of this Sacrament. O most indulgent God! grant that I may so receive the body of thine only Son, Jesus Christ our Lord, as to deserve to be incorporated with his mystical body, and be numbered amongst its members. O most loving Father! grant that I may one day be permitted to contemplate through all eternity, face to face, thy beloved Son, whom now, in my pilgrimage, I am about to receive concealed under the sacramental veils. Who liveth and reigneth with thee in the unity of the Holy Ghost, God, for ever. Amen.

### PRAYER OF ST. AMBROSE.

O MY most loving Lord Jesus Christ, I a poor sinner, presuming not on mine own merits, but trusting to thy mercy and goodness, am filled with fear when I approach this banquet of thy most sacred body and blood. I have defiled both my soul and body by many sins, and have not kept a strict guard over my heart and my tongue. Wherefore, O God of goodness and majesty, I, a wretched creature, entangled as I am, have recourse to thee, the Fountain of life, I fly to thee that I may be healed, I have recourse to thy protection, and I ardently desire to receive him as my Saviour, whom I fear to look upon as my Judge. To thee, O Lord, I lay open my wounds: to thee I disclose my shame. I acknowledge my many grievous sins, on account of which I am filled with fear. I trust in thy mercy which is unbounded. Look down, therefore, upon me with eyes of pity, O Lord Jesus, eternal King, God-Man crucified for man. Graciously hear me, who have placed my hope in thee, have mercy on me so full of misery and sin, for thou art the full and overflowing Fountain of mercy. Hail, saving Victim, offered up for me and for all men upon the tree of the cross! Hail, noble and precious blood, flowing from the wounds of Jesus, my crucified Lord, and washing away the sins of the whole world! Remember, O Lord, thy creature, whom thou hast redeemed with thy precious blood. I am grieved because I have offended thee by sin: I desire to make amends for my past misconduct. Remove far from me, O most bountiful Father, all my sins, that being purified both in soul and body, I may be made worthy to receive the Holy of Holies; and grant that this devout participation of thy body and blood may be to me the remission of all my sins, the perfect cleansing of my faults, the means of banishing all evil thoughts, the renewal of devout affections, the advancement of good works, as well as the strongest defence for soul and body against the snares of my enemies. Amen.

When you approach Holy Communion your dress ought to be becoming and modest, and your whole deportment expressive of veneration and respect for the presence of your Lord and Saviour Jesus Christ, who, in this holy Sacrament, has humbled and annihilated himself for you, that he may come to visit you and abide with you.

When about to communicate, go to the rails, take up the cloth and hold it before you. Whilst the Clerk says the *Confiteor*, humbly confess your sins, and beg God's pardon for them. When the Priest turns round to give the absolution, receive it with your head bowed down, as from the hand of the invisible High Priest, whom you are going to receive.

When the Priest holds up the blessed Sacrament with these words, *Ecce Agnus Dei, &c. Behold the Lamb of God, behold him who taketh away the sins of the world*, humbly beg, with a lively confidence in the merits of the death and passion of Jesus, that He would take away your sins.

When the Priest repeats three times, *Domine non sum dignus, &c. Lord, I am not worthy that thou shouldst enter under my roof, but only say the word and my soul shall be healed*, repeat the same with him in your heart, and humble yourself exceedingly through the sense of your unworthiness and sins; but let this be joined with a lively confidence in him, who can raise you up, and perfectly heal your soul by his only word.

When the Priest gives you the blessed Sacrament, saying, *May the body of our Lord Jesus Christ preserve thy soul to everlasting life, Amen*, receive it with a lively faith, a profound humility, and a heart inflamed with love. At the time of your receiving, let your head be erect, your mouth opened moderately wide, and your tongue a little advanced, so as to rest upon your under lip, that the Priest may conveniently convey the blessed Sacrament into your mouth; which being done shut your mouth; let the sacred Host moisten a little upon your tongue and then swallow it as soon as you can conveniently. If the Host should chance to adhere to the roof of your mouth, be not disturbed; do not put your finger into your mouth, but gently and quietly remove it with your tongue. Return to your place, and endeavour to entertain as well as you can, the Guest whom you have received.

Spend at least a quarter of an hour after communion in devotions suitable to that occasion. It would be a great abuse to turn your back immediately upon your Saviour, by going away, as some do, and thinking no more of Him whom they have received.

### ASPIRATIONS AFTER COMMUNION.

BEHOLD, O Lord, I have thee now, who hast all things; I possess thee who possessest all things, and who canst do all things: take off my heart then, O my God and my All, from everything else but thee: let my heart be fixed on thee alone, let me ever repose in thee, where alone my treasure is, the sovereign truth, true happiness, and every good.

Let my soul, O Lord, feel the sweetness of thy presence. Let me taste how sweet thou art; that being allured by thy love, I may never more hunt after worldly joys;

is this to me that my Lord, and so great a God, whom heaven and earth cannot contain, should come into this poor cottage, this house of clay of my earthly habitation? Oh, that I could give thee a hearty welcome! that I could entertain thee as I ought! Thy loving kindness invites me to thy embraces, and I would willingly say with the spouse in the Canticle, "*I have found him whom my soul loveth, I have held him, and will not let him go.*" (Cant. iii. 4). But awe for so great a Majesty checks me, and the sense of my great unworthiness and innumerable sins keeps me back. No, my soul, it is only the feet of thy Saviour that thou canst presume to embrace; it is there thou must remain with Magdalen, and wish that like her, thou couldst wash them with thy tears. Oh, that thou couldst be so happy!

But what return shall I make thee, O Lord, for all that thou hast done for me! Behold, when I had no being at all, thou hast created me; and when I was gone astray, and lost in my sins, thou hast redeemed me, by dying for me; all that I have, all that I am is thy gift; and now, after all thy other favours, thou hast given me thyself; blessed be thy Name for ever. Thou art great, O Lord, and exceedingly to be praised; great are thy works, and of thy wisdom there is no end: but thy tender mercies, thy bounty and goodness to me, are above all thy works; these I desire to confess and extol for ever. Bless, then, thy Lord, O my soul, and let all that is within thee praise and magnify his Name. Bless thy Lord, O my soul, and see thou never forgettest all that he hath done for thee. O all ye works of the Lord, bless the Lord, praise and glorify him for ever. O all ye Angels of the Lord, bless the Lord, praise and glorify his holy Name. Bless the Lord, all ye Saints, and let the whole Church of heaven and earth join in praising and giving him thanks for all his mercies and graces to me; and so, in some measure, supply for what is due from me. But as all this still falleth short of what I owe thee for thine infinite love, I offer to thee, O eternal Father, this same Son of thine, whom thou hast given me, and Him, I am sure, thou wilt accept. Look not, then, upon my insensibility and ingratitude, but upon the face of thy Christ, and with him, and through him, receive this offering of my poor self, which I desire to make thee.

o

### PRAYER OF ST. THOMAS OF AQUIN.

I GIVE thee thanks, most holy Lord, Almighty Father, and eternal God, who hast deigned, not for any merits of mine, but solely through the condescension of thy mercy, to satisfy me a sinner and thine unworthy servant, with the most precious body and blood of thy Son, Jesus Christ our Lord. I implore thee, let not this holy Communion be to me a condemnation unto punishment, but a saving plea unto forgiveness; let it be to me the armour of faith, and the shield of good will. Let it prove the emptying out of my vices, the extinction of my concupiscence and lust, the increase in me of charity and patience, of humility and obedience, and of all virtues; a strong defence against the snares of all mine enemies visible and invisible; a bond of indissoluble union with thee, the one true God, and an earnest of final perseverance. And I beseech thee that thou wouldst deign to conduct me a sinner to that ineffable banquet where thou with thy Son and the Holy Ghost art to thy Saints true light, fulness of content, everlasting joy, gladness without alloy, and perfect bliss. Through Jesus Christ our Lord. Amen.

(A Plenary Indulgence to be obtained by all the faithful, who, after having confessed their sins with contrition, and received the Holy Communion, shall devoutly recite the following prayer before a representation of Christ crucified, and pray for the intentions of the Sovereign Pontiff.)

EN Ego, O bone et dulcissime Jesu ! ante conspectum tuum genibus me provolvo, ac maximo animi ardore te oro atque obtestor ut meum in cor vividos fidei, spei, et charitatis sensus, atque veram peccatorum meorum pœnitentiam, eaque emendandi firmissimam voluntatem velis imprimere, dum magno animi affectu et dolore, tua quinque Vulnera mecum ipse considero, et mente contemplor, illud præ oculis habens, quod jam in ore ponebat suo David Propheta, de te, O bone Jesu ! *Foderunt manus meas et pedes meos : dinumeraverunt omnia ossa mea.* (Ps. xxi. 17.)

BEHOLD, O good and most sweet Jesus, I cast myself upon my knees in thy sight, and with the most fervent desire of my soul I pray and beseech thee that thou wouldst impress upon my heart lively sentiments of faith, hope, and charity, with true repentance for my sins, and a most firm desire of amendment, whilst with deep affection and grief of soul I ponder within myself, and mentally contemplate thy five most precious wounds; having before my eyes that which David spake of thee, O good Jesus ! in prophecy: " *They have dug my hands and feet; they have numbered all my bones.*"(Ps. xxi. 17.)

## ANIMA CHRISTI.

| | |
|---|---|
| Anima Christi, sanctifica me. | Soul of Christ, sanctify me. |
| Corpus Christi, salva me. | Body of Christ, save me. |
| Sanguis Christi, inebria me. | Blood of Christ, inebriate me. |
| Aqua lateris Christi, lava me. | Water from the side of Christ, wash me. |
| Passio Christi, conforta me. | Passion of Christ, strengthen me. |
| O bone Jesu, exaudi me. | O good Jesus, hear me. |
| Intra tua vulnera absconde me. | Within thy wounds hide me. |
| Ne permittas me separari a te. | Never permit me to be separated from thee. |
| Ab hoste maligno defende me. | From the wicked enemy defend me. |
| In hora mortis meæ voca me, | At the hour of my death call me, |
| Et jube me venire ad te; | And bid me come to thee; |
| Ut cum Sanctis tuis laudem te, | That with thy Saints I may praise thee, |
| In sæcula sæculorum. Amen. | For ever and ever. Amen. |

---

It is a useful practice, when you communicate, to make an intention to gain whatever Indulgences are offered to you on that day by the Church, either on occasion of the Feast itself, or on account of any exercise of devotion you are in the habit of practising.

## HYMN.

Ad quem diu suspiravi,
  Jesum tandem habeo;
Hunc amplector quem optavi,
  Quem optavi teneo.
Omnes meæ exultate
  Facultates animæ;
Exultate, triumphate,
  Et ingressu plaudite.

Tristis eram et abjectus,
  Eram sine gaudio,
Quia aberat dilectus
  Quem præ cunctis diligo;
Sed ut venit et intravit
  Animæ tugurium,
O quam dulce permeavit
  Meum cor solatium!

Non sic terras umbris tectas
  Gratus sol illuminat,
Non sic æstibus dejectas
  Nimbus herbas recreat;
Sicut animam languentem
  Refocillat Dominus,
Hanc tristantem et torpentem
  Novis donat viribus.

Felix dies, felix hora
  Qua me, Jesu, visitas;
Pulchra nimis et decora
  Lux ad me qua properas.
Qui te tenet habet satis,
  Quia qui te possidet
Uberem felicitatis
  Veræ fontem obtinet.

Quis non tuam admiretur
  Bonitatem, Domine,
Si quod facis meditetur
  Serio examine?
Ad te ruo, ad me ruis,
  Et me sinis protinus
Immiscere meos tuis
  Amplexus amplexibus.

Nihil eram, me creasti
  Ex obscuro nihilo,
Divinæque me donasti
  Rationis radio.
Pro me nasci voluisti
  In deserto stabulo,
Et finire morte tristi
  Vitam in patibulo.

Præter dona quibus ditas
  Me diebus singulis,
Dapes hodie mellitas
  Datis addis gratiis.
O voluptas cordis mei,
  Jesu dilectissime,
In me regna, Fili Dei,
  Regna, regna libere!

In me proprium amorem
  Tam potenter eneces,
Ut te amem et adorem
  Solum quia dignus es.
In me tolle quod est puris
  Grave tuis oculis,
Ut sic arctius venturis
  Tibi jungar sæculis.

Oriente sole mane,
  Occidente vespera,
Bone Jesu, mecum mane,
  Mecum semper habita :
Nil a te, nec mors nec vita,
  Nil a te me separet;
Unio sit infinita
  Quam vis nulla terminet.

Canam donec respirabo
  Gratiarum cantica,
Millies hæc iterabo
  In cœlesti patria.
Quando te remoto velo
  Sicut es aspiciam,
Et cum Angelis in cœlo
  In æternum diligam.   Amen.

### O DEUS EGO AMO TE.

O GOD! Thou who art the object of my love,
Not for the hopes of endless joys above,
Nor for the fear of endless pains below,
Which those who love thee not must undergo :
For me, and such as me thou once didst bear
The ignominious cross, the nails, the spear;
A thorny crown transpierced thy sacred brow,
What bloody sweats from every member flow!
For me in torture thou resign'st thy breath,
Nail'd to the cross, and savedst me by thy death;
Say, can these sufferings fail my heart to move?
What but thyself can now deserve my love?
Such as then was, and is thy love to me,
Such is, and shall be still, my love to thee.
Thy love, O Jesus, may I ever sing,
O God of love, kind Parent, dearest King!
                                          Amen.

## Sacrament of Confirmation.

*When the Apostles had heard that Samaria had received the word of God, they sent unto them Peter and John; who when they were come, prayed for them, that they might receive the Holy Ghost. For he was not, as yet, come upon any of them; but they were only baptised in the Name of the Lord Jesus. Then they laid their hands upon them, and they received the Holy Ghost.* (Acts viii. 14, 15, 16, 17.)

Confirmation is a sacrament, by which the faithful who have already been made children of God by their baptism, receive the Holy Ghost, that they may become strong and perfect Christians, and soldiers of Jesus Christ. It is called Confirmation from its effects: these are a fortifying grace, by which those who are confirmed are strengthened, so that they may not fear to profess the true faith; and a certain dedication or consecration of the soul, as his temple, by the Holy Ghost.

This sacrament stamps upon the soul a mark, which is called a character, that can never be effaced: hence this sacrament can be received but once; and it would be a sacrilege to attempt to receive it a second time; for this reason the faithful are bound to take great care to come to this sacrament duly disposed.

The dispositions which the Christian must bring with him to receive worthily the sacrament of Confirmation, are, first, purity of conscience, at least from all mortal sin, for the Holy Ghost will not come to a soul in which Satan reigns by mortal sin; secondly,

ORDER OF CONFIRMATION. 297

a sincere desire of giving himself up to the Holy Ghost, to follow the influence of divine grace, to be the temple of God for ever, and, by his assistance, answer all the obligations of a soldier of Christ.

### ORDER OF CONFIRMATION.

*The Bishop, standing with his face towards those to be confirmed, with his hands joined upon his breast, says:—*

Spiritus Sanctus superveniat in vos, et virtus Altissimi custodiat vos a peccatis.

May the Holy Ghost come down upon you, and the power of the Most High keep you from sin.

℟. Amen.

℟. Amen.

*Then making the Sign of the Cross, he says:*

℣. Adjutorium nostrum in nomine Domini.

℣. Our help is in the name of the Lord.

℟. Qui fecit cœlum et terram.

℟. Who hath made heaven and earth.

℣. Domine, exaudi orationem meam.

℣. O Lord, hear my prayer.

℟. Et clamor meus ad te veniat.

℟. And let my cry come unto thee.

℣. Dominus vobiscum.

℣. The Lord be with you.

℟. Et cum spiritu tuo.

℟. And with thy spirit.

*With his hands extended towards those to be confirmed, he says:—*

OREMUS.

LET US PRAY.

Omnipotens sempiterne Deus, qui regenerare dignatus es

O Almighty and everlasting God, who hast vouchsafed to re-

o 5

hos famulos tuos ex aqua et Spiritu Sancto, quique dedisti eis remissionem omnium peccatorum; emitte in eos septiformem Spiritum tuum, sanctum Paraclitum, de Cœlis.

℞. Amen.
℣. Spiritum sapientiæ et intellectus.

℞. Amen.
℣. Spiritum consilii et fortitudinis.

℞. Amen.
℣. Spiritum scientiæ et pietatis.

℞. Amen.
Adimple eos spiritu timoris tui, et consigna eos signo cru✠cis Christi, in vitam propitiatus æternam. Per eumdem Dominum nostrum Jesum Christum Filium tuum: qui tecum vivit, et regnat in unitate ejusdem Spiritus Sancti, Deus, per omnia sæcula sæculorum.

℞. Amen.

generate these thy servants, by water and the Holy Ghost, and who hast given them the remission of their sins; send forth upon them thy sevenfold Spirit, the holy Paraclete, from heaven.

℞. Amen.
℣. The Spirit of wisdom and understanding.

℞. Amen.
℣. The Spirit of counsel and of fortitude.

℞. Amen.
℣. The Spirit of knowledge and of piety.

℞. Amen.
Replenish them with the spirit of thy fear, and sign them with the sign of the cross ✠ of Christ, in thy mercy, unto life eternal, through the same Jesus Christ thy Son, our Lord, who liveth and reigneth with thee in the unity of the same Holy Spirit, one God, world without end.

℞. Amen.

ORDER OF CONFIRMATION. 299

Here the Bishop inquires the name of each person to be confirmed, which should be the name of some Saint whom each one chooses for his patron: he then makes the sign of the cross on the forehead of each one to be confirmed, with the holy chrism, saying:—

N., Signo te signo cru✠cis, et confirmo te chrismate salutis. In nomine Pa✠tris, et Fi✠lii, et Spiritus✠ Sancti.

N., I sign thee with the sign of the cross✠, and I confirm thee with the chrism of salvation. In the name of the Fa✠ther and of the Son✠, and of the Holy✠Ghost.

℟. Amen.  ℟. Amen.

The Bishop then gives the person confirmed a gentle blow on the cheek, saying:—

Pax tecum.  Peace be with you.

After all have been confirmed, the Bishop washes his hands, and in the meantime the following anthem is sung:—

Confirma hoc, Deus, quod operatus es in nobis, a templo sancto tuo quod est in Jerusalem.

Confirm, O God, that which thou hast wrought in us, from thy holy temple, which is in Jerusalem.

℟. Gloria Patri, &c.  ℟. Glory be to the Father, &c.

After repeating the Anthem *Confirma hoc*, the Bishop, laying aside his mitre, stands facing the altar, and prays as follows:—

℣. Ostende nobis, Domine, misericordiam tuam.

℣. Show us, O Lord, thy mercy.

℟. Et salutare tuum da nobis.

℟. And grant us thy salvation.

℣. Domine, exaudi orationem meam.

℣. O Lord, hear my prayer.

℟. Et clamor meus ad te veniat.

℣. Dominus vobiscum.

℟. Et cum spiritu tuo.

OREMUS.

DEUS, qui Apostolis tuis Sanctum dedisti Spiritum, et per eos, eorumque successores, cæteris fidelibus tradendum esse voluisti; respice propitius ad humilitatis nostræ famulatum; et præsta, ut eorum corda, quorum frontes sacro chrismate delinivimus, et signo sanctæ Crucis signavimus, idem Spiritus Sanctus in eis superveniens, templum gloriæ suæ dignanter inhabitando perficiat. Qui, cum Patre et eodem Spiritu Sancto, vivis et regnas Deus, in sæcula sæculorum.

℟. Amen.

℟. And let my cry come unto thee.

℣. The Lord be with you.

℟. And with thy spirit.

LET US PRAY.

O GOD, who didst give the Holy Ghost to thy Apostles, and hast been pleased to ordain that by them, and by their successors, He should be given to the rest of the faithful; mercifully look down upon what we, thy poor servants, have done; and grant that the hearts of these thy faithful, whose foreheads we have anointed with thy sacred chrism, and signed with the sign of the holy Cross, may, by the same Holy Ghost coming down upon them, and by his vouchsafing to dwell in them, be made the temple of his glory. Who with the Father and the same Holy Ghost, livest and reignest God, world without end.

℟. Amen.

Then the Bishop gives his blessing to all present, in these words:—

| | |
|---|---|
| Ecce sic benedicetur omnis homo, qui timet Dominum. | Behold, thus shall every man be blessed, who feareth the Lord. |
| Bene✠dicat vos Dominus ex Sion, ut videatis bona Jerusalem omnibus diebus vitæ vestræ, et habeatis vitam æternam. | May the Lord bless ✠ you out of Sion, that you may see the good things of Jerusalem all the days of your life; and that you may live with him for all eternity. |
| ℟. Amen. | ℟. Amen. |

## Hymns to the Holy Ghost.

### VENI, CREATOR.

| | |
|---|---|
| VENI, Creator Spiritus, | COME, Holy Ghost, Creator, come, |
| Mentes tuorum visita; | From thy bright heavenly throne; |
| Imple superna gratia | Come, take possession of our souls, |
| Quæ tu creasti pectora. | And make them all thine own. |
| Qui diceris Paraclitus, | Thou who art call'd the Paraclete, |
| Altissimi donum Dei, | Best gift of God above; |
| Fons vivus, ignis, charitas, | The living spring, the living fire, |
| Et spiritalis unctio. | Sweet unction and true love. |

Tu septiformis munere,　　Thou who art seven-
　　　　　　　　　　　　　　fold in thy grace,
Digitus paternæ dex-　　Finger of God's right
　teræ,　　　　　　　　　　　hand;
Tu rite promissum Pa-　　His promise teaching
　tris,　　　　　　　　　　　little ones
Sermone ditans guttu-　　To speak and under-
　ra.　　　　　　　　　　　　stand.

Accende lumen sensi-　　O Guide our minds with
　bus,　　　　　　　　　　　thy blest light,
Infunde amorem cordi-　　With love our hearts
　bus,　　　　　　　　　　　inflame;
Infirma nostri corporis　And with thy strength,
　　　　　　　　　　　　　　which ne'er decays,
Virtute firmans perpeti.　Confirm our mortal
　　　　　　　　　　　　　　frame.

Hostem repellas lon-　　Far from us drive our
　gius,　　　　　　　　　　　hellish foe,
Pacemque dones pro-　　True peace unto us
　tinus;　　　　　　　　　　bring;
Ductore sic te prævio,　And through all perils
　　　　　　　　　　　　　　lead us safe
Vitemus omne noxi-　　Beneath thy sacred
　um.　　　　　　　　　　　wing.

Per te sciamus da Pa-　Through thee may we
　trem,　　　　　　　　　　the Father know,
Noscamus atque Fili-　Through thee the eter-
　um,　　　　　　　　　　　nal Son;
Teque utriusque Spi-　And thee the Spirit
　ritum　　　　　　　　　　of them both,
Credamus omni tem-　Thrice blessed Three
　pore.　　　　　　　　　　in One.

## VENI, SANCTE SPIRITUS.

| | |
|---|---|
| Deo Patri sit gloria, | All glory to the Father be, |
| Ejusque soli Filio, | With his co-equal Son, |
| Cum Spiritu Paraclito, | The like to thee, Great Paraclete, |
| Nunc, et per omne sæculum: Amen. | Till time itself is done. Amen. |

### VENI, SANCTE SPIRITUS.

| | |
|---|---|
| VENI, Sancte Spiritus, | HOLY Spirit, Lord of light, |
| Et emitte cœlitus | From thy clear celestial height, |
| Lucis tuæ radium. | Thy pure beaming radiance give : |
| Veni, Pater pauperum, | Come, thou father of the poor, |
| Veni, Dator munerum, | Come with treasures which endure, |
| Veni, lumen cordium. | Come, thou light of all that live. |
| Consolator optime, | Thou, of all consolers best, |
| Dulcis hospes animæ, | Visiting the troubled breast, |
| Dulce refrigerium. | Dost refreshing peace bestow ; |
| In labore requies, | Thou in toil art comfort sweet ; |
| In æstu temperies, | Pleasant coolness in the heat ; |
| In fletu solatium. | Solace in the midst of woe. |

O lux beatissima,  
Reple cordis intima,  
Tuorum fidelium.  
Sine tuo numine,  
Nihil est in homine,  
Nihil est innoxium.

Light immortal! light divine!  
Visit thou these hearts of thine,  
And our inmost being fill:  
If thou take thy grace away,  
Nothing pure in man will stay;  
All his good is turn'd to ill.

Lava quod est sordidum,  
Riga quod est aridum,  
Sana quod est saucium.  
Flecte quod est rigidum,  
Fove quod est frigidum,  
Rege quod est devium.

Heal our wounds, our strength renew;  
On our dryness pour thy dew;  
Wash the stains of guilt away.  
Bend the stubborn heart and will;  
Melt the frozen, warm the chill;  
Guide the steps that go astray.

Da tuis fidelibus,  
In te confitentibus,  
Sacrum septenarium.  
Da virtutis meritum,

Thou, on those who evermore  
Thee confess and thee adore,  
In thy sevenfold gifts descend:  
Give them comfort when they die;

VENI, SANCTE SPIRITUS. 305

Da salutis exitum,

Da perenne gaudium. Amen.

Give them life with thee on high,

Give them joys which never end. Amen.

*Ant.* Veni, Sancte Spiritus, replet uorum corda fidelium, et tui amoris in eis ignem accende.

*Ant.* Come, Holy Spirit, fill the hearts of thy faithful, and kindle in them the fire of thy love.

℣. Emitte Spiritum tuum, et creabuntur.

℣. Send forth thy Spirit, and our hearts will be regenerated.

℞. Et renovabis faciem terræ.

℞. And thou shalt renew the face of the earth.

OREMUS.

LET US PRAY.

DEUS, qui corda fidelium Sancti Spiritus illustratione docuisti, da nobis in eodem Spiritu recta sapere, et de ejus semper consolatione gaudere. Per Dominum nostrum Jesum Christum Filium tuum, qui tecum vivit et regnat in unitate ejusdem Spiritus Sancti Deus. Per omnia sæcula sæculorum. Amen.

O GOD, who hast taught the hearts of the faithful by the light of the Holy Spirit, grant that we may, by the gift of the same Spirit, be always truly wise, and ever rejoice in his consolations. Through our Lord Jesus Christ, thy Son, who liveth and reigneth with thee in the unity of the same Holy Spirit, God; world without end. Amen.

# The Sacrament of Extreme Unction.

INSTRUCTIONS AND DEVOTIONS FOR THE SICK.

Of this holy Sacrament St. James, the Apostle, thus speaks: "*Is any man sick among you? Let him bring in the Priests of the church, and let them pray over him, anointing him with oil in the name of the Lord. And the prayer of faith shall save the sick man, and the Lord shall raise him up; and if he be in sins, they shall be forgiven him.*" (James v. 14, 15.)

The priest in administering this sacrament anoints the five principal senses of the body: the eyes, the ears, the nostrils, the lips, the hands, and the feet, because these may have been employed during life in offending God. At each anointing he pronounces these words: "*May the Lord by this holy anointing, and by his own most tender mercy, pardon thee, whatever sin thou hast committed by thy sight, hearing, &c.*"

The sick person should endeavour to prepare himself to receive this sacrament by acts of sincere contrition for all his sins, by great confidence in the tender mercies of his Redeemer, and by a perfect resignation of himself to the holy will of God.

If you are attacked by any serious illness, let your first care be to send for your spiritual physician, and settle the state of your soul. This is much better done in the beginning of sickness than afterwards, when the strength of fever, or the quality of the remedies may render a person absolutely unfit for so great a work. Sickness is often sent as a punishment for sin, and therefore a sincere repentance and confession of sin are often a more effectual means of recovery than any other.

If you have not your will already made, let this also be done in the beginning of your sickness, that so, having settled your temporal affairs you may apply your soul without disturbance to the spiritual.

Take proper care for the discharge of your debts, and all other obligations incumbent upon you; endeavour to do this in the beginning of your sickness. Forgive all those who have in any way injured you, and ask pardon of those whom you have injured.

Aim, as much as you can, at a penitential spirit during your sickness; often cry to God for mercy, and make frequent acts of contrition for your sins. St. Augustine used to say that no Christian, however innocent his life, ought to venture to die in any other state than that of a penitent.

ACTS OF THE MOST NECESSARY VIRTUES PROPER TO BE INCULCATED IN TIME OF SICKNESS.

LORD, I accept this sickness from thy hands, and resign myself in all things to thy blessed will, whether it be for life or death. Not my will, but thine be done; thy will be done on earth as it is in heaven.

Lord, I submit to all the pains and uneasiness of this my illness: my sins have deserved much more. Thou art just, O Lord, and thy judgment is right.

Lord, I offer up to thee all that I now suffer, or may have yet to suffer, to be united to the sufferings of my Redeemer, and sanctified by his passion.

I adore thee, O my God, and my all, as my first beginning and last end; and I desire to pay thee the best homage I am able, and to bow down all the powers of my soul to thee.

Lord, I desire to praise thee for ever, in sickness as well as in health; I desire to join my heart and voice with the whole church of heaven and earth, in blessing thee for ever.

I give thee thanks from the bottom of my heart, for all thy mercies and blessings bestowed upon me, and thy whole church, through Jesus Christ thy Son; and above all, for thy having loved me from all eternity, and redeemed me with his precious blood. Oh, let not that blood be shed for me in vain.

Lord, I believe all those heavenly truths which thou hast revealed, and which thy holy Catholic church believes and teaches. Thou art the sovereign Truth, who neither canst deceive nor be deceived: and thou hast promised the Spirit of Truth to guide thy church in all truth. In this faith I resolve, through thy grace, both to live and die. O Lord, strengthen and increase this my faith.

O my God, all my hopes are in thee: and through Jesus Christ, my Redeemer, and through his passion and death, I hope for mercy, grace, and salvation from thee. In thee, O Lord, have I put my trust, let me never be confounded.

O sweet Jesus, receive me into thine arms, in this day of my distress: hide me in thy wounds, bathe my soul in thy precious blood.

I love thee, O my God, with my whole heart and soul, above all things; at least, I desire so to love thee. Oh, come now and take full possession of my whole soul, and teach me to love thee for ever.

I desire to be dissolved, and to be with Christ.

Oh, when will thy kingdom come? O Lord, when wilt thou perfectly reign in all hearts? When shall sin be no more?

I desire to embrace every one with perfect charity for the love of thee. I forgive, from my heart, all who have in any way offended or injured me, and ask pardon of all whom I have in any way offended.

them to communicate after having broken their fast. The sick person will therefore use his best endeavour to make a worthy preparation for this blessed Sacrament.

A SHORT EXERCISE IN PREPARATION FOR THE HOLY VIATICUM.

1. My heart is ready, O God, my heart is ready; not my will, but thine be done. O my Lord, I resign myself entirely to thee, to receive death at the time, and in the manner it shall please thee to send it.

2. I most humbly ask pardon for all my sins committed against thy sovereign goodness, and repent of them all from the bottom of my heart.

3. I firmly believe whatsoever the holy Catholic Church believes and teaches; and by thy grace I will die in this belief.

4. I hope to possess eternal life by thy infinite mercy, and by the merits of my Saviour Jesus Christ.

5. O my God, I desire to love thee as my sovereign good above all things, and to despise this miserable world: I desire to love my neighbour as myself, for the love of thee, and to forgive all injuries from my heart.

6. O my divine Jesus, how great is my desire to receive thy sacred body! Oh,

come now into my soul: grant that I may worthily receive thee before my death. I desire to unite this communion with all the worthy communions which shall be made in thy holy church, even to the end of time.

7. Grant me the grace, O my divine Saviour, perfectly to efface all the sins I have committed by any of my senses, by applying daily to my soul thy blessed merits, and the holy unction of thy precious blood.

8. Holy Virgin, Mother of God, defend me from my enemies in my last hour, and present me to thy divine Son. Glorious St. Michael, prince of the heavenly host, and thou, my Angel Guardian, and you, my blessed Patrons, intercede for me, and assist me in this last and dreadful passage.

9. O my God, I renounce all the temptations of the enemy, and in general whatsoever may displease thee. I accept of thy divine appointments with regard to myself, and entirely abandon myself to them as most just and equitable.

10. O Jesus, my divine Saviour, be thou a Jesus to me, and save me. O my God, hiding myself with a humble confidence in thy wounds, I give up my soul

into thy divine hands. Oh, receive it into the bosom of thy mercy. Amen.

#### A PRAYER BEFORE EXTREME UNCTION.

THOU hast mercifully provided remedies, O Lord, for all our necessities: grant me grace so to make use of them, that my soul may receive all those good effects which thou hast appointed in their institution. I desire to be anointed as thou hast commanded by thine Apostle; grant, I beseech thee, that by this holy unction, and the prayers of the Church, I may partake of that spirit with which Christ suffered on the cross, for thy glory and for the destruction of sin. Give me true patience to support all the pains and inconveniences of my sickness; an inward strength to resist all the temptations of the enemy; that true light, by which I may be conducted through the shadow of death to eternal happiness: and, if my health be expedient for thy glory, let this sacrament be the means to restore it. Behold I approach to it with a firm faith and confidence in thy goodness, that thou wilt not forsake me in this time of my distress, but that thou wilt stand by me by thy grace, and defend me from all evil, and prepare my soul for a happy passage.

SHORT ACTS BEFORE ANOINTING.

My eyes have seen vanities, but now let them be shut to the world, and open to thee alone, my Jesus: and pardon me all the sins which I have committed by my sense of sight.

My ears have been open to detraction, profaneness, and unprofitable discourses; let me now give ear to thy word, to thy commandments, and thy calls, and pardon me, O Jesus, all the sins which I have committed by my sense of hearing.

I have taken delight in the perfumes of this world, which are nothing but corruption: now let my heart and prayers ascend like incense in thy sight, and pardon me all the sins which I have committed by my sense of smell.

My tongue has in many ways offended both in speaking and tasting, now let its whole business be to cry for mercy; pardon me, dear Jesus, all the sins which I have committed by words, or by any excess in eating or drinking.

My hands have offended in contributing to many follies, injurious to myself and my neighbour: now let them be lifted up to heaven, in testimony of a penitent heart: and pardon me, O Lord, all the sins which

I have committed by the ill use of my hands.

My feet have gone astray in the paths of vanity and sin: now let me walk in the way of thy commandments : and forgive me, O Lord, all the sins which I have committed by my disordered steps.

By this holy anointing and the power of thy grace, O God, forgive all my sins, and convert my heart wholly to thee, that I may cheerfully submit to death, in punishment of my offences, and so enter into thine eternal rest. Amen.

### A PRAYER AFTER EXTREME UNCTION.

O MY God, it is by thee that I have been created, redeemed, and sanctified : it is thou who hast preserved me from many dangers, both of soul and body; it is thou who hast nourished me with the adorable sacrament of thy body and blood, and granted me the grace to receive the rites of thy Church, preferably to so many others, who have been carried off by a sudden death, without being favoured with such succours and graces as thou hast bestowed upon me, a most ungrateful sinner. For these and all other blessings, I return thee most sincere thanks. Oh, that I had the hearts and tongues of all men and angels, how willingly would I employ them all in praising, loving, and glorifying thee. To thee I resign my heart. Into thy hands, O Lord, I commend my spirit. Receive me, O dear Jesus, in thy mercy, into those loving arms, which were extended on the cross, for my redemption, and admit me to the embraces of thine infinite charity. I desire not to be freed from my pains, since thou knowest what is best for me. Suffer me never to murmur, but grant me patience to bear whatever thou wilt, and as long as thou pleasest. Should it be thy will to inflict greater punishments on my weak body and languishing soul than those which I now suffer, my heart is ready, O Lord, to accept them, and to suffer in whatever manner and measure that may be most conformable to thy divine will.

This one grace I most humbly beg of thee, that I may die the death of the just, and be admitted, after the sufferings and tribulations of this transitory and sinful life, into the kingdom of thy glory, there to see and enjoy thee in the company of the blessed for ever. Amen.

### THE LAST BLESSING AND PLENARY INDULGENCE.

As the hour of death approaches, that awful hour on which so much depends, the pious Christian should fervently prepare to receive the Last Blessing and Plenary Indulgence granted to those who are near their end. The dying Christian should remember well that, in order to receive the benefit of this Plenary Indulgence and Blessing, it is requisite that he concur on his part, by renouncing and detesting all his sins, by accepting with patience and resignation whatever he may have yet to suffer, and by offering up his pains and death, in union with the sufferings and death of his Redeemer in satisfaction for his sins.

During the time the Priest is conferring this solemn blessing, the following Prayer may be repeated.

O MY God, I once more renounce and detest all my sins. Have mercy on me, O God, according to thy great mercy. I cast myself into the arms of thy holy love, and I resign myself to thy blessed will. Receive me, I beseech thee, into the number of thy servants, that I may praise thee for ever. Father, into thy hands I commend my spirit. Lord Jesus, receive my soul. Amen.

## THE RECOMMENDATION OF A SOUL THAT IS JUST DEPARTING.

Lord have mercy on him (or her).
*Christ have mercy on him.*
Lord have mercy on him.
Holy Mary, *pray for him.*
All ye holy Angels and Archangels,
Holy Abel,
All ye choirs of the Just,
Holy Abraham,
St. John the Baptist,
St. Joseph,
All ye holy Patriarchs and Prophets,
St. Peter,
St. Paul,
St. Andrew,
St. John,
All ye holy Apostles and Evangelists,
All ye holy Disciples of our Lord,
All ye holy Innocents,
St. Stephen,
St. Lawrence,
All ye holy Martyrs,
St. Sylvester,
St. Gregory,
St. Augustine,
All ye holy Bishops and Confessors,
St. Benedict,
St. Francis,

*Pray for him (or her).*

All ye holy Monks and Hermits,
St. Mary Magdalen,
St. Lucy,
All ye holy Virgins and Widows,
All ye men and women, Saints of God,
*intercede for him (or her).*

*Pray, &c.*

Be merciful unto him, *Spare him, O Lord.*
Be merciful unto him, *Deliver him, O Lord.*
Be merciful unto him,
From thy wrath,
From the dangers of eternal death,
From an evil death,
From the pains of hell,
From all evil,
From the power of the devil,
By thy Nativity,
By thy Cross and Passion,
By thy Death and Burial,
By thy glorious Resurrection,
By thy admirable Ascension,
By the grace of the Holy Ghost, the Comforter,
In the day of Judgment,

*Deliver him (or her), O Lord.*

We sinners *beseech thee hear us.*
That thou spare him,
*We beseech thee hear us.*
Lord have mercy on him.
*Christ have mercy on him.*
Lord have mercy on him.

Go forth, O Christian soul, from this world, in the name of God the Father Almighty, who created thee; in the name of Jesus Christ, the Son of the living God, who suffered for thee; in the name of the Holy Ghost who sanctified thee; in the name of the Angels and Archangels; in the name of the Thrones and Dominations; in the name of the Principalities and Powers; in the name of the Cherubim and Seraphim; in the name of the Patriarchs and Prophets; in the name of the holy Apostles and Evangelists; in the name of the holy Martyrs and Confessors; in the name of the holy Monks and Hermits; in the name of the holy Virgins and of all the Saints of God: may thy place be this day in peace, and thine abode in holy Sion. Through Christ our Lord. Amen.

O God most merciful, O God most clement, O God, who, according to the multitude of thy mercies, blottest out the sins of penitents, and graciously remittest the guilt of their past offences; mercifully regard this thy servant N., and vouchsafe to hear him, who, in all the sincerity of his heart, begs for the remission of all his sins. Make good, O most merciful

Father, whatever hath been corrupted in him through human frailty, or vitiated through the deceit of the enemy; and associate him, as a member of redemption, to the unity of the body of the Church. Have compassion, O Lord, on his sighs; have compassion on his tears; and admit him who hath no hope but in thy mercy, to the sacrament of thy reconciliation. Through Christ our Lord. Amen.

I recommend thee, dear brother, to the Almighty God, and commit thee to his care, whose creature thou art, that when thou shalt have paid the debt of all mankind by death, thou mayst return to thy Maker, who formed thee out of the dust of the earth. When, therefore, thy soul shall depart from the body, may the resplendent multitude of the Angels meet thee; may the court of the Apostles meet thee; may the triumphant army of the Martyrs, clad in white robes, come out to meet thee; may the glorious company of the illustrious Confessors encompass thee; may the choir of joyful Virgins receive thee; and mayst thou meet with a blessed repose in the bosom of the Patriarchs; may Jesus Christ appear to thee with a mild and cheerful countenance, and order thee a place amongst those who are to stand before him for ever. Mayst thou never know the horror of darkness, the roaring of flames, or racking torments. May the most wicked enemy, with all his evil spirits, be forced to give way; may he tremble at thine approach in the company of Angels, and fly away into the vast chaos of eternal night. Let God arise, and let his enemies be scattered; and let them that hate him flee from before his face: as smoke vanishes, so let them vanish away: as wax melteth before the fire, so let sinners perish at the presence of God; and let the just feast and rejoice before God. May, then, all the legions of hell be confounded and put to shame; and may none of the ministers of Satan dare to stop thee in thy way. May Christ, who was crucified for thee, deliver thee from torments. May Christ, who vouchsafed to die for thee, deliver thee from eternal death. May Christ, the Son of the living God, place thee in the ever-verdant gardens of his paradise: and may He, the true Shepherd, acknowledge thee as one of his flock. May he absolve thee from all thy sins, and place thee at his right hand, in the company of his elect. Mayst thou see thy Redeemer face to face, and standing always in his presence, behold with happy eyes the most clear truth. Mayst thou be placed among the companies of the blessed, and enjoy the sweetness of the contemplation of thy God for ever. R̟. Amen.

Receive, O Lord, thy servant into the place of salvation, which he hopeth to obtain through thy mercy. R̟. Amen.

Deliver, O Lord, the soul of thy servant from all dangers of hell, and from all pain and tribulation. R̟. Amen.

Deliver, O Lord, the soul of thy servant, as thou didst deliver Enoch and Elias from the common death of the world. R̟. Amen.

Deliver, O Lord, the soul of thy servant, as thou didst deliver Abraham from the midst of the Chaldeans. R̟. Amen.

Deliver, O Lord, the soul of thy servant, as thou didst deliver Job from all his afflictions. R̟. Amen.

Deliver, O Lord, the soul of thy servant, as thou didst deliver Isaac from being sacrificed by his father. R̟. Amen.

Deliver, O Lord, the soul of thy servant, as thou didst deliver Lot from Sodom and the flames of fire. R̟. Amen.

Deliver, O Lord, the soul of thy servant, as thou didst deliver Moses from the hands of Pharaoh, king of Egypt. ℟. Amen.

Deliver, O Lord, the soul of thy servant, as thou didst deliver Daniel from the lions' den. ℟. Amen.

Deliver, O Lord, the soul of thy servant, as thou didst deliver the three children from the fiery furnace, and from the hands of an unmerciful king. ℟. Amen.

Deliver, O Lord, the soul of thy servant, as thou didst deliver Susanna from her false accusers. ℟. Amen.

Deliver, O Lord, the soul of thy servant, as thou didst deliver David from the hands of Saul and Goliah. ℟. Amen.

Deliver, O Lord, the soul of thy servant, as thou didst deliver Peter and Paul out of prison. ℟. Amen.

And as thou didst deliver that blessed Virgin and Martyr St. Thecla, from most cruel torment, so vouchsafe to deliver the soul of this thy servant, and bring it to the participation of thy heavenly joys. Amen.

We commend to thee, O Lord, the soul of thy servant N., and we beseech thee, O Lord Jesus Christ, the Saviour of the world, not to refuse to admit into the company of thy Patriarchs, a soul for which in thy mercy, thou wast pleased to come down upon earth. Acknowledge him as thy creature, not made by strange gods, but by thee, the only living and true God: for there is no other God besides thee, and none that can equal thy works. Let his soul rejoice in thy presence, and remember not his former iniquities and excesses, the unhappy effects of passion or evil concupiscence; for although he has sinned, yet he has not renounced the Father, Son, and Holy Ghost; but has believed, and has had a zeal for God, and faithfully worshipped Him who made all things.

Remember not, O Lord, we beseech thee, the sins of his youth and his ignorances, but according to thy great mercy, be mindful of him in thy heavenly glory. May the heavens be opened to him, and may the Angels rejoice with him. Receive, O Lord, thy servant into thy kingdom. Let St. Michael, the Archangel of God, who is the chief of the heavenly host, conduct him. Let the holy Angels of God come to meet him, and carry him to the city of the heavenly Jerusalem. May St. Peter, the Apostle to whom God gave the keys of the kingdom of heaven, receive him. May St. Paul, the Apostle who was a vessel of election, assist him. May St. John, the chosen Apostle of God to whom were revealed the secrets of heaven, intercede for him. May all the holy Apostles, to whom our Lord gave the power of binding and loosing, pray for him. May all the Saints and Elect of God, who in this world have suffered torments for the name of Christ, intercede for him, that being delivered from the bonds of the flesh, he may be admitted to the glory of the kingdom of heaven, by the bounty of our Lord Jesus Christ, who, with the Father and the Holy Ghost, liveth and reigneth for ever and ever. Amen.

O Lord Jesus Christ, who, by the mouth of thy holy Prophet, hast said, I have loved thee with an everlasting love, therefore have I drawn thee to myself taking pity on thee: by that divine love which brought thee down from heaven to suffer all the torments of thy passion for our redemption, we humbly beseech thee to offer to thy eternal Father that same love, in behalf of the soul of this thy servant N., and deliver him from all the sufferings which he has deserved on account of his sins;

and save his soul in this hour of its departure out of his body. Open to him the gates of life, introduce him into thy heavenly paradise, and make him rejoice with thy Saints; that he may live with thee in the bond of eternal love, and be inseparably united to thy Saints and to thee, who, with the Father and the Holy Ghost, livest and reignest God, world without end. Amen.

The soul being departed, the following is to be said:

COME to his assistance all ye Saints of God: meet him all ye Angels of God; receive his soul and present it now before its Lord.

May Jesus Christ receive thee, and the Angels conduct thee to thy place of rest. May the Angels of God receive his soul, and present it now before its Lord.

℣. Eternal rest give to him, O Lord: and let perpetual light shine upon him.

℟. May the Angels of God present him now before his Lord.

℣. Lord have mercy on him.
℟. Christ have mercy on him.
℣. Lord have mercy on him.
Our Father, &c.

℣. And lead us not into temptation.
℟. But deliver us from evil. Amen.
℣. Eternal rest give to him, O Lord.
℟. And let perpetual light shine upon him.
℣. From the gates of hell,
℟. Deliver his soul, O Lord.
℣. May he rest in peace.
℟. Amen.
℣. O Lord, hear my prayer.
℟. And let my cry come to thee.

LET US PRAY.

To thee, O Lord, we recommend the soul of thy servant N., that being dead to this world he may live to thee; and whatever sins he has committed in this life through human frailty, do thou in thy most merciful goodness, pardon. Through our Lord Jesus Christ. Amen.

Then may be added the following Prayer for those who are present.

GRANT, O God, that while we lament the departure of this thy servant, we may always remember that we are most certainly to follow him. Give us grace to prepare for that last hour by a good life, that we may not be surprised by a sudden and unpro-

℣. Requiescat in pace.

℟. Amen.

℣. Domine, exaudi orationem meam.

℟. Et clamor meus ad te veniat.

℣. Dominus vobiscum.

℟. Et cum spiritu tuo.

OREMUS.

ABSOLVE, quæsumus Domine, animam famuli tui N. ab omni vinculo delictorum, ut in resurrectionis gloria, inter Sanctos et electos tuos resuscitatus respiret.

℟. Amen.

℣. May he rest in peace.

℟. Amen.

℣. O Lord, hear my prayer.

℟. And let my cry come unto thee.

℣. The Lord be with you.

℟. And with thy spirit.

LET US PRAY.

ABSOLVE, we beseech thee, O Lord, the soul of thy servant N. from all the bonds of his sins, that, rising again in the glory of the resurrection, he may enjoy repose among thy Saints and elect.

℟. Amen.

[Then Mass is celebrated, at the end of which the Priest, placing himself at the feet of the deceased, opposite the processional Cross, proceeds to say the Prayer, *Non intres in judicium* (Enter not into judgment), as follows]:—

If Mass is not celebrated, he proceeds at once as follows:

NON intres in judicium cum servo tuo, Domine, quia nullus apud te justificabitur homo, nisi per te omnium peccatorum ei

ENTER not into judgment with thy servant, O Lord, for in thy sight shall no man be justified, unless through thee the remis-

tribuatur remissio. Non ergo eum, quæsumus, tua judicialis sententia premat, quem tibi vera supplicatio fidei Christianæ commendat : sed gratiâ tuâ illi succurrente, mereatur evadere judicium ultionis, qui dum viveret, insignitus est signaculo Sanctæ Trinitatis : qui vivis et regnas in sæcula sæculorum.

sion of all his sins be granted unto him. Let not, therefore, we beseech thee, the sentence of thy judgment weigh upon him, whom the true supplication of Christian faith doth commend unto thee ; but by the succour of thy grace, may he merit to escape the judgment of vengeance, who, while he lived, was marked with the seal of the Holy Trinity : who livest and reignest for ever and ever.

℟. Amen.

℟. Amen.

*Then, a Chorister beginning, the Clergy standing round chant the following Response :—*

℟. Libera me, Domine, de morte æterna, in die illa tremenda : * Quando cœli movendi sunt et terra : † Dum veneris judicare sæculum per ignem.

℟. Deliver me, O Lord, from eternal death, in that tremendous day : When the heavens shall be moved, and the earth : When thou shalt come to judge the world by fire.

℣. Tremens factus sum ego, et timeo, dum discussio venerit, atque ventura ira : Quando, &c.

℣. I am in fear and trembling, until the trial cometh, and the wrath to come: When, &c.

## BURIAL OF THE DEAD.

*Benediction of the Grave, if it has not previously been blessed.*

**OREMUS.**

Deus, cujus miseratione animæ fidelium requiescunt, hunc tumulum benedicere ✠ dignare, eique Angelum tuum sanctum deputa custodem : et quorum quarumque corpora hic sepeliuntur, animas eorum ab omnibus absolve vinculis delictorum ; ut in te semper, cum Sanctis tuis, sine fine lætentur. Per Christum Dominum nostrum.

℟. Amen.

**LET US PRAY.**

O God, by whose compassion the souls of the faithful find rest, vouchsafe to bless ✠ this grave, and assign thereto thy holy Angel for a guard ; and absolve from all the bonds of sin the souls of those whose bodies are here buried, that with thy Saints they may ever rejoice in thee for all eternity. Through Christ our Lord.

℟. Amen.

*The Prayer being said, the Priest sprinkles the grave with holy water, and afterwards incenses the coffin and the grave. Then he intones the Antiphon :*

*Ant.* Ego sum.   *Ant.* I am.

*And the Benedictus (see after Benediction of the Blessed Sacrament) is then sung.*

*Ant.* Ego sum resurrectio et vita, qui credit in me etiam si mortuus fuerit, vivet, et omnis qui vivit, et credit in me, non morietur in æternum.

*Ant.* I am the resurrection and the life. He that believeth in me, though he were dead, yet shall he live, and every one that liveth, and believeth in me, shall not die for ever.

*Then the Priest says:*

| | |
|---|---|
| Kyrie eleison. | Lord have mercy on us. |
| *Christe eleison.* | *Christ have mercy on us.* |
| Kyrie eleison. | Lord have mercy on us. |
| Pater noster. | Our Father, &c. |

*In the meantime, standing in his place, he sprinkles the corpse.*

℣. Et ne nos inducas in tentationem.

℟. Sed libera nos a malo.

℣. A porta inferi. (pag. 331.)

℣. And lead us not into temptation.

℟. But deliver us from evil.

℣. From the gate of hell (*as in* p. 331.)

### OREMUS.

FAC, quæsumus, Domine, hanc cum servo tuo defuncto (*vel* famula tua defuncta) misericordiam, ut factorum suorum in pœnis non recipiat vicem, qui (*vel* quæ) tuam in votis tenuit voluntatem; ut sicut hic eum (*vel* eam) vera fides junxit fidelium turmis, ita illic eum (*vel* eam) tua miseratio societ Angelicis Choris. Per Christum Dominum nostrum.

℟. Amen.

℣. Requiem æternam dona ei Domine.

### LET US PRAY.

GRANT, O Lord, we beseech thee, this mercy unto thy servant deceased, that, having in intention kept thy will, he may not suffer in requital of his deeds: but that, as here a true faith joined him unto the company of the faithful, so there thy compassion may associate him with the Choir of Angels. Through Christ our Lord.

℟. Amen.

℣. Eternal rest give unto him, O Lord.

℟. Et lux perpetua luceat ei.

℣. Requiescat in pace.

℟. Amen.

℣. Anima ejus, et animæ omnium fidelium defunctorum per misericordiam Dei requiescant in pace.

℟. Amen.

℟. And may perpetual light shine upon him.

℣. May he rest in peace.

℟. Amen.

℣. May his soul, and the souls of the faithful departed, through the mercy of God, rest in peace.

℟. Amen.

On returning from the burial is recited the Antiphon *Si iniquitates observaveris* with the Psalm *De profundis;* after which the Antiphon *Si iniquitates* is repeated.

## Prayers for the Dead.

### A PRAYER FOR THE FAITHFUL DEPARTED.

O GOD, the Creator and Redeemer of all the faithful, grant to the souls of thy servants departed, the remission of all their sins, that through pious supplications, they may obtain the pardon which they have always desired. Who livest and reignest with God the Father, in the unity of the Holy Ghost, world without end. Amen.

### ON THE DAY OF A PERSON'S DECEASE OR BURIAL.

O GOD, whose property is always to have mercy and to spare, we humbly beseech thee for the soul of thy servant *N.*, which thou hast this day commanded to depart out of this world, that thou wouldst not deliver it into the hands of the enemy, nor forget it unto the end, but wouldst command it to be received by thy holy Angels, and conducted to Paradise, its true country; that, as in thee it hath hoped and believed, it may not suffer the pains of hell, but may take possession of eternal joys. Through Christ our Lord. Amen.

### ON THE ANNIVERSARY OF A PERSON'S BURIAL.

O GOD, the Lord of mercy and pardon, grant to the soul of thy servant *N.*, the anniversary of whose burial we commemorate, a place of refreshment, a happy rest, and the brightness of light. Through Christ our Lord. Amen.

### FOR ONE LATELY DECEASED.

ABSOLVE, we beseech thee, O Lord, the soul of thy servant *N.* from every bond of sin, that, being raised in the glory of the resurrection, he may be refreshed among thy Saints and Elect. Through Christ our Lord. Amen.

### FOR A BISHOP OR PRIEST.

O GOD, who, amongst apostolic priests, hast adorned thy servant *N*. with the pontifical (*or* sacerdotal) dignity, grant, we beseech thee, that he may also be associated with them in everlasting fellowship. Through Christ our Lord. Amen.

### FOR FATHER AND MOTHER.

O GOD, who hast commanded us to honour our father and mother, have compassion, in thy mercy, on the souls of my father and mother; forgive them their sins, and grant that I may see them in the joy of eternal brightness. Through Christ our Lord. Amen.

### FOR FRIENDS AND BENEFACTORS.

O GOD, bountiful in forgiving, and lovingly desirous of man's salvation, we humbly beseech thy mercy in behalf of our friends, relations, and benefactors, who have passed from this world, that, through the intercession of blessed Mary, ever Virgin, and all the Saints, thou wouldst permit them to come to the full participation of everlasting happiness. Through Christ our Lord. Amen.

# Indulgences attached to Devotions for the Faithful Departed.

**THE OFFICE OF THE DEAD.**

1°. 100 days Indulgence to all the faithful, as often as they shall devoutly say, of obligation, this office, on the days prescribed by the rubrics of the Roman Breviary.

2°. 50 days Indulgence to all the faithful, every time they say it out of their own devotion. A.

**THE DE PROFUNDIS (AFTER NIGHTFALL).**

1°. 100 days Indulgence, if, at the sound of the bell, at the first hour after nightfall, the faithful shall say this Psalm devoutly on their knees, with the following ℣. and ℟.:—

℣. Requiem æternam, &c.

℟. Et lux, &c.

℣. Requiescant in pace.

℟. Amen.

℣. Eternal rest, &c.

℟. And let, &c.

℣. May they rest in peace.

℟. Amen.

2°. Plenary Indulgence once a year, on any one day of their choice, to those who perform this pious exercise exactly during the course of the year, provided they have confessed and communicated.

N.B.—Those who cannot read, or do not know by heart the De Profundis, may gain the same Indulgences by reciting the Our Father and Hail Mary, with the ℣. and ℟., as above.

Where no bell is sounded, these same Indulgences may be gained by those who after nightfall recite the above prayers. A.

**FIVE TIMES THE OUR FATHER, HAIL MARY, &c.**

FIVE times the Our Father, and five times the Hail Mary, with the Versicle, *Eternal Father, we pray thee, help the souls of thy servants whom thou hast redeemed with the blood of Jesus Christ.*

℣. Eternal rest give to them, O Lord.
℟. And may perpetual light shine upon them.
℣. May they rest in peace.
℟. Amen.

1°. 300 days Indulgence to all the faithful who, being contrite in heart, and devoutly meditating on the Passion of our Lord Jesus Christ, shall recite the above prayers for the faithful departed.

2°. Plenary Indulgence, on usual conditions, on any one day in each month.

## Dies Iræ.

Dies iræ, dies illa,
Solvet sæclum in favilla,
Teste David cum Sibylla.

Quantus tremor est futurus,
Quando Judex est venturus,
Cuncta stricte discussurus!

Tuba mirum spargens sonum
Per sepulchra regionum,
Coget omnes ante thronum.

Mors stupebit, et natura,
Cum resurget creatura,
Judicanti responsura.

Liber scriptus proferetur,
In quo totum continetur,
Unde mundus judicetur.

Judex ergo cum sedebit,
Quidquid latet, apparebit:
Nil inultum remanebit.

Quid sum miser tunc dicturus?
Quem patronum rogaturus,
Cum vix justus sit securus?

Rex tremendæ majestatis,
Qui salvandos salvas gratis,
Salva me, fons pietatis.

Recordare, Jesu pie,
Quod sum causa tuæ viæ:
Ne me perdas illa die.

Quærens me, sedisti lassus;
Redemisti, crucem passus:
Tantus labor non sit cassus.

Juste Judex ultionis,
Donum fac remissionis
Ante diem rationis.

Ingemisco tamquam reus:
Culpa rubet vultus meus:
Supplicanti parce, Deus.

Qui Mariam absolvisti,
Et latronem exaudisti,
Mihi quoque spem dedisti.

Preces meæ non sunt dignæ:
Sed tu bonus fac benigne,
Ne perenni cremer igne.

Inter oves locum præsta,
Et ab hœdis me sequestra,
Statuens in parte dextra.

Confutatis maledictis,
Flammis acribus addictis,
Voca me cum benedictis.

Oro supplex et acclinis,
Cor contritum quasi
  cinis:
Gere curam mei finis.

Lacrymosa dies illa,
Qua resurget ex fa-
  villa
Judicandus homo reus.

Huic ergo parce, Deus:
Pie Jesu Domine,
Dona eis requiem.
      Amen.

# Devotions in Honour of the Sacred Heart of Jesus.

*"I came to send fire on the earth, and what will I, but that it be kindled."*—Luc. xii. 49.

DEVOTION towards the most Sacred Heart of our Lord Jesus Christ is with reason called a treasure of true sanctity; but it is a hidden treasure, which, whoever finds shall have life, and shall obtain from our Lord the salvation of many.

We read expressly in the life of the Blessed Mary Margaret Alacocque, through whom this treasure has been made known to our times, that our Lord once said to her in a vision:

"My Heart shall dilate itself to pour profusely the gifts of divine love on all such persons as shall devote themselves to me by a special service.

"Whoever shall pay this homage of devotion to my Heart, and exert himself to extend widely the practice of this devotion, shall be blessed with a singular gift of softening the hearts of the most obdurate sinners."

Oh, how great would be the power of Priests and labourers in the vineyard of the Lord, if they but knew the great influence they possess herein! Beyond measure would then be the fruit with which they would return laden.

Any one of the faithful who visits a picture of the Sacred Heart, exposed for public veneration in a Church or Oratory, or upon any altar, and prays before it for some time, according to the intention of the Sovereign Pontiff, gains each time an Indulgence of seven years and seven quarantines, applicable to the Souls in Purgatory. (Pius VI. 1799.)

## Act of Consecration to the Sacred Heart of Jesus.

To thee, O Sacred Heart of Jesus, I devote and offer up my life, thoughts, words, actions, pains, and sufferings. May I be no longer employed, save only in loving, serving, honouring, and glorifying thee. Wherefore, O most Sacred Heart! be thou the sole object of my love, the protector of my life, the pledge of my salvation, and my secure refuge at the hour of my death. Be thou, O most bountiful

Heart! my justification at the throne of God, and screen me from his anger, which I have so justly merited. In thee I place all my confidence, and, convinced as I am of my own weakness, I rely entirely on thy bounty. Destroy in me all that is displeasing and offensive to thee. Imprint thyself like a divine seal on my heart, that I may ever remember my obligations never to be separated from thee. May my name also, I beseech thee, by thy tender bounty, ever be fixed and engraved in thee, O Book of Life! and may I be a victim consecrated to thy glory, ever burning with the flames of thy pure love, and entirely penetrated with it for eternity. In thee I place all my happiness, this is all my desire, to live and die in no other quality but that of thy devoted servant. Amen.

## Litany of the Sacred Heart of Jesus.

LORD have mercy on us.
*Christ have mercy on us.*
Lord have mercy on us.
Christ hear us.
*Christ graciously hear us.*

God the Father of heaven,
God the Son, Redeemer of the world,
God the Holy Ghost,
Holy Trinity, one God,
Heart of Jesus,

*Have mercy on us.*

## SACRED HEART OF JESUS. 347

Heart of Jesus, hypostatically united to the Eternal Word,
Heart of Jesus, Sanctuary of the Divinity,
Heart of Jesus, Tabernacle of the most holy Trinity,
Heart of Jesus, Temple of all sanctity,
Heart of Jesus, Fountain of all grace,
Heart of Jesus, most meek,
Heart of Jesus, most humble,
Heart of Jesus, most obedient,
Heart of Jesus, most chaste,
Heart of Jesus, Furnace of divine love,
Heart of Jesus, Source of contrition,
Heart of Jesus, Abyss of wisdom,
Heart of Jesus, Ocean of goodness,
Heart of Jesus, Throne of mercy,
Heart of Jesus, Model of all virtues,
Heart of Jesus, sorrowful in the garden, unto death,
Heart of Jesus, filled with reproaches,
Heart of Jesus, wounded for our sins,
Heart of Jesus, made obedient even unto death upon the cross,
Heart of Jesus, pierced by a lance,
Heart of Jesus, Refuge of sinners,
Heart of Jesus, Strength of the weak,
Heart of Jesus, Comfort of the afflicted,
Heart of Jesus, Support of the tempted,
Heart of Jesus, Perseverance of the just,
Heart of Jesus, Hope of the dying,
Heart of Jesus, Joy of the blessed,
Heart of Jesus, Delight of all saints,

*Have mercy on us.*

Lamb of God, who takest away the sins of the world,
*Spare us, O Jesus.*
Lamb of God, who takest away the sins of the world,

*Graciously hear us, O Jesus.*

Lamb of God, who takest away the sins of the world,

*Have mercy on us, O Jesus.*

℣. O most Sacred Heart of Jesus, have mercy on us.

℟. That we may worthily love thee with our whole hearts.

LET US PRAY.

GRANT, we beseech thee, Almighty God, that we who glorying in the most Sacred Heart of thy beloved Son, commemorate the choicest gifts which his love hath bestowed upon us, may both delight in so doing, and may enjoy the fruits thereof. Through the same Jesus Christ our Lord. Amen.

---

THROUGH thy Sacred Heart, O Jesus! overflowing with all sweetness, we recommend to thee ourselves and all our concerns, our parents, relations, superiors, benefactors, friends, and enemies; take under thy protection this house, city (or county), and kingdom; extend this thy care to all such as are under any affliction, and to those who are in their last agony; cast an eye of compassion on the obstinate sinner, on the poor suffering souls in purgatory, as also on those who are engaged and united with us in this holy Confraternity of honouring and worshipping thee. Bless these in particular, O bountiful Jesus! and bless them according to the extent of thy infinite goodness, mercy, and charity. Amen.

### Act of Reparation to the Sacred Heart of Jesus.

O MOST amiable and adorable Heart of Jesus, glowing with charity, and inflamed with zeal for the interest of thy Father, and for the salvation of mankind! O Heart, ever sensible of our misery, and ever ready to afford us relief; the real Victim of love in the holy Eucharist, and a propitiatory Sacrifice for sin on the altar of the Cross! seeing that the greater number of Christians make no other return for this thy mercy than contempt of thy favours, forgetfulness of their own obligations, and ingratitude to the best of benefactors; is it not just that we, thy servants, penetrated with the deepest sense of the indignities offered to thee, should, as far as we are able, make an act of humble reparation of honour to thy most sacred Majesty? Prostrate, therefore, in body, and humbled in mind, before heaven and earth, we solemnly declare our sincere detestation and abhorrence of such conduct. Intense was the bitterness which the multitude of our sins brought on thy tender Heart; great the weight of our iniquities, which pressed thy face to the earth in the Garden of Olives; and inconceivable thy anguish, when, expiring through love, grief, and agony, on Mount Calvary, thou didst in thy last breath pray for sinners, and invite them to repentance. This we know, O dear Redeemer! and would most willingly atone for these thy sufferings by our own, or share with thee in thine.

O merciful Jesus, ever present on our altars, and with a Heart open to receive all who labour and are burdened : O adorable Heart, source of true contrition, give to our hearts the spirit of sincere repentance, and to our eyes a fountain of tears, that we may weep for our own sins, and for the sins of the world. Pardon, divine Jesus! all the injuries, reproaches, and outrages, done thee through the course of thy holy life and bitter passion. Pardon all the impieties, irreverences, and sacrileges which have been committed against thee in the Sacrament of the Eucharist from its first institution. Graciously receive the small tribute of our sincere repentance as an agreeable offering in thy sight, and in return for the benefits we daily receive from the altar, where thou art a living and continual sacrifice, and in union with that bloody holocaust, thou didst present to thy Eternal Father, on Mount Calvary, from the Cross.

Sweet Jesus, give thy blessing to the ardent desire we now entertain, and to the holy resolution we have taken, of ever loving and adoring thee with our whole hearts in the sacrament of love, the Eucharist; that thus we may repair by a true conversion of heart, and a becoming zeal for thy glory, our past negligence and infidelity. Be thou, O adorable Heart! who knowest the clay of which we are formed, be thou our Mediator with thy heavenly Father, whom we have so grievously offended; strengthen our weakness, confirm our resolutions, and with thy charity, humility, meekness, and patience, cancel our many sins; be thou our support, our refuge, and our strength, that nothing henceforth, in life or death, may separate us from thee. Amen.

### Prayer of St. Gertrude.

HAIL, O Sacred Heart of Jesus, living and quickening Source of Eternal Life, infinite Treasury of the Divinity, burning Furnace of divine Love: thou art my Refuge and my Sanctuary. O my amiable Saviour! consume my heart with that burning fire with which thine is ever inflamed: pour down on my soul those graces, which flow from thy love, and let my heart be so united with thine, that our wills may be one, and my will in all things conformed to thine. May thy will be the standard and rule equally of my desires and of my actions. Amen.

## Confraternity of the Sacred Heart of Jesus.

THE great ends of the Confraternity are Reparation and Thanksgiving; Reparation for all the injuries which our divine Redeemer has received from man, in his Sacred Passion, and in the most Blessed Sacrament of the Altar; Thanksgiving for his love and all the favours bestowed upon us by him, especially in those two great Mysteries.

### OFFERING

*To be made on the day of admission into the Confraternity, and renewed at other times, as devotion may suggest.*

I, *N. N.*, in order to increase more and more the glory of Jesus, who died on the cross for us, and of his inflamed Heart, which burns with love towards us in the most Holy Sacrament of the Altar, and to repair the offences which are committed against him in that Sacrament of Love, do unite myself with the other members of this pious Association : and my desire is to partake of the sacred Indulgences which are granted to it, in satisfaction for my sins, and to succour the holy Souls in Purgatory. Amen.

### PRAYERS

*To be recited daily by the Associates for the Intentions of the Confraternity.*

ONE Our Father, Hail Mary, and Creed, with the following aspiration :—

O Sacred Heart of Jesus, I implore,
That I may ever love thee more and more.

It is further recommended,

1°. To communicate every month.

2°. To recite the Litany of the Sacred Heart with the Act of Reparation on Fridays.

3°. To pray often for the Associates, alive and dead.

### PLENARY INDULGENCES

*Granted to the Associates on the usual conditions of Confession, Communion, and Prayer for the Pope's intentions.*

1°. On the day of admission.

2°. On the Feast of the Sacred Heart of Jesus (Friday after the octave of Corpus Christi), or on the following Sunday.

3°. On the first Friday or Sunday of the month.

4°. On one other day of each month at choice.

5°. At the hour of death.

6°. On Christmas Day, Holy Thursday, Easter Sunday, Ascension Day, and on each of the six Fridays or Sundays preceding the Feast of the Sacred Heart of Jesus.

7°. On the Feasts of our Blessed Lady's Immaculate Conception, Nativity, Annunciation, Purification, and Assumption.

8°. On the Feasts of All Saints, All Souls, St. Joseph, SS. Peter and Paul, and St. John the Evangelist.

9°. Once a month, for reciting morning, noon and night, the Glory be to the Father, &c. thrice, to thank the blessed Trinity for the graces and favours bestowed on the Blessed Virgin Mary.

There are also several partial Indulgences, and all are applicable to the Souls in Purgatory.

## Devotion to the Agonizing Heart of Jesus.

THE end of this Devotion is—

1°. To pay a tribute of homage to the sufferings which the Heart of Jesus endured for the salvation of souls throughout the whole course of his life, and especially during his sacred passion.

2°. To obtain through the merits of this long agony the grace of a happy death for those who, in number about 80,000, die each day throughout the world—a number in nothing exaggerated.

## SACRED HEART OF JESUS.

### A PRAYER

*To be said daily in behalf of those who are in their agony, and of all those who are that day to die.*

O CLEMENTISSIME Jesu amator animarum, obsecro te per agoniam Cordis tui sacratissimi et per dolores Matris tuæ Immaculatæ, lava in Sanguine tuo peccatores totius mundi, nunc in agonia positos et hodie morituros. Amen.

Cor Jesu in agonia factum, miserere morientium.

O MOST merciful Jesus, lover of souls, I beseech thee by the agony of thy most Sacred Heart, and by the grief of thy Immaculate Mother, purify in thy Blood all sinners who are in their agony, and who are this day to die. Amen.

Agonizing Heart of Jesus, have pity on the dying !

An Indulgence of 100 days may be gained each time this Prayer is recited, and a Plenary Indulgence once a month, on usual conditions. A. Resc. Feb. 2, 1850.

### PIOUS PRACTICE.

OFFER up, together with this prayer, some of your daily actions to the Agonizing Heart of Jesus, in behalf of those who are this day in their agony.

## Guard of Honour of the Sacred Heart of Jesus.

PATRONS: The Blessed Virgin, under the title of Our Lady of the Sacred Heart, St. Joseph, St. Francis of Assisium, St. Francis of Sales, The Blessed Margaret Mary Alacocque.

*My Heart hath expected reproach and misery. And I looked for one that would grieve together with me, but there was none: and for one that would comfort me, and I found none.* (Psalm lxviii. 21.)

### OBJECT OF THE ASSOCIATION.

It is to respond to this sorrowful complaint of our Lord, that the Guard of Honour has been organized.

The members who compose it shall, by their devotedness and their love, strive to console the Heart of Jesus, drowned in grief at the forgetfulness and ingratitude of men, for whom he suffered so much, whom he loves so ardently, and by whom he is so little loved.

Like respectful and loving children who try to console their tender father, and to make amends to him for all that their ungrateful and unnatural brothers cause him to suffer, the Guards of Honour succeed each other by turns before their Saviour Jesus, to offer to his most tender heart, respect, love, devotedness, and consolation.

### ORGANIZATION OF THE ASSOCIATION.

The associates choose, once for all, one hour in the day which best suits them. At the beginning of this Hour of Guard, without in any way changing their ordinary occupations, the Associates station themselves in spirit at the Post of Love, the Tabernacle; there they offer to Jesus all their thoughts, words, actions, and above all, the desire they have to console his tender Heart by their fidelity and their love.

During the course of the Hour, the Associates try to think a little oftener of our Lord, make at least an act of love; and if they can, a little sacrifice. But nothing, absolutely nothing, is prescribed, or of obligation; nothing but a good will is required, the Associates being free to follow the impulse of their heart and their piety in sanctifying this blessed hour.

NOTE.—If the Associates forget their Hour of Guard, they can resume it as soon as they perceive their omission.

The Heart of Jesus will heap grace upon grace, blessing upon blessing, on those faithful and compassionate souls who shall fulfil this mission of devotedness and love.

#### OFFERING OF THE HOUR OF GUARD.

DIVINE Jesus, I offer thee this Hour of Guard, during which, in union with [*Here name the Patrons of the Hour chosen*] I desire most particularly to love thee; to glorify thee, and above all to console thy adorable Heart, for the forgetfulness and ingratitude of men. Accept, for this end, my thoughts, words, actions, and sufferings. Above all, receive my heart, which I give thee without reserve, entreating thee to consume it in the fire of thy pure love.

May the Sacred Heart of Jesus be everywhere loved.

O my Jesus, I desire to love thee during this hour for all those hearts which do not love thee.
Our Lady of the Sacred Heart, protect the Guard of Honour.

## The Apostleship of Prayer.

THE Apostleship of Prayer has for its end to unite so thoroughly all Christian hearts with the Heart of Jesus, as to lead them to appropriate to themselves all his intentions, and, ceasing to think solely of themselves, to unite with him in the great interests that are the objects of his intercession, namely, for the extension of the divine glory, the conversion of sinners, the advancement of the just, and the triumph of the Church.

In order to gain the Indulgences granted to the Apostleship of Prayer, it is sufficient that those who have been admitted, whether individually or collectively, to this Association, offer their actions each day for the intentions of the Sacred Heart of Jesus. This offering, which manifestly excludes no private intention, may be made by reciting the Prayer of the Association to the Sacred Heart, that is, the Pater, Ave and Creed, with the Aspiration: *Heart of Jesus, burning with love of me, inflame my heart with love of Thee.* It will be well to renew these intentions in reciting the Angelus, and still better to unite ourselves with the Masses that are said every hour of the day in some part or other of the world, and to say, at least in the interior of the heart, at the beginning of our actions : *Divine Heart of Jesus, I offer thee this action for all the intentions for which thou immolatest thyself at this moment, on the altar, to God thy Father.*

This renewal of intentions cannot fail to augment considerably the merit of the different actions of the day; nevertheless, in order to render these actions meritorious, and to have a share in the privileges of the Apostleship of Prayer, the general offering made at the beginning of the day is sufficient.

INDULGENCES

*That may be gained by the Associates of the Apostleship of Prayer.*

(Pius IX.—26th Feb. 1861.)

I.—PLENARY INDULGENCES.

N.B.—In order to gain these Indulgences, it is necessary to confess, receive the Holy Communion, and pray for the intentions of the Sovereign Pontiff.

(1°) On the day of admission. (2°) On the Feast of the Sacred Heart of Jesus, or the Sunday immediately following. (3°) On the first Friday of each month, and one other day at the choice of the Associates, on condition that they have recited each day of the month the prayer of the Association, that is the Pater, Ave and Creed, with the Aspiration,

*Heart of Jesus, burning with love of me, inflame my heart with love of Thee!* (The Indulgence of the first Friday may be transferred to the first Sunday.) (4°) Another Friday or other day of each month, equally at the choice of the Associates, on condition that they pray for the intentions of the Sovereign Pontiff in a public church. (5°) On the Feasts of Christmas, Holy Thursday, Easter Sunday, Ascension, the Immaculate Conception, the Nativity of the Blessed Virgin, the Annunciation, the Purification, and the Assumption; on the Feasts of St. Joseph Spouse of the Blessed Virgin, of the holy Apostles, SS. Peter and Paul, of St. John the Evangelist, of St. Gregory the Great (12th March), of All Saints, and on the Commemoration of the Souls of the faithful departed, on condition that they visit a church in which the Association of the Sacred Heart is established. (6°) On the six Fridays or the six Sundays preceding the Feast of the Sacred Heart, on condition that they visit a church where this feast is celebrated. (7°) A Plenary Indulgence is granted to those who have been admitted to the *perpetual adoration*, any day they may select, on condition that they spend on that day about an hour in exercises of piety, renewing their baptismal engagements and other good resolutions, and that they pray in a public church for the intentions of the Sovereign Pontiff. (8°) Those who engage on any day of each month to make a visit to the Blessed Sacrament, and to pray for a quarter of an hour, endeavouring to appease the Divine Majesty, gain a Plenary Indulgence on Holy Thursday, and also another on the day on

## SACRED HEART OF JESUS.

which they perform this exercise. (9°) Also a Plenary Indulgence is gained at the hour of death, by invoking the holy name of Jesus, at least with the heart, if it cannot be done with the lips.

There are also many Partial Indulgences attached to the Apostleship of Prayer.

Another advantage which the Associates of the Apostleship of Prayer will doubtless value much, is the special participation granted to them in the prayers and good works of the religious of the Society of Jesus, of the Society of Mary, of the two Congregations of the Sacred Heart, of the regular clerics called Theatines, and of the religious of both sexes of La Trappe.

The Associate, when inscribing his or her name on the ticket, may choose the day on which to gain the Indulgence attached to the admittance into the Association. The day of the year, as also the day of each month, may be selected on which to perform the exercise of the perpetual worship. But this devotion is by no means of obligation.

# Devotions to the Immaculate Heart of Mary.

### Act of Consecration to the Immaculate Heart of Mary.

O HOLY Mother of God (page 192.)

---

### Litany of the Immaculate Heart of Mary.

LORD have mercy on us.
*Christ have mercy on us.*
Lord have mercy on us.
Christ hear us.
*Christ graciously hear us.*
God the Father of heaven, *have mercy on us.*
God the Son, Redeemer of the world, *have mercy on us.*
God the Holy Ghost, *have mercy on us.*
Holy Trinity one God, *have mercy on us.*
Heart of Mary,
Heart of Mary, according to the Heart of Jesus,
Heart of Mary, united to that of Jesus,
Heart of Mary, organ of the Holy Ghost,
Heart of Mary, sanctuary of the Divinity,
Heart of Mary, tabernacle of God Incarnate,

} *Pray for us.*

Heart of Mary, always exempt from sin,
Heart of Mary, full of grace,
Heart of Mary, blessed amongst all hearts,
Heart of Mary, throne of glory,
Heart of Mary, abyss of humility,
Heart of Mary, holocaust of divine love,
Heart of Mary, nailed to the cross of Jesus,
Heart of Mary, comfort of the afflicted,
Heart of Mary, refuge of sinners,
Heart of Mary, hope of the agonizing,
Heart of Mary, seat of mercy,

} *Pray for us.*

Lamb of God, who takest away the sins of the world, *spare us, O Lord.*

Lamb of God, who takest away the sins of the world, *graciously hear us, O Lord.*

Lamb of God, who takest away the sins of the world, *have mercy on us.*

℣. Pray for us, O holy Mother of God.

℟. That we may be made worthy of the promises of Christ.

LET US PRAY.

O ALMIGHTY and eternal God, who, in the heart of the Blessed Virgin Mary, didst prepare a fitting dwelling-place for thy Son, grant mercifully, that we who devoutly commemorate this most pure heart, may live in accordance with its desires: Through Christ our Lord. Amen.

## Confraternity of the Holy and Immaculate Heart of Mary.

THE Arch-Confraternity was founded at Paris, in the Church of Notre Dame des Victoires, December 3rd, 1836, and approved of by Pope Gregory XVI. on the 24th April, 1838, with the privilege of aggregating to itself other like Confraternities.

The principal end of this Confraternity is to pray for the conversion of sinners; and the extraordinary conversions which have been wrought by means of it, are a clear proof how pleasing this institution is to Almighty God.

### PRAYERS

*To be recited daily by the Associates, in order to attain the ends of the Confraternity.*

To thee, O my God, I offer up, through the Holy and Immaculate Heart of the ever Blessed Virgin Mary, all my thoughts, words, and actions, more particularly every exercise of devotion performed for the conversion of all who are unhappily engaged in sin or error; and for the sanctification of those who are members of this pious Association.

Holy Mary, Refuge of Sinners, pray for us.

O Mary, conceived without sin, pray for us who have recourse to thee.

Hail Mary, &c.

The Associates are recommended: (1°) To communicate once a month. (2°) To recite the Beads once a week. (3°) To wear, as a badge, the medal of the Immaculate Conception, commonly called the "Miraculous Medal." (4°) To say often the Memorare (page 19.)

PLENARY INDULGENCES

*Granted to the Associates on the usual conditions of Confession, Communion and Prayer for the Pope's intentions.*

(1°) On the day of their admission. (2°) On the anniversary of their Baptism. (3°) On two days every month at the choice of each one: (applicable to the Souls in Purgatory.) (4°) At the hour of their death. (5°) On the Sunday before Septuagesima, the principal solemnity of the Arch-Confraternity. (6°) On the Feast of our Lord's Circumcision (Jan. 1). (7°) On the Feasts of our Blessed Lady's Purification, Annunciation, Dolours, Assumption, Nativity, and Immaculate Conception. (8°) On the Feast of St. Paul's Conversion (Jan. 25). (9°) On that of St. Mary Magdalen (July 22). (10°) Also on the Feast of St. Joseph (March 19); on that of St. John Baptist (June 24); and on that of St. John the Evangelist (Dec. 27.)

# Occasional Devotions.

## The Devotions of the Quarant Ore;
### OR, FORTY HOURS' PRAYER.

THIS devotion continues for forty hours, in memory of the forty hours during which the body of our Lord remained in the sepulchre. It was begun at Milan in 1534, and was introduced into Rome, by St. Philip Neri in 1548, and sanctioned by Pope Clement VIII., who issued a solemn Bull respecting it, November 25th, 1592.

To promote this devotion, Pope Clement XIII. granted a Plenary Indulgence to all those who, confessing their sins and receiving the Holy Communion, should visit any church or chapel where this devotion was being performed.

To gain this Indulgence it is required:—(1°) To visit the Blessed Sacrament once each day during the three days of exposition; and (2°) to to receive the Holy Communion on one of the three days; but not necessarily in the same church or chapel in which the Blessed Sacrament is exposed.

Pope Paul V. also granted an Indulgence of ten years and ten quarantines for every visit made to the Blessed Sacrament thus exposed.

These Indulgences are applicable to the Souls in Purgatory.

The forms of Prayers used in this devotion are, the Litany of the Saints, Collects, &c.,

to which may be added the Litany of the Blessed Virgin, the Psalm Miserere, and the Te Deum.

## A Devotion in Honour of the Sacred Heart of Jesus,

*In Reparation for the Injuries offered to the Blessed Sacrament.*

### A HYMN.

To Jesus' heart all burning
  With fervent love for men,
My heart with fondest yearning
  Shall raise its joyful strain.

### CHORUS.

While ages course along,
  Blest be, with loudest song,
The Sacred Heart of Jesus
  By every heart and tongue.

O Heart for sinners riven,
  By sheer excess of love ;
The spear through thee was driven,
  'Twas sin of mine that drove.

O heart for me on fire
  With love no tongue can speak,
My yet untold desire
  God gives me for thy sake.

Too true, I have forsaken
  Thy flock by wilful sin,
Yet, now let me be taken
  Back to thy fold again.

As thou art meek and lowly,
    And ever pure of heart,
So may my heart be wholly
    Of thine the counterpart.

Away with earthly passion,
    Away with glittering pelf,
In my heart's consecration
    I yield thee all myself.

Would that to me were given
    The pinions of the dove,
I'd speed athwart the heaven,
    My Jesus' love to prove.

Within the cleft I'll cower
    Of Jesus' wounded side,
In sunshine or in shower,
    Securely there I'll hide.

When life away is flying,
    And earth's false glare is done,
Still Sacred Heart in dying
    I'll say, I'm all thine own.

*Priest.* In the name of the Father, and of the Son, and of the Holy Ghost. Amen.

Our Father. Hail Mary. I believe.

### FIRST SORROW.

*Priest.* The first sorrow of the Sacred Heart of Jesus—the sorrow that is felt at the first sacrilegious Communion ever made.

To be sung three times.

*Priest.* Adoremus in æternum

℟. Sanctissimum Sacramentum.

*Priest.* Let us consider in the first sorrow of the Sacred Heart of Jesus, the first sacrilegious Communion ever made.

Here the Priest may briefly speak on the subject of the first sacrilegious Communion ever made.

The Priest will then say,

O SACRED banquet, wherein Christ is made our food: wherein the remembrance of his Passion is renewed, the soul is filled with grace, and there is given us the pledge of future glory.

Blessed be Jesus in the most Holy Sacrament of the Altar.

℟. Blessed be Jesus in the most Holy Sacrament of the Altar.

*Priest.* Blessed be the Sacred Heart of Jesus.

℟. Blessed be the Sacred Heart of Jesus.

*Priest.* Blessed be the Immaculate Heart of Mary.

℞. Blessed be the Immaculate Heart of Mary.

*Priest.* O Sacred Heart of Jesus, I implore.

℞. That I may love thee ever more and more.

*Priest and* ℞. Our Father. Hail Mary. Glory, &c.

(Sing to the air of the Stabat Mater:)

Heart of Jesus, Joy of Heaven,
Refuge of mankind forgiven,
 Grant us to atone thy wrongs.

### SECOND SORROW.

*Priest.* The second sorrow of the Sacred Heart of Jesus—the sorrow that it feels at the injuries done to the Blessed Sacrament by Unbelievers.

To be sung three times.

*Priest.* Adoremus in æternum
℞. Sanctissimum Sacramentum.

*Priest.* Let us consider in the second sorrow of the Sacred Heart of Jesus the injuries done to the Blessed Sacrament by Unbelievers.

To be sung.

Heart of Jesus, Joy of Heaven,
Refuge of mankind forgiven,
 Grant us to atone thy wrongs.

*Priest.* O sacred banquet, &c. (page 369.)

THIRD SORROW.

*Priest.* The third sorrow of the Sacred Heart of Jesus—the sorrow that it feels at the injuries done to the Blessed Sacrament by Heretics.

To be sung three times.

*Priest.* Adoremus in æternum
℟. Sanctissimum Sacramentum.

*Priest.* Let us consider in the third sorrow of the Sacred Heart of Jesus the injuries done to the Blessed Sacrament by Heretics.

To be sung.

Heart of Jesus, Joy of Heaven,
Refuge of mankind forgiven,
Grant us to atone thy wrongs.

*Priest.* O sacred banquet, &c. (page 369.)

FOURTH SORROW.

*Priest.* The fourth sorrow of the Sacred Heart of Jesus — the sacrilegious Communions of bad Catholics.

To be sung three times.

*Priest.* Adoremus in æternum
℟. Sanctissimum Sacramentum.

*Priest.* Let us consider in the fourth sorrow of the Sacred Heart of Jesus the sacrilegious Communions of bad Catholics.

*Priest.* O Sacred banquet, &c. (page 369.)

To be sung.

Heart of Jesus, Joy of Heaven,
Refuge of mankind forgiven,
 Grant us to atone thy wrongs.

### FIFTH SORROW.

*Priest.* The fifth sorrow of the Sacred Heart of Jesus—the injuries done to the Blessed Sacrament by the neglect of tepid Catholics.

To be sung three times.

*Priest.* Adoremus in æternum

R⁊. Sanctissimum Sacramentum.

*Priest.* Let us consider in the fifth sorrow of the Sacred Heart of Jesus the injuries done to the Blessed Sacrament by the neglect of tepid Catholics.

*Priest.* O Sacred banquet, &c. (page 369.)

To be sung.

Heart of Jesus, Joy of Heaven,
Refuge of mankind forgiven,
 Grant us to atone thy wrongs.

*Ant.* I looked for one that would grieve together with me but there was none: and for one that would comfort me and I found none.

℣. I am come to cast fire on the earth:

℟. And what will I, but that it be kindled?

℣. The Lord be with you.

℟. And with thy spirit.

LET US PRAY.

GRANT we beseech thee Almighty God, that we, who while we glory in the most holy Heart of thy beloved Son, call to mind the choicest gifts of his love, may rejoice alike in their effects and in their reward: Through the same Christ our Lord.

℟. Amen.

*Priest.* May the souls of the faithful, through the mercy of God, rest in peace.

℟. Amen.

## The Way of the Cross.

Those who perform devoutly the "Way of the Cross" may gain all the Indulgences granted to the faithful who visit in person the sacred places in Jerusalem.

CONDITIONS.—1. To go from one station to another as far as the number of persons engaged in the devotion and space will admit. 2. To meditate, according to their abilities, on the Passion. A.

*The Priests and Acolyths, kneeling before the altar, say as follows:*

O JESUS, our adorable Saviour, behold us prostrate at thy feet, imploring thy mercy for ourselves, and for the souls of all the faithful departed. Vouchsafe to apply to us the infinite merits of thy passion, on which we are now about to meditate. Grant that while we trace this path of sighs and tears, our hearts may be so touched with contrition and repentance, that we may be ready to embrace with joy, all the crosses and sufferings and humiliations of this our life and pilgrimage.

℣. Domine, labia mea aperies.

℟. Et os meum annuntiabit laudem tuam.

℣. Deus, in adjutorium meum intende.

℟. Domine, ad adjuvandum me festina.

℣. Gloria Patri, &c.

℟. Sicut erat, &c.

℣. Thou shalt open my lips, O Lord.

℟. And my mouth shall declare thy praise.

℣. O God, come to my assistance.

℟. O Lord, make haste to help me.

℣. Glory be, &c.

℟. As it was, &c.

*Then, moving in procession to the First Station, the following* ℣. *and* ℟. *are said or sung:*

| | |
|---|---|
| ℣. Adoramus te, Christe, et benedicimus tibi. | ℣. We adore thee, O Christ, and we bless thee. |
| ℟. Quia per sanctam Crucem tuam redemisti mundum. | ℟. Because by thy holy Cross thou hast redeemed the world. |

*This* ℣. *and* ℟. *are repeated before each Station.*

## First Station.
### JESUS CHRIST CONDEMNED TO DEATH.

*The Priest reads:*

LEAVING the house of Caiphas, where he had been blasphemed, and the house of Herod, where he had been mocked, Jesus is dragged before Pilate, his back torn with scourges, his head crowned with thorns: and He, who on the last day will judge the living and the dead, is himself condemned to a disgraceful death.

### PRAYER.

IT was for us that thou didst suffer, O dear Jesus; it was for our sins thou wast condemned to die. Oh, grant that we may detest them from the bottom of our hearts, and by this repentance obtain thy mercy and pardon.

### AN ACT OF CONTRITION.

O GOD, we love thee with our whole hearts, and above all things, and are heartily sorry that we have offended thee. May we never offend thee any more. Oh, may we love thee without ceasing, and make it our delight to do in all things thy most holy will.

| | |
|---|---|
| Pater, &c. Ave, &c. | Our Father, &c. Hail Mary, &c. |
| Gloria Patri, &c. | Glory be to the Father, &c. |
| ℣. Miserere nostri, Domine. | ℣. Lord have mercy on us. |
| ℟. Miserere nostri. | ℟. Have mercy on us. |
| ℣. Fidelium animæ, per misericordiam Dei, requiescant in pace. | ℣. May the souls of the faithful, through the mercy of God, rest in peace. |
| ℟. Amen. | ℟. Amen. |

*This Act of Contrition is repeated after each Station.*

*While passing from one Station to another, a verse of the Stabat Mater is sung or said. (See after the last Station.)*

## Second Station.

### JESUS RECEIVES THE CROSS.

| | |
|---|---|
| ℣. Adoramus te, &c. | ℣. We adore thee, &c. |
| ℟. Quia, &c. | ℟. Because, &c. |

*Priest.*

A HEAVY cross is laid upon the bruised shoulders of Jesus. He receives it with meekness, nay, with a secret joy, for it is the instrument with which he is to redeem the world.

## THE WAY OF THE CROSS. 377

**PRAYER.**

O JESUS! grant us, by virtue of thy cross, to embrace with meekness and cheerful submission the difficulties of our state, and to be ever ready to take up our cross and follow thee.

Act of Contrition, &c. (page 375.)

Pater, Ave, &c., as before.

### Third Station.

**JESUS FALLS THE FIRST TIME UNDER THE WEIGHT OF THE CROSS.**

℣. Adoramuste, &c.    ℣. We adore thee, &c.
℞. Quia, &c.    ℞. Because, &c.

*Priest.*

BOWED down under the weight of the cross, Jesus slowly sets forth on the way to Calvary, amidst the mockeries and insults of the crowd. His agony in the garden has exhausted his body; he is sore with blows and wounds; his strength fails him; he falls to the ground under the cross.

**PRAYER.**

O JESUS! who for our sins didst bear the heavy burden of the cross, and didst fall under its weight, may the thought of thy sufferings make us watchful over ourselves, and save us from any grievous sin.

Act of Contrition, &c. (page 375.)

Pater, Ave, &c., as before.

## Fourth Station.

JESUS IS MET BY HIS BLESSED MOTHER.

℣. Adoramus te, &c.   ℣. We adore thee, &c.
℞. Quia, &c.     ℞. Because, &c.

*Priest.*

STILL burdened with his cross, and wounded yet more by his fall, Jesus proceeds on his way. He is met by his Mother. What a meeting must that have been! What a sword of anguish must have pierced that Mother's heart! What must have been the compassion of that Son for his holy Mother!

PRAYER.

O JESUS! by the compassion which thou didst feel for thy Mother, have compassion on us, and give us a share in her intercession. O Mary, most afflicted Mother, intercede for us, that, through the sufferings of thy Son, we may be delivered from the wrath to come.

Act of Contrition, &c. (page 375.)

Pater, Ave, &c., as before.

## Fifth Station.

THE CROSS IS LAID UPON SIMON OF CYRENE.

℣. Adoramus te, &c.   ℣. We adore thee, &c.
℞. Quia, &c.     ℞. Because, &c.

THE WAY OF THE CROSS.

*Priest.*

As the strength of Jesus fails, and he is unable to proceed, the executioners seize and compel Simon of Cyrene to carry his Cross. The virtue of that cross changed his heart, and from a compulsory task it became a privilege and a joy.

**PRAYER.**

O LORD Jesus! may it be our privilege also to bear thy cross; may we glory in nothing else; by it may the world be crucified unto us, and we unto the world; may we never shrink from sufferings, but rather rejoice to be counted worthy to suffer for thy name's sake.

Act of Contrition, &c. (page 375.)

Pater, Ave, &c., as before.

## Sixth Station.

THE FACE OF JESUS IS WIPED BY VERONICA.

℣. Adoramus te, &c.    ℣. We adore thee, &c.

℟. Quia, &c.    ℟. Because, &c.

*Priest.*

As Jesus proceeds on the way, covered with the sweat of death, a woman, moved with compassion, makes her way through the crowd, and wipes his face with a handkerchief. As a reward for her piety, the impression of his sacred countenance is miraculously imprinted upon the handkerchief.

#### PRAYER.

O Jesus! may the contemplation of thy sufferings move us with the deepest compassion, make us detest our sins, and kindle in our hearts more fervent love of thee. So assist us by thy grace, that we may never fall again into sin.

Act of Contrition, &c. (page 375.)

Pater, Ave, &c., as before.

### Seventh Station.

#### JESUS FALLS A SECOND TIME.

℣. Adoramus te, &c.     ℣. We adore thee, &c.

℟. Quia, &c.     ℟. Because, &c.

#### *Priest.*

THE pain of his wound, and the loss of blood increasing at every step of his way, again his strength fails him, and Jesus falls to the ground a second time.

#### PRAYER.

O Jesus! falling again under the burden of our sins, and of thy sufferings for them, how often have we grieved thee by our repeated infidelities! Oh, may we rather die than ever offend thee again!

Act of Contrition, &c. (page 375.)

Pater, Ave, &c., as before.

## Eighth Station.

THE WOMEN OF JERUSALEM MOURN FOR OUR LORD.

℣. Adoramus te, &c.   ℣. We adore thee, &c.
℟. Quia, &c.   ℟. Because, &c.

*Priest.*

AT the sight of the sufferings of Jesus, some holy women in the crowd are so touched with sympathy, that they openly grieve for him. Jesus, knowing the things that were to come to pass upon Jerusalem, because of its rejection of him, turns to them, and says, "Daughters of Jerusalem, weep not over me, but weep for yourselves and for your children." (*Luke* xxiii. 28.)

PRAYER.

O LORD Jesus, we will grieve both for thee and for ourselves; for thy sufferings, and for our sins which caused them. Oh, teach us so to mourn, that we may be comforted, and escape those dreadful judgments prepared for all who in this life reject or neglect thee.

Act of Contrition, &c. (page 375.)

Pater, Ave, &c., as before.

## Ninth Station.

JESUS FALLS THE THIRD TIME UNDER THE CROSS.

℣. Adoramus te, &c.   ℣. We adore thee, &c.
℟. Quia, &c.   ℟. Because, &c.

## Twelfth Station.

### JESUS DIES UPON THE CROSS.

℣. Adoramus te, &c.    ℣. We adore thee, &c.

℞. Quia per, &c.    ℞. Because, &c.

*Priest.*

FOR three hours has Jesus hung upon his cross; his blood has run in streams down his body, and bedewed the ground; and, in the midst of excruciating sufferings, he has pardoned his murderers, promised the bliss of Paradise to the good thief, and committed his blessed Mother and beloved Disciple to each other's care. All is now consummated; and meekly bowing down his head, he gives up the ghost.

### PRAYER.

O JESUS! we devoutly embrace that honoured cross where thou didst love us even unto death. In that death we place all our confidence. Henceforth let us live only for thee; and in dying for thee, let us die loving thee, and in thy sacred arms.

Act of Contrition, &c. (page 375.)

Pater, Ave, &c., as before.

## Thirteenth Station.

### JESUS IS LAID IN THE ARMS OF HIS SACRED MOTHER.

℣. Adoramus te, &c.    ℣. We adore thee, &c.

℞. Quia, &c.    ℞. Because, &c.

*Priest.*

THE multitude have left the heights of Calvary, and none remain save the beloved disciple and the holy women, who, at the foot of the cross, are striving to stem the grief of Christ's inconsolable Mother. Joseph of Arimathea and Nicodemus take down the body of her divine Son from the cross, and deposit it in her arms.

PRAYER.

O THOU, whose grief was boundless as an ocean that hath no limits, Mary, Mother of God, give us a share in thy most holy sorrow for the sufferings of thy Son, and have compassion on our infirmities. Accept us as thy children with the beloved disciple. Shew thyself a mother unto us; and may He, through thee, receive our prayer, who for us vouchsafed to be thy Son.

Act of Contrition, &c. (page 375.)

Pater, Ave, &c., as before.

## Fourteenth Station.

JESUS IS LAID IN THE SEPULCHRE.

℣. Adoramuste, &c.   ℣. We adore thee, &c.
℟. Quia per, &c.   ℟. Because, &c.

*Priest.*

THE body of her dearly beloved Son is taken from his Mother, and laid by the disciples in the tomb. The tomb is closed, and there the lifeless body remains until the hour of its glorious resurrection.

### PRAYER.

WE, too, O God, will descend into the grave whenever it shall please thee, as it shall please thee, and wheresoever it shall please thee. Let thy just decrees be fulfilled; let our sinful bodies return to their parent dust; but do thou, in thy great mercy, receive our immortal souls, and when our bodies have risen again, place them likewise in thy kingdom, that we may love and bless thee for ever and ever. Amen.

Act of Contrition, &c. (page 375.)
Pater, Ave, &c., as before.

*The Benediction is then given, after which the following Antiphon and Prayer are sung.*

Ant. Christus factus est pro nobis obediens usque ad mortem, mortem autem crucis.

Ant. Christ was made for us obedient unto death, even the death of the cross.

### OREMUS.

RESPICE, quæsumus, Domine, super hanc familiam tuam, pro qua Dominus noster Jesus Christus non dubitavit manibus tradi nocentium, et crucis subire tormentum. Qui tecum vivit et regnat in unitate Spiritus Sancti, Deus, per omnia sæcula sæculorum.

R̲. Amen.

### LET US PRAY.

LOOK down, O Lord, we beseech thee, upon this thy family, for which our Lord Jesus Christ did not refuse to be delivered into the hands of wicked men, and to endure the torments of the cross. Who liveth and reigneth with thee in the unity of the Holy Ghost, God for ever and ever.

R̲. Amen.

*When the Benediction is given with the Cross of the Passion, the following order is to be observed.*

**Benediction with the Cross of the Passion.**

*Cantor.* Jube, Domine, benedicere.
*Priest.* Benedicat vos Dominus noster Jesus Christus, qui pro nobis flagellatus est, crucem portavit, et fuit crucifixus.
℟. Amen.

*Cantor.* Grant us, O Lord, a blessing.
*Priest.* May our Lord Jesus Christ bless us, who for us was scourged, loaded with his cross, and crucified.
℟. Amen.

## Stabat Mater.
(100 days Indulgence for each devout recital. A.)

STABAT Mater dolorosa,
Juxta crucem lacrymosa,
  Dum pendebat Filius.

At the Cross her station keeping,
Stood the mournful Mother weeping
  Close to Jesus to the last.

Cujus animam gementem,
Contristatam, et dolentem
  Pertransivit gladius.

Through her heart, his sorrow sharing,
All his bitter anguish bearing,
  Now at length the sword had pass'd.

O quam tristis et afflicta
Fuit illa benedicta
  Mater Unigeniti !

Oh, how sad and sore distress'd
Was that Mother highly blest
  Of the sole-begotten One!

Quæ mœrebat, et do-
  lebat,
Et tremebat, cum vide-
  bat,
  Nati pœnas inclyti.

Christ above in tor-
  ment hangs;
She beneath beholds
  the pangs
  Of her dying glori-
  ous Son.

Quis est homo qui non
  fleret,
Christi Matrem si vi-
  deret
  In tanto supplicio?

Is there one who would
  not weep,
Whelm'd in miseries so
  deep
  Christ's dear Mother
  to behold?

Quis non posset con-
  tristari,
Piam Matrem contem-
  plari,
  Dolentem cum Filio?

Can the human heart
  refrain
From partaking in her
  pain,
  In that Mother's
  pain untold?

Pro peccatis suæ gentis

Vidit Jesum in tor-
  mentis,
  Et flagellis subdi-
  tum.

Bruis'd, derided, curs'd,
  defil'd,
She beheld her tender
  child
  All with bloody
  scourges rent.

Vidit suum dulcem
  Natum,
Moriendo, desolatum,
  Dum emisit spiri-
  tum.

For the sins of his own
  nation,
Saw him hang in deso-
  lation,
  Till his spirit forth
  he sent.

## STABAT MATER.

| | |
|---|---|
| Eia Mater, fons amoris, | O thou Mother, fount of love! |
| Me sentire vim doloris | Touch my spirit from above, |
| Fac, ut tecum lugeam: | Make my heart with thine accord: |
| | |
| Fac ut ardeat cor meum, | Make me feel as thou hast felt, |
| In amando Christum Deum, | Make my soul to glow and melt |
| Ut sibi complaceam. | With the love of Christ my Lord. |
| | |
| Sancta Mater, istud agas, | Holy Mother! pierce me through, |
| Crucifixi fige plagas | In my heart each wound renew |
| Cordi meo valide. | Of my Saviour crucified: |
| | |
| Tui Nati vulnerati, | Let me share with thee his pain, |
| Tam dignati pro me pati, | Who for all my sins was slain, |
| Pœnas mecum divide. | Who for me in torments died. |
| | |
| Fac me tecum pie flere | Let me mingle tears with thee, |
| Crucifixo condolere, | Mourning Him who mourn'd for me, |
| Donec ego vixero. | All the days that I may live: |

Juxta crucem tecum
stare,
Et me tibi sociare

In planctu desidero.

By the Cross with thee
to stay,
There with thee to
weep and pray,
Is all I ask of thee
to give.

Virgo virginum præ-
clara,
Mihi jam non sis
amara,
Fac me tecum plan-
gere.

Virgin of all virgins
best!
Listen to my fond re-
quest:
Let me share thy
grief divine;

Fac ut portem Christi
mortem,
Passionis fac consor-
tem,
Et plagas recolere.

Let me, to my latest
breath,
In my body bear the
death
Of that dying Son
of thine.

Fac me plagis vulne-
rari,
Fac me cruce inebriari.

Et cruore Filii.

Wounded with his
every wound,
Steep my soul till it
hath swoon'd
In his very blood
away:

Flammis ne urar suc-
census,
Per te, Virgo, sim
defensus,
In die judicii.

Be to me, O Virgin,
nigh,
Lest in flames I burn
and die,
In his awful judg-
ment day.

| | |
|---|---|
| Christe, cum sit hinc exire, | Christ, when thou shalt call me hence |
| Da per Matrem me venire. | Be thy Mother my defence, |
| Ad palmam victoriæ. | Be thy cross my victory: |
| | |
| Quando corpus morietur, | While my body here decays, |
| Fac ut animæ donetur | May my soul thy goodness praise, |
| Paradisi gloria. Amen. | Safe in Paradise with thee. Amen. |

## Month of May.

IT is a well-known devotion, to consecrate to the most holy Mary the month of May, as the month most beautiful and full of bloom in the whole year.

Pope Pius VII., in order to animate all Christian people to the practice of a devotion so tender and agreeable to the most blessed Virgin, and calculated to be of such great spiritual benefit to themselves, granted, by a Rescript of March 21, 1815, (kept in the *Segretaria* of his Eminence the Cardinal-Vicar,) to all the faithful of the Catholic world, who either in public or in private, should, during this month, honour the Blessed Virgin with some special homage or devout prayers.

1°. The Indulgence of 100 days for each day.

2°. The Plenary Indulgence once in this month; to be gained on that day when, having confessed and communicated, they shall pray to God for the Holy Church, &c.

These Indulgences were confirmed for ever by the same holy Pontiff, June 18, 1822.

---

# Devotions of the Ten Sundays in honour of St. Ignatius of Loyola.

GRACIOUSLY yielding to the humble prayer of F. Lawrence Ricci, General of the Society of Jesus, our most Holy Father, Pope Clement XIII., granted to all the faithful of both sexes, who, being truly sorry for their sins, and having confessed them, and received holy Communion, shall by fervent meditation, prayer, or other exercises of Catholic piety, sanctify the ten consecutive Sundays before the Feast of St. Ignatius, or any other ten Sundays of the year, in honour of the same Saint and for the glory of God, and shall devoutly visit a Church of the Society of Jesus, a Plenary Indulgence on each of the said Sundays. And his Holiness wished this said grant to remain in force for all future times.

Given at Rome by the Secretary of the Sacred Congregation of Indulgences, the 27th January, 1767.

## DEVOTIONS RECOMMENDED FOR EACH SUNDAY.

PERFORM your actions in imitation of those of St. Ignatius, and offer them to God in union with the desires and merits of this Saint.

Recite ten times the Our Father, Hail Mary, and Glory be to the Father, &c., or at least ten times Glory be to the Father, &c., to obtain the virtue which you propose to yourself, in honour of St. Ignatius, together with the following Antiphon and Prayer :—

*Ant.* This man, despising the world, and triumphing over earthly things, heaped up riches in heaven, both by word and work.

℣. The Lord hath loved and adorned him.

℟. A garment of glory he hath put on him.

### LET US PRAY.

O GOD, who, for the increase of the greater glory of thy name, hast, by blessed Ignatius, strengthened thy Church-militant with new auxiliaries, graciously vouchsafe that we, assisted by his prayers, and imitating his virtues, combating here on earth, may obtain with him an everlasting crown in heaven: Through Jesus Christ our Lord. Amen.

# A Novena; or Nine Days' Devotion to St. Francis Xavier,

### APOSTLE OF THE INDIES.

THIS Novena generally commences on the 4th and ends on the 12th of March, upon which latter day, in the year of our Lord, 1622, Pope Gregory XV. canonized the Saint.

### LITANY OF ST. FRANCIS XAVIER.

LORD have mercy on us.
*Christ have mercy on us.*
Lord have mercy on us.
Christ hear us.
*Christ graciously hear us.*
God, the Father of heaven, *have mercy on us.*
God the Son, Redeemer of the world, *have mercy on us.*
God the Holy Ghost, *have mercy on us.*
Holy Trinity one God, *have mercy on us.*

Holy Mary,
Holy Father Ignatius,
St. Francis Xavier, most worthy son of St. Ignatius,
St. Francis Xavier, Apostle of the Indies,
St. Francis Xavier, announcing peace to men,

} *Pray for us.*

Vessel of election, carrying the name of Jesus to the Gentiles,
Vessel full of divine grace,
Defender of the faith,
Enemy of infidelity,
Destroyer of idols,
Chosen instrument of the Eternal Father for the advancement of his glory,
Faithful follower and companion of Jesus Christ,
Pillar of the Church of God,
Light of infidels,
Master of the faithful,
Mirror of true piety,
Guide in the way of virtue and perfection,
Pattern of apostolical spirit and sanctity,
Light of the blind,
Curer of the lame,
Help of the shipwrecked,
Health of the sick,
Protector in time of plague, famine, and war,
Whose power the devils obeyed,
Wonderful worker of miracles,
Refuge of the miserable,
Comfort of the afflicted,

*Pray for us.*

Splendour of the East,
Tabernacle of incorruption,
Treasury of divine love,
Glory of the Society of Jesus,
Xavier most poor,
Xavier most chaste,
Xavier most obedient,
Xavier most humble,
Xavier most desirous of the cross
 and labours of Christ,
Xavier most zealous for God's glory
 and the good of souls,
Angel in life and manners,
Patriarch in affection and care for
 God's people,
Prophet in gift and spirit,
Apostle in dignity and merit,
Martyr in desiring to die for Christ,
Confessor in virtue and profession of
 life,
Virgin in body and mind,
} *Pray for us.*

Lamb of God, who takest away the sins of the world, *spare us, O Lord.*
Lamb of God, who takest away the sins of the world, *graciously hear us, O Lord.*
Lamb of God, who takest away the sins of the world, *have mercy on us.*
Christ hear us.
*Christ graciously hear us.*

Lord have mercy on us.
*Christ have mercy on us.*
Lord have mercy on us.
Our Father, &c.

℣. Pray for us, St. Francis Xavier.

℟. That we may be made worthy of the promises of Christ.

### LET US PRAY.

O GOD, who didst vouchsafe by the preaching and miracles of St. Francis Xavier, to join unto thy Church the countries of the Indies, grant, we beseech thee, that we, who reverence his glorious merits, may also imitate his example. Through Jesus Christ our Lord. Amen.

### LET US PRAY.

O LORD Jesus Christ, true God and Man, my Creator and Redeemer, for thy sake, and because I love thee above all things, I am sorry that I have offended thee, and I firmly resolve to confess my sins, perform the penance that shall be enjoined me, and make restitution and satisfaction wherever it shall be due from me. For the love of thee, I forgive all my enemies; to thee I offer up my life, actions, and sufferings, in satisfaction for my sins; and I trust in thy goodness and infinite mercy that thou wilt forgive me, through the merits of thy precious blood and passion, and that thou wilt also give me grace to amend my life, and to persevere in thy service unto my death. Amen.

Most glorious St. Francis Xavier, Apostle of the Indies, if it be for the glory of God, and to thy honour, that I obtain what I ask for in this Novena, intercede for me with God, that he may grant this my petition; if not, obtain for me that which is most conformable to his holy will and most useful to my soul. Amen.

Here say the "Our Father," and "Hail Mary," three times, and the following prayer to St. Francis Xavier :—

Most holy father, St. Francis Xavier, who didst receive praise from the mouths of innocent children, I most humbly implore thy bountiful charity through the most precious blood of Jesus, and the Immaculate Conception of our blessed Lady Mother of God, to obtain of God for me, that at the approach of my last hour, my heart may be separated from all worldly thoughts and distractions, and be so fixed in the most ardent love of him and the desire of a happy eternity, that laying aside all earthly things which hitherto have distracted me, I may most diligently seek and truly find that one thing necessary, to die and rest in peace, under the protection of the most holy Virgin Mary, in the wounds of Jesus, her most beloved Son, in the sweet embraces of my God, and in thy presence, holy Saint, through whose intercession I hope to obtain this mercy. But yet, whilst it shall please the divine Providence to preserve my life, I beseech thee, my most loving protector and most affectionate father, to obtain for me, of his divine Majesty, that I may live as I would wish to have lived at the hour of my death, ever imitating thy virtues, and fulfilling the most holy will of God; that so my death may be a passage into life everlasting. I also beseech thee to obtain for me that which I ask in this Novena, if it be for the glory of God, and the good of my soul. Amen.

*Here you are to ask St. Francis Xavier for the particular favour you desire to obtain.*

### PRAYER OF ST. FRANCIS XAVIER FOR THE CONVERSION OF INFIDELS.

ETERNAL God, Creator of all things, remember that thou alone didst create the souls of infidels, framing them to thine own image and likeness ; and yet behold, O God, how to thy dishonour they are daily falling into hell. Remember thy only Son Jesus Christ, who suffered for them, most bountifully shedding his precious blood; permit him not any longer to be despised by infidels, but being appeased by the prayers of thine elect, the Saints, and of the Church, the most blessed Spouse of thy Son, vouchsafe to be mindful of thy mercy ; and, forgetting their idolatry and infidelity, cause them also to know him whom thou didst send, Jesus Christ, thy Son our Lord, who is our health, life, and resurrection, through whom we are made free and are saved, to whom be all glory for ever. Amen.

*Ant.* Fare thee well, good and faithful servant; because thou hast been faithful over a few things, I will place thee over many things ; enter into the joy of thy Lord.

℣. Our Lord hath guided the just man by right ways.

℟. And hath showed him the kingdom of God.

**LET US PRAY.**

O GOD, who didst vouchsafe, by the preaching and miracles of St. Francis Xavier, to join unto thy Church the countries of the Indies, grant, we beseech thee, that we who reverence his glorious merits, may also imitate his example: Through Jesus Christ our Lord. Amen.

### A COMMEMORATION OF ST. IGNATIUS OF LOYOLA.

*Ant.* This man, despising the world, and triumphing over earthly things, heaped up riches in heaven both by word and work.

℣. The Lord hath loved and adorned him.

℟. A garment of glory he hath put on him.

**LET US PRAY.**

O GOD, who, for the increase of the greater glory of thy name, hast, by blessed Ignatius, strengthened thy Church-militant with new auxiliaries, graciously vouchsafe that we, assisted by his prayers, and imitating his virtues, combating here on earth, may obtain with him an everlasting crown in heaven: Through Jesus Christ our Lord. Amen.

### COMMEMORATION OF ST. GREGORY THE GREAT, APOSTLE OF ENGLAND.

*Ant.* O most excellent Doctor, light of the holy church, blessed Gregory, lover of God's law, supplicate the Son of God for us.

℣. The Lord hath chosen him a priest unto himself.

℟. To offer up unto him the sacrifice of praise.

**LET US PRAY.**

O God, who hast bestowed the rewards of eternal life on the soul of thy servant Gregory, mercifully grant that we, who are depressed with the weight of our sins, may by his prayers be delivered: Through Jesus Christ our Lord. Amen.

## Devotions of the Six Sundays in Honour of St. Aloysius.

The six Sundays of St. Aloysius are kept in memory of the six years this Saint spent in the Society of Jesus. To nourish so salutary a devotion approved in heaven by many favours spiritual and temporal, Clement XII. granted a Plenary Indulgence on each of these Sundays, to all who practice this devotion.

## IN HONOUR OF ST. ALOYSIUS. 403

In order to gain this Indulgence, it is requisite that these six Sundays should be kept consecutively; and that on each of them, the faithful being truly penitent, and having communicated, should spend some time in pious meditations or vocal prayer, or other works of piety in honour of the Saint.

### LITANY OF ST. ALOYSIUS.

LORD have mercy on us.
*Christ have mercy on us.*
Lord have mercy on us.
Christ hear us.
*Christ graciously hear us.*
God, the Father of Heaven, *have mercy on us.*
God the Son, Redeemer of the world, *have mercy on us.*
God the Holy Ghost, *have mercy on us.*
Holy Trinity one God, *have mercy on us.*
Holy Mary,
Holy Mother of God,
Holy Virgin of Virgins,
St. Aloysius,
Most beloved of Christ,
The delight of the Blessed Virgin,
Most chaste youth,
Angelical youth,
Most humble youth,
Model of young students,
Despiser of riches, } *Pray for us.*

Enemy of vanities,
Scorner of honours,
Honour of princes,
Flower of innocence,
Ornament of the religious state,
Mirror of mortification,
Mirror of perfect obedience,
Lover of Evangelical poverty,
Most affectionately devout,
Most zealous observer of the rules,
Most desirous of the salvation of souls,
Faithful adorer of the Eucharist,
Particular client of St. Ignatius,

} *Pray for us.*

Be merciful to us, O Lord, *and spare us.*
Be merciful to us, O Lord, *and hear us.*

From the concupiscence of the eyes,
From the concupiscence of the flesh,
From the pride of life,
By the merits and intercession of St. Aloysius,
By his angelical purity,
By his sanctity and glory,

} *O Lord, deliver us.*

Lamb of God, who takest away the sins of the world, *spare us, O Lord.*

Lamb of God, who takest away the sins of the world, *graciously hear us, O Lord.*

Lamb of God, who takest away the sins of the world, *have mercy on us.*

IN HONOUR OF ST. ALOYSIUS. 405

Christ hear us.
*Christ graciously hear us.*
℣. Pray for us, St. Aloysius.
℟. That we may be made worthy of the promises of Christ.

LET US PRAY.

O GOD, the distributor of heavenly gifts, who didst join in the angelical youth Aloysius, wonderful innocence of life, with an equal severity of penance; grant through his merits and prayers, that we, who have not followed the example of his innocence, may imitate his practice of penance. Through our Lord Jesus Christ. Amen.

One of the following Prayers, according to the Sunday, may be recited next.

FIRST SUNDAY.

MOST amiable Penitent! who by real grief and continual tears for thy sins, hast taught me how I should deplore mine, behold a humble suppliant at thy feet, conscious of many and grievous sins, yet averse to a due repentance. Obtain for thy client some share at least in that grief, which forced from thee so many tears, and flung thy innocent soul into such agonies.

I am indeed unworthy of such a favour: but God, whom I have offended, and to whose justice I can make no other atonement, is most worthy, to whom I should offer a sacrifice of a humble and contrite heart. Grant then, that being mindful of my iniquities, I may grieve for them, and may deem them, as they are, my only and greatest evil; that by this means and through thy intercession, I may hope to obtain the reward promised to true penitents, the pardon of all my sins: Through our Lord Jesus Christ. Amen.

### SECOND SUNDAY.

Most mortified and most innocent Aloysius! I am confounded when I behold the wide disparity between the innocence of thy life and the guilt of mine. Thou didst treat thy pure and undefiled body with the utmost rigour and severity; I indulge and pamper my rebellious flesh with so great an indulgence. How wisely didst thou comply with the inspirations of thy divine Teacher, by whose direction thou didst exact that rigorous account of thyself. How foolishly do I yield to the suggestions of the enemy of my salvation in seeking self-ease and satisfaction. Obtain for me, I beseech thee, a holy hatred of myself, that inflamed with a just indignation at the guilt of my past disorderly life, I may have the resolution to enter into the narrow path of self-denial, which leads to bliss, and inflict on myself the punishment due to my sins. Suffer me not, O most loving Patron, to stray hereafter, or by relapsing into my former disorders, to return into the broad way which inevitably leads to perdition. Obtain a ray of heavenly grace to guide my steps, and to convince me, that the inordinate cravings of my body and senses are the most dangerous of my enemies : may I, encouraged by thy example, be ever upon the watch to observe their movements, and by a just severity keep them under due subjection; that thus victorious over myself, I may be entitled to the crown of glory promised to those who conquer themselves.

### THIRD SUNDAY.

FLOWER of innocence, most angelical youth! my soul rejoices at thy purity, so particular and above nature, which no grievous crime nor breath of impure thought could ever affect or sully. Confounded at the multitude of my crimes, let me address thee and humbly sue for pardon. I am sorry for, and abhor whatever is displeasing in thy most pure sight. Obtain for me of God, unsullied purity of body and mind. May whatever is unclean be abominable in my eyes. May I have resolution to guard and shut all the passages of my soul against its entrance; this I now resolve, relying with confidence on the patronage and the protection of the Immaculate Virgin Mary. "*Let my heart be undefiled, that I may not be confounded.*" (Ps. cxviii. 80.) Amen.

### FOURTH SUNDAY.

O MOST amiable patron, Aloysius! cast an eye of pity and compassion on thy poor client, if, considering the disparity and the irregularity of my life, I may style myself thine. Thy disengagement from the world and thy union with God are a continual reproach to me, in my attachment to the one, and my indifference to the other. I am truly poured out like water, lost in the pursuit of vain objects, and dissipated in my own unprofitable wanderings. I grieve to find myself so far from God, so much attached to the world. My soul has forgotten God, her Saviour, and her strong support she has not remembered; obtain therefore for me a small share of that union with God which thou didst ever enjoy. May I seriously keep in view, and take delight in such things as are eternal: may I regulate my conduct by the light and maxims of the Gospel, and not by the false dictates of worldly prudence. Let those be "*a lamp to my feet, and a light to my paths.*" (Ps. cxviii. 105.)

FIFTH SUNDAY.

ZEALOUS and loving promoter of the eternal welfare of souls, holy Aloysius! if it be true, as most certainly it is, that charity never ceases, and though born in time is perfected in eternity; why may I not, emboldened by the great charity for which thou wast so remarkable while upon earth, presume on thy favour and interest now in heaven. As thy most humble client, I beseech thee to obtain for me some spark of that pure and disinterested charity, which gave life to all thy actions. For, though a Christian, I am still unskilled how to love my neighbour as becomes a follower of Christ: I am still unacquainted

T

with the method and measure of love enforced by divine command: still inexperienced how to love him for God's sake only, and more inclined to follow the dictates of nature than the guidance of divine grace. I beg of thee, therefore, to exert, thy powerful intercession, that I may be actuated hereafter by no other motive than a well-ordered charity. Kindle in my heart, by thy powerful mediation, that pure flame which consumed thine; that as thy precious and happy death was the reward of a life spent in charity, so the practice of the same virtue may prove my comfort and security in my last moment, on which depends a happy or unhappy eternity. Amen.

SIXTH SUNDAY.

HOLY youth, example of divine charity, Aloysius! how singular was thy happiness, who didst live but for the love of thy heavenly Spouse and in his chaste embraces. To whom more properly can I recommend my cold heart? Oh, may I receive some heat and influence from that sacred fire, which inflamed and consumed thee. May I henceforward know and ever love God, my only good. I confess with confusion, that I have been defective in this part of my duty, and though I have often been warned by the just reproaches of my conscience, and admonished by the tender invitations of my amiable Saviour, I have ever been disobedient; I have refused to place my affections on God, my Creator and Redeemer; and at the same time in a prodigal manner, I have squandered them away on base and contemptible objects. I acknowledge and lament my fault, my folly and my blindness. O blessed Aloysius, by that seraphic love which consumed thy heart, and which thou didst endeavour to instil into others, obtain for me this favour and mercy, that I may ever live in the love and grace of God, and die in the same. Amen.

Here recite six times the Our Father, the Hail Mary and Glory, &c.

### PRAYER.

ANGELICAL youth, most loving protector, and powerful advocate, Aloysius! as thy most unworthy servant and client, yet sensible of the power which thou enjoyest with God, the just reward of thy merit, I humbly prostrate myself before thee. I rejoice, not only for the renown of thy name, illustrious upon earth by frequent and glorious prodigies; but also for the sublime pre-eminence with which God has been pleased to crown thy virtues in heaven. Praise and glory be to the most sacred Trinity, who embellished thy soul with a most admirable innocence and with so many most heroic virtues. Blessed be the Eternal Father, who is well pleased in thee, his adopted child, adorned with such singular prerogatives. Blessed be God the Son, who sees in thee such abundant fruits of his precious blood and passion. Blessed be the Holy Ghost, who resided in thee after a particular manner, and inflamed thy heart with an ardent love and charity. By these singular favours, by thy innocence and penance equally admirable, by that love of God which burnt in thy breast, and his towards thee: in fine, by the unspeakable bliss and happiness thou enjoyest in heaven, give me leave, in a suppliant manner, to entreat thee to obtain for me a true contrition and repentance, an undefiled purity of heart, and a conscience free from sin. Be thou ever present to me, protect and defend me as well in life as in death, when my weakness will stand most in need of thy powerful assistance.

Let me also, my dear and indulgent patron, most earnestly beg the particular grace of *N.N.* This I confidently hope to obtain through thy holy intercession. O Queen of Heaven, Virgin Mother, who didst so much love Aloysius, intercede with thy only begotten Son, that under thy patronage, some weight may be added to my poor and unworthy prayers: grant this my request, founded not on my own, which are none, but on the merits of St. Aloysius. O most holy Virgin, may all know and be sensible, that thou wouldst have Aloysius honoured and respected, and that as a true Mother, thou embracest such as have recourse to his protection and patronage. May the number of the faithful who honour thee, O Queen of Angels, and the angelical Aloysius, here on earth be daily increased, and may they yet more praise and glorify thee and him in heaven, for all eternity. Amen.

## Devotions in Honour of St. Stanislas Kostka.

AT the repeated prayer of the Father Pro-curator of the Venerable Congregation called *Pii Operarii* (Pious Labourers) here in Rome, to propagate amongst the faithful the devotion towards St. Stanislas Kostka, as especially calculated to augment the love of our blessed Lady, Pope Pius VIII., by two decrees, April 3 and May 1, 1821, and Leo XII., by two other decrees, Jan. 21 and Feb. 25, 1826 (all of which were published by the S. Congr. of Indulgences, May 13, 1826), granted—

1°. The Plenary Indulgence on the Feast of the Saint, Nov. 13, or on that Sunday on which, for the convenience of the people, this feast shall be celebrated *de licentia Ordinarii*, to all the faithful who, having confessed and communicated, shall visit the church or public oratory where it is celebrated, and pray according to the intention of the Sovereign Pontiff.

2°. The Indulgence of seven years and seven quarantines on every one of the ten Sundays before his feast, kept in honour of the ten months of novitiate made by the saint; to be gained by visiting the church or oratory where these Sundays are kept, and praying as above.

3°. The Indulgence of 100 days every day of the Novena preceding his feast, for assisting devoutly at the said Novena with contrite heart and praying as above.

4°. The Indulgence of 100 days, once a day, to all who shall say a Pater and Ave before a picture of the saint exposed in any church or public oratory, and pray as above.

5°. The Plenary Indulgence may be gained by the faithful by practising this exercise for a month continuously, on any one day in the month when, after Confession and Communion, they shall pray as above. Whoever, by reason of a lawful impediment, shall be unable to say in Church the Pater and Ave described, may say it wherever he likes on the days he is hindered, and gain this Plenary Indulgence.

6°. The Indulgence of 100 days, in addition to the seven years and seven quarantines granted for the above-named ten Sundays, to all who, being contrite in heart, shall assist at the day's Retreat called the Retreat of St. Stanislas, wherever it is made once in the week, and shall pray according to the mind of the Sovereign Pontiff.

All these Indulgences, at first granted for the kingdom of the Two Sicilies, were afterwards extended to the Pontifical States for any church or public oratory where the devotion to St. Stanislas is or shall be introduced, as appears from the decree above named, Feb. 25, 1826; and the same Pope Leo XII., by another decree of the S. Congr. of Indulgences, March 3, 1827, made them available for the whole Catholic world, even for private monastic churches and oratories of seminaries, colleges, conservatories, monasteries and houses of retreat for both sexes.

Furthermore, Pope Pius IX., by an autograph Rescript, kept in the Segretaria of the S. Congr. of Indulgences, dated March 22, 1847, granted—

7°. The Indulgence of 300 days, to be gained once a day by all the faithful who, in honour of this Saint shall say the three following Prayers for Purity, Charity, and a Good Death, adding to each, one Pater, one Ave, and one Gloria.

And the same Pope, by a decree of the same S. Congr., of July 10, 1854, has vouchsafed to add—

8°. The Plenary Indulgence to all the faithful who shall say these Prayers, with the Pater, Ave, and Gloria, once a day for a month together; to be gained by them on that day in each month when, after having confessed and communicated, they shall visit a church or public oratory, and pray there, for a time, according to the mind of his Holiness.

THE PRAYER FOR PURITY.

My most pure patron Stanislas, Angel of purity, I rejoice with thee for that marvellous gift of virginal purity which graced thy spotless heart; I humbly pray thee, obtain for me strength against all impure temptations, and inspire me with constant watchfulness to guard my purity, that virtue most glorious in itself, and most acceptable to God.

Pater. Ave. Gloria.

THE PRAYER FOR CHARITY.

My most loving patron Stanislas, seraph of charity, I rejoice with thee for the burning flame of love which ever kept thy pure and innocent heart elevated to, and united with its God ; I humbly pray thee, kindle in me a flame of the love of God so brightly burning, as to consume away all earthly love, and set me all on fire with his love alone.

Pater. Ave. Gloria.

THE PRAYER FOR A GOOD DEATH.

My most tender and most mighty patron Stanislas, Angel of purity and seraph of charity, I rejoice with thee for thy most happy death, originating in thy desire to contemplate Mary assumed to heaven, and caused at last by a gushing burst of love for her. I give thanks to Mary, because she willed to accomplish thy desires ; and I pray thee, gracious Saint, by all the lustre of thy happy death, be thou my advocate and my patron at death. Intercede with Mary for me, to obtain for me a death, if not all happiness like thine, yet calm and peaceful, under the safe conduct of her my advocate, and thee my special patron.

Pater. Ave. Gloria.

# The Scapular of our Lady of Mount Carmel.

### I. THE CONDITIONS AND THE PROMISES.

No peculiar obligation is contracted by being invested with the Brown Scapular: but all right to participate in its Indulgences are forfeited if the Scapular be laid aside. This right may, however, be regained by merely resuming the Scapular: it is not necessary that it should be again blessed. Those who wear it till death may piously hope that the Blessed Virgin will preserve them from the danger of dying in bad dispositions, according to the promise she made to St. Simon Stock. In order to participate in the *Sabbatine Indulgence*, that is to say, in order to obtain the help promised by our Lady to the members of the Confraternity of the Scapular, on the Saturday following the day of their death, it is further necessary to recite every day the Little Office of the Blessed Virgin, or (for those who cannot read) to abstain every Wednesday of the year. Priests who give the Scapular ordinarily have the power of substituting some other pious work in place of these.

### II. PLENARY INDULGENCES.

(1°) On the day of admission. (2°) On the Feast of our Lady of Mount Carmel (July 16th), or on any day of the Octave. (3°) At the hour of death. (4°) On the Feasts of the Immaculate Conception, the Nativity, the Presentation, the Annunciation, the Visitation, the Purification, and the Assumption of the Blessed

Virgin. (5°) On the Feasts of St. Joseph, St. Simon Stock (May 16th), St. Anne, St. Michael, St. Teresa. (6°) On every Wednesday of the year.

N.B.—All the Indulgences are applicable to the Souls in Purgatory, on the usual conditions.

Besides the above there are also many partial Indulgences. A.

# The Scapular of the Immaculate Conception.

### I. CONDITIONS.

In order to gain the numerous Indulgences granted to this Scapular, it is necessary to pray for the reformation of manners, and the conversion of sinners; no fixed prayers are imposed. St. Andrew Avellino recommends twelve Paters and Aves in honour of the twelve special privileges granted to the Blessed Virgin, and three Glorias in honour of the Blessed Trinity.

### II. PLENARY INDULGENCES.

*(The usual conditions, Confession, Communion and prayers for the Pope's Intention.)*

(1°) On the day of admission. (2°) At the hour of death. (3°) At the close of an annual retreat. (4°) On the first Sunday of every month. (5°) On the Saturdays of Lent. (6°) On Passion Sunday, and the Friday of Passion Week. (7°) On the Wednesday, Thursday, and Friday of Holy Week. (8°) On the first and last days of the Novena before Christmas day.

(9°) On the Feasts of Christmas day, Easter Sunday, Ascension day, Whit Sunday, and Trinity Sunday. (10°) On the Feasts of the Immaculate Conception, the Nativity, the Annunciation, the Purification, the Assumption, and the Feast of our Lady of the Angels (August 2nd). (11°) On the Feasts of St. Joseph (March 19th), the Finding of the Cross (May 3rd), St. John Baptist (June 24th), SS. Peter and Paul (June 29th), St. Augustine (Aug. 28th), St. Michael (Sep. 29th), the Angel Guardians (Oct. 2nd), St. Teresa (Oct. 15th), All Saints (Nov. 1st). (12°) On the Feast of St. Cajetan (Aug. 7th), and on the Feasts of the other Saints belonging to the Order of Theatines (March 24th, April 12th, June 17th, November 10th, December 13th). (13°) During the 40 hours' adoration, once a year. (14°) On one day each year, left to the choice of each member.

Further, twice each month, the members may, by praying in the church of the Theatines, or, in places where they have no Church, in any other which may have an Altar dedicated to our Lady, gain the Indulgences attached to the Holy Sepulchre, or to the other holy places in Palestine.

Further, as often as the members say six Paters, Aves, and Glorias, in any place whatever, or at any time whatever, in honour of the most Holy Trinity, and of the Blessed Virgin conceived without sin, to obtain the triumph of the Church, the extirpation of heresy, and peace between Christian Princes, they may gain all the Indulgences of the seven Churches in Rome, of the Portiuncula, of Jerusalem, and of St. James of Compostella.

*These latter Indulgences are very great. Confession and Communion are not prescribed to gain them.*

ALL these Indulgences are applicable to the Souls in Purgatory. Further, the Altar at which Mass is offered up for the repose of a person invested with a Scapular of the Immaculate Conception is privileged, that is to say, the Mass offered has a Plenary Indulgence attached to it for the benefit of the dead person.

The Sovereign Pontiffs have granted many other Indulgences to the Blue Scapular. The list is too long for insertion: they may be gained by offering up to God, in the morning, an intention to gain them all. A.

The members of the Apostleship of Prayer will gladly wear these several Scapulars, as powerful weapons, to secure the triumph of the noble cause in which they are engaged. Confident in the intercession of Mary, trusting to the promises attached to the definition of the Immaculate Conception, strong in the infinite merits of the sacred blood of their Redeemer, assisted by the prayers of those blessed Souls in Purgatory, to whom the Gates of Heaven were opened by the numerous Indulgences granted to these Scapulars, they will pray with redoubled hope, and redoubled power, for the conversion of sinners and for the triumph of the Church.

## The Agnus Dei.

### OF THE CEREMONIES USED BY THE ROMAN PONTIFFS IN THE BLESSING AND CONSECRATING THE MOULDS OF WAX, CALLED "AGNUS DEI."

THE ceremonial of the Roman Church, with which the Sovereign Pontiff is wont to bless and consecrate the impressions in wax, commonly called "Agnus Dei," is very ancient.

The "Agnus Dei" are made of pure white virgin wax, by which is signified Christ's human nature assumed by divine power, in the spotless womb of the Virgin Mary, without admixture or stain of sin. The image of a lamb is impressed upon them, as a token of that Immaculate Lamb who was slain for the redemption of man upon the altar of the cross. Blessed water is made use of, for this is the element by which many great mysteries and miracles have been worked by God both in the Old and the New Testament. Balm is mingled with the water, by which is signified the good odour of Christ, redolent in the actions and conversation of the faithful. Holy chrism is added, by which everything specially dedicated to divine worship, as churches, altars, and priests, are prepared and consecrated, and by which also is signified charity, the first of all the virtues.

In this water, previously blessed, and then mingled with balm and chrism, the "Agnus Dei" are immersed; and both before and after the immersion, the Sovereign Pontiff prays earnestly to God with solemn prayers, that he may be pleased to bless, sanctify, and consecrate these moulds in wax, and impart to them such power, that whosoever with true faith and sincere piety shall make use of them, may obtain many spiritual and temporal benefits.

And that benefits and gifts of graces are granted and bestowed by God the giver of all good to the faithful, in virtue of the blessing communicated to these forms of wax, and by the prayers, especially which the Vicar of Christ, the Roman Pontiff, in the name of the whole Church, says over them in their consecration, is a thing firmly and entirely to be believed, and has been very often confirmed by many and striking miracles. And if the desired effect be not always obtained, it is to be attributed either to the weak or little faith or devotion of those who were then, or to some other secret cause known to God and allowed of by him.

(Rome, from the Printing Office of the Rev. Apostolical Consistory, 1828.)

*A Prayer that may be said by those who carry about them an "Agnus Dei."*

O MY Lord Jesus Christ, the true Lamb, who takest away the sins of the world, by thy mercy, which is infinite, pardon my iniquities, and by thy sacred Passion preserve me this day from all sin and evil. I carry about me this holy Agnus in thy honour, as a preservative against mine own weakness, and as an incentive to the practice of that meekness, humility, and innocence which thou hast taught us. I offer myself up to thee as an entire oblation, in memory of that sacrifice of love which thou didst offer for me on the cross, and in satisfaction for my sins. Accept this oblation, I beseech thee, O my God, and may it be acceptable to thee, in the odour of sweetness. Amen.

## Devotion of the Bona Mors;

OR PRAYERS FOR OBTAINING A HAPPY DEATH, THROUGH THE PASSION OF JESUS CHRIST.

IN the name of the Father, and of the Son, and of the Holy Ghost. Amen.

Open thou our mouths, O Lord, to bless thy holy name; cleanse our hearts from all vain, evil, and distracting thoughts; enlighten our understandings and inflame our wills, that we may worthily perform this holy exercise with attention and devotion, and may deserve to be heard in the presence of thy divine Majesty. Who with God the Father, in the unity of the Holy Ghost, liveth and reigneth God, world without end. Amen.

Lord have mercy on us.
*Christ have mercy on us.*
Lord have mercy on us.

Holy Mary,
All ye holy Angels and Archangels,
St. Abel,
All ye Choirs of the Just,
St. Abraham,
St. John the Baptist,
St. Joseph,
All ye holy Patriarchs and Prophets,
St. Peter,
St. Paul,
St. Andrew,
St. John,
All ye holy Apostles and Evangelists,
All ye holy Disciples of our Lord,
All ye holy Innocents,
St. Stephen,
St. Lawrence,
All ye holy Martyrs,
St. Sylvester,
St. Gregory,
St. Austin,
All ye holy Bishops and Confessors,
St. Benedict,
St. Francis,
All ye holy Monks and Hermits,
St. Mary Magdalen,
St. Lucy,
All ye holy Virgins and Widows,

} *Pray for us.*

All ye Saints of God,
*Intercede for us.*

Be merciful unto us,
*Spare us, O Lord.*
Be merciful unto us,
*Hear us, O Lord.*
From thy anger,
From the peril of death,
From an evil death,
From the pains of hell,
From all evil,
From the power of the devil,
By thy Nativity,
By thy Cross and Passion,
By thy Death and Burial,
By thy glorious Resurrection,
By thy admirable Ascension,
By the grace of the Holy Ghost the Paraclete,
In the day of judgment,
} *O Lord deliver us.*

We sinners,
*Beseech thee to hear us.*
That thou wouldst spare us,
That thou wouldst vouchsafe to bring us unto true penance,
That thou wouldst vouchsafe to grant eternal rest to all the faithful departed,
} *We beseech thee, hear us.*

Lord have mercy on us.
Christ have mercy on us.
Lord have mercy on us.

## LET US PRAY.

WE beseech thy clemency, O Lord, that thou wouldst vouchsafe so to strengthen thy servants in thy grace, that at the hour of death the enemy may not prevail over them, but that they may deserve to pass with thy Angels into everlasting life. Through our Lord Jesus Christ thy Son, who with thee liveth and reigneth in the unity of the Holy Ghost, God, world without end. Amen.

Almighty and most gracious God, who for thy thirsting people didst bring forth from the rock a stream of living water, draw forth from the hardness of our hearts tears of compunction, that we may bewail our sins, and receive remission of them from thy mercy. Through Christ our Lord. Amen.

O Lord Jesus Christ, Redeemer of the world, behold, prostrate at thy feet, an ungrateful and perfidious creature. O my God, I have offended thee exceedingly in thought, in word, and in deed. My heinous crimes fixed thee to the bloody cross. To rescue me from eternal damnation, thou didst endure an agony of three hours on Mount Calvary. How much I am displeased with myself, how grieved at having offended thee, a God of infinite goodness, of infinite charity! I am astonished at thy unwearied patience in supporting a provoking sinner. With my whole heart I detest my sins; and because I love thee, and will love thee above all created things, I steadfastly purpose, by the help of thy grace, never more to offend thee, and rather to die than to commit one mortal sin. Amen.

O Jesus, who during thy prayer to the Father in the garden, wast so filled with sorrow and anguish that there came forth from thee a bloody sweat: have mercy on us.

℟. Have mercy on us, O Lord; have mercy on us.

O Jesus, who wast betrayed by the kiss of a traitor into the hands of the wicked, seized and bound like a thief, and abandoned by thy disciples: have mercy on us.

℟. Have mercy on us, O Lord; have mercy on us.

O Jesus, who by the unjust council of the Jews wast sentenced to death, led like a malefactor before Pilate, scorned and derided by the impious Herod: have mercy on us.

℟. Have mercy on us, O Lord; have mercy on us.

O Jesus, who wast stripped of thy garments, and most cruelly scourged at the pillar: have mercy on us.

℟. Have mercy on us, O Lord; have mercy on us.

O Jesus, who wast crowned with thorns, buffeted, struck with a reed, blindfolded, clothed with a purple garment, in many ways derided, and overwhelmed with reproaches: have mercy on us.

℟. Have mercy on us, O Lord; have mercy on us.

O Jesus, who wast less esteemed than the murderer Barabbas, rejected by the Jews, and unjustly condemned to the death of the cross: have mercy on us.

℟. Have mercy on us, O Lord; have mercy on us.

O Jesus, who wast loaded with a cross, and led to the place of execution as a lamb to the slaughter: have mercy on us.

℟. Have mercy on us, O Lord; have mercy on us.

O Jesus, who wast numbered among thieves, blasphemed and derided, made to drink of gall and vinegar, and crucified

deplore beyond all imaginable evils, because they offend thee, O infinite Goodness: and I resolve never more to sin. Vouchsafe to convert all sinners, and to make them understand the heinousness and the enormity of mortal sin.

Our Father, &c. Hail Mary, &c. Glory be to the Father, &c.

O Lord Jesus Christ, I adore the sacred wound of thy right foot. I thank thee for the pain which thou didst endure with so much love and charity. I condole with thee in thy sufferings, and with thy afflicted Mother. Grant me strength against all temptations, and prompt obedience in the execution of thy holy will. Comfort, O Jesus, the poor, the miserable, the afflicted, and all who are tempted or persecuted. Most just Judge, govern those who administer justice, and assist all those who labour in the care of souls.

Our Father, &c. Hail Mary, &c. Glory be to the Father, &c.

O Lord Jesus Christ, I adore the sacred wound of thy left hand. I thank thee for the pain which thou didst endure with so much love and charity. I condole with thee in thy sufferings, and with thy afflicted Mother. Preserve me from the pains of hell; grant me patience in the adversities of this life, and conformity in all things to thy blessed will. I offer unto thee all my sufferings both of mind and body, in satisfaction for my sins, which have so often deserved eternal torments. Pardon all my enemies, and all those who bear ill will against me. Grant patience to the sick, and restore them to health : support with thy assisting grace all who are in their agony, that they may not perish.

Our Father, &c. Hail Mary, &c. Glory be to the Father, &c.

O Lord Jesus Christ, I adore the sacred wound of thy right hand. I thank thee for the pain which thou didst endure with so much love and charity. I condole with thee in thy sufferings, and with thy afflicted Mother. Grant me a resolute will to seek those things which concern my salvation, as also the grace of final perseverance, that I may secure the enjoyment of that glory which was purchased at the price of thy most precious blood. Grant likewise, O Jesus, peace and relief to the souls in purgatory, and daily advance towards perfection thy holy servants in this world, more especially those who are of this confraternity.

Our Father, &c. Hail Mary, &c. Glory be to the Father, &c.

O Lord Jesus Christ, I adore the sacred wound in thy blessed side. I thank thee for the infinite love manifested towards us at the opening of thy sacred heart. Grant me a pure and perfect charity, that loving all things for thy sake, and thee above all things, I may breathe my last in the purest sentiments of divine love. Protect thy holy Catholic Church, direct thy governing Vicar upon earth, all ecclesiastical orders, and all pious persons who are instrumental in the conversion of souls. Preserve in thy holy service all Christian kings and princes. Bring back into the way of salvation all those who have gone astray, whether through malice or ignorance; and subject unto thy sacred yoke all infidels, heretics, and enemies of thy holy name.

Our Father, &c. Hail Mary, &c. Glory be to the Father, &c.

LET US PRAY.

O LORD Jesus Christ, God of my heart; by those five wounds which thy love for us inflicted on thee, succour thy servants whom thou hast redeemed with thy precious blood. Amen.

Most merciful Redeemer ; by thy unspeakable torments, and by the grief which thou wast pleased to suffer for me, especially when thy soul was separated from thy body, I humbly beseech thee to secure my soul at the hour of its departure, and to comfort me then, as thou didst comfort the penitent thief, with the blessed assurance that I shall be with thee in Paradise. Amen.

Let us say thrice the Our Father and thrice the Hail Mary, in memory of the three hours our Redeemer hung upon the cross, for the souls of the faithful departed of this Congregation.

Let us say once the Our Father and the Hail Mary, for those who are in the deplorable state of mortal sin.

Let us likewise say once the Our Father and the Hail Mary, that the person of this Congregation who is to die next may depart happily, strengthened with the holy Sacraments of the Church.

Let us dispose ourselves, by acts of perfect contrition and of pure love of God, to receive profitably the Benediction of our Lord and Saviour in the adorable Sacrament of the Altar.

O MERCIFUL Redeemer, and God of infinite patience! great is my confusion when I appear in thy divine presence, because I have so frequently preferred contemptible creatures to thee, the Almighty Creator of the universe. I utterly detest my presumption in sinning in thy most pure sight. I acknowledge that I am a criminal, and I plead guilty at the bar of thy dread tribunal. Thou mightest have been glorified in thy justice, by striking me suddenly dead, and by condemning me to eternal flames for the base indignities I have offered thee; but thou wast pleased to be glorified in the high prerogative of thy mercy, by inviting me to repentance. I abhor all my crimes of thought, word, and deed, not merely for the fear of punishment, and for the hope of reward, but chiefly for thy sake, and because thou dost infinitely detest them. O God of majesty and mercy, look upon the sacred marks in thy hands, feet, and side, which thou dost still retain in thy glorified body, that they may plead in my behalf. By that tender love which induced thee to create, to redeem, and to sanctify me, unite thy infinite merits to my profound misery. Strengthen my weakness, confirm this my resolution of never more offending thee; rather let me lose everything, even life itself, than lose thy favour by mortal sin. My heart was created for thee, and I love thee better than myself. Every day of my life, and especially that on which I shall expire, I will strive to love and to serve thee for thy own sake, my God and my Creator. O Saviour of perishing mankind, who openest thy hand, and fillest every creature with benediction, give me now such a blessing as thou didst bestow on thy beloved Disciples, when ascending in triumph from the mountain of Olives; that I may live and die in these happy dispositions. Amen.

## Confraternity of the Bona Mors.

THE Arch-Confraternity was founded at Rome, in the Church of the Gesu, and approved of by Pope Benedict XII., on the 22nd September, 1729.

The great end of the Confraternity is devotion to the Passion of our Lord Jesus Christ, and to the Dolours of the Blessed Virgin Mary, in order to obtain the grace of a happy death.

### PRAYERS

*To be recited daily by the Associates for the intentions of the Confraternity.*

THRICE the Our Father, and the Hail Mary, in memory of the three hours our dear Redeemer hung upon the cross, with the following aspirations:

Lord, into thy hands I commend my soul, and the souls of all who are now, or may hereafter be in their agony.

Mary, Mother of Grace, Mother of Mercy, protect us against our enemy, and receive our souls at the hour of death.

The Associates are recommended: (1°) To communicate once a month, praying for a happy death for all the Members. (2°) To attend the prayers for a happy death, which are publicly recited in many churches and chapels once a month. (3°) To have a crucifix, and a picture of the Blessed Virgin Mary.

PLENARY INDULGENCES

*Granted to the Associates on the usual conditions of Confession, Communion, and Prayers for the Pope's Intentions.*

(1°) On the day of admission. (2°) At the hour of death. (3°) Once a month, on any Friday or Sunday in each month, if, having confessed and communicated, the Members shall assist at the Benediction of the Blessed Sacrament. (4°) On the Feasts of our Lord's Nativity, Epiphany, Resurrection, and Ascension; on Whit-Sunday, Trinity Sunday, and Corpus Christi. (5°) On the Feast of our Lady's Immaculate Conception, Nativity, Annunciation, Purification, and Assumption. (6°) On the Feasts of the Nativity of St. John the Baptist, of St. Joseph, of All Saints, and of each of the Twelve Apostles. A.

## PARTIAL INDULGENCES.

(1°) Of seven years and seven forty days for assisting at the Benediction of the Most Holy Sacrament, on the evenings of the Fridays or Sundays above mentioned. (2°) Of one year; 1. For visiting the sick; 2. For visiting those in prison; 3. For hearing Mass on week days; 4. For evening examination of conscience; 5. For attending a funeral.

# Occasional Prayers.

### FOR THE HOLY CATHOLIC CHURCH.

DEFEND, O Lord, thy servants, we beseech thee, from all dangers both of body and soul; and, by the intercession of the blessed and glorious Virgin Mary, Mother of God, of the blessed Apostles Peter and Paul, of blessed *N.*, and of all thy Saints, mercifully grant us the blessings of peace and safety; that all adversities and errors being removed, thy Church may freely and securely serve thee: Through our Lord Jesus Christ. Amen.

### FOR THE POPE.

O GOD, the Pastor and Ruler of all the faithful, mercifully look upon thy servant *N.*, whom thou hast been pleased to appoint the pastor of thy Church; grant, we beseech thee, that both by word and example he may edify those over whom he is placed; and, together with the flock committed to his care, may obtain everlasting life: Through, &c.

### FOR BISHOPS, AND THE PEOPLE COMMITTED TO THEM.

ALMIGHTY and everlasting God, who alone dost great marvels, send down upon thy servants, the Bishops of thy Church [*especially N. our Bishop*], and all congregations committed unto them, the spirit of thy saving grace; and that they may truly please thee, pour upon them the continual dew of thy blessing: Through, &c.

FOR A CONGREGATION OR FAMILY.

DEFEND, we beseech thee, O Lord, by the intercession of the Blessed Mary, ever Virgin, this thy family from all adversity; and mercifully protect us, now prostrate before thee with our whole hearts, from all the snares of our enemies: Through, &c.

PRAYER FOR PEACE.

(100 days Indulgence for each devout recital. Plenary Indulgence once a month on usual conditions. A.)

*Ant.* Give peace, O Lord, in our days for there is none other that fighteth for us, but only thou, our God.

℣. Peace be in thy strength, O Lord.

℟. And plenty in thy strong places.

LET US PRAY.

O GOD, from whom come all holy desires, all right counsels and just works, grant unto us, thy servants, that peace

u 5

which the world cannot give, that our hearts may be devoted to thy service, and delivered from the terror of our enemies, we may pass our time in peace beneath thy protection: Through Christ our Lord. Amen.

### IN ANY TRIBULATION.

O ALMIGHTY God, despise not thy people who cry unto thee in their affliction, but for the glory of thy name, turn away thine anger, and help us in our tribulations: Through, &c.

### PRAYER OF CHILDREN FOR THEIR PARENTS.

O MERCIFUL God, who visitest the iniquities of parents on their children to the third and fourth generation, and showest mercy unto thousands of those who love thee and keep thy commandments, pour down thy blessings on my father and my mother; reward, I beseech thee, O Lord, all their labours and tender solicitude for my welfare, by the remission of their sins, and deliver them from the punishments which remain due to them. Endue them with such fortitude and resignation to thy divine will, as may enable them to bear patiently all the trials of this life; may thy heavenly grace make them fruitful in good works, and may they, like the holy Patriarchs, enjoy the blessings of a long, happy, and peaceable life, and find in their children the consolation and support of their old age. May the precious inheritance of their virtues descend to their children, that thus both may be inseparably united in the enjoyment of eternal life. Amen.

**PRAYER FOR A FRIEND.**

O GOD, who, by the grace of the Holy Spirit, has poured into the hearts of thy faithful the gifts of charity; grant to thy servant, for whom we implore thy mercy, health of both body and soul; that he may love thee with all his strength, and cheerfully perform those things which are pleasing unto thee: Through, &c.

**FOR A DECEASED FRIEND.**

O GOD, the Creator and Redeemer of all the faithful, grant to the soul of thy servant departed the remission of all his sins, that through pious supplications he may obtain that pardon which he has always desired; who livest and reignest with God the Father, in the unity of the Holy Ghost, God, world without end. Amen.

## Prayers to the S. John Berchmans,

*In memory of the five years that he lived in Religion, and which may serve for a Novena or other devotion in his honour.*

O GLORIOUS patron, blessed John Berchmans, I implore of thee, by thy angelic modesty and composure, to obtain for me the grace to put a rein on the freedom of my senses, that being kept duly under control, they may not wander on dangerous objects to the injury of my soul.

Our Father. Hail Mary. Glory, &c.

O MOST pure saint, I beg of thee, by thy admirable innocence and purity of life, to obtain for me the grace to mortify my inordinate passions, that having conquered and subdued them, I may enjoy true peace and purity of heart.

Our Father. Hail Mary. Glory, &c.

O GREAT Saint, model of obedience, I beg of thee, by thy most exact obedience to all the rules of thy Institute, to obtain for me the grace to observe the holy laws of God, and the duties of my state, that thus I may attain perfection and my eternal salvation.

Our Father. Hail Mary. Glory, &c.

O MOST amiable Saint, model of charity, I beg of thee by thy burning love for God, to obtain for me the grace to detach my heart from every undue affection to the fleeting things of this life, that, cleansed and purified, it may seek solely its Lord and its God.

Our Father. Hail Mary. Glory, &c.

O MOST devout Saint, model of fervent prayer, I beg of thee by thy tender devotion to the holy Mother of God, and to the angelic Saint Aloysius, to obtain for me the grace to foster and to increase within myself a similar devotion, that, honouring Mary and Aloysius here on earth, I may merit hereafter, to praise and thank them for ever with thee in heaven. I also earnestly beg of thee to obtain for me the special grace that I ask in this Novena, if it be for the glory of God and the good of my soul.

Our Father. Hail Mary. Glory, &c.

PRAYER.

O ADMIRABLE Saint, mirror of modesty, of purity, of regularity, of charity and devotion, I choose thee, this day, as my special advocate and protector with God: and placing my confidence in thee, I beg of thee to obtain for me strength and courage, to copy in my own life the example of thy virtues.

Intercede earnestly for youth, and shielding them from the many dangers they have to encounter in these unhappy times, lead them, after thy example, to grow up modest in deportment, pure in morals, obedient to the divine law, fervent in piety, and devoted to religion.

In fine, enkindle in the minds of all those who invoke thy intercession, a lively desire for their eternal salvation, that, having faithfully combated here on earth, they may come to triumph with thee in heaven, for all eternity. Amen.

℣. Pray for us, O blessed John.

℟. That we may be made worthy of the promises of Christ.

LET US PRAY.

O GOD, who didst place the wonderful sanctity of the Blessed John, thy Confessor, in the perfect observance of religious discipline, and in innocence of life, grant through his merits and prayers, that faithfully fulfilling the commandments of thy law, we may attain purity of mind and body. Through Jesus Christ, our Lord. Amen.

## PRAYER OF B. JOHN BERCHMANS TO HIS GUARDIAN ANGEL.

O HOLY Angel, dear to God, who through the divine disposition didst take me under thy holy guardianship from the very first moment of my existence, and who never ceasest to enlighten, to defend, and to guide me, I venerate thee as my patron, I love thee as my guardian, I submit myself entirely to thy direction, and I give myself entirely to thee to be governed by thee. I beg and implore of thee by the love of Jesus Christ, that, however ungrateful I may be to thee, and stubborn to thy admonitions, thou wilt yet not abandon me, but wilt rather kindly lead me back when straying from the right path, wilt instruct me in my ignorance, raise me in my falls, console me in my afflictions, and sustain me in my trials, until finally, thou shalt bring me to share in heaven thy eternal happiness. Amen.

## Vespers for Sundays and Festivals.

Pater noster, Ave Maria, *in secret.*

℣. Deus, in adjutorium meum intende.
℟. Domine, ad adjuvandum me festina.
℣. Gloria Patri, et Filio, et Spiritui Sancto.
℟. Sicut erat in principio, et nunc, et semper, et in sæcula sæculorum. Amen.
Alleluia.

*From Septuagesima to Palm Sunday, inclusively, is said:*

Laus tibi Domine, Rex æternæ gloriæ.

*Ant.* Dixit Dominus.

*In Paschal Time, the Psalms are all said under this one Antiphon:* Alleluia.

Psalm cix.

Dixit Dóminus, Dómino meo: * Sede a dextris meis:

Donec ponam inimícos tuos : * scabéllum pedum tuórum.

Virgam virtútis tuæ emíttet Dóminus ex Sion : * domináre in médio inimicórum tuórum.

Tecum princípium in die virtútis tuæ, in splendóribus Sanctórum : * ex útero ante lucíferum génui te.

Jurávit Dóminus, et non pœnitébit eum : * Tu es sacerdos in ætérnum, secúndum órdinem Melchisedech.

Dóminus a dextris tuis : * confrégit in die iræ suæ reges.

Judicábit in natiónibus, implébit ruínas: * conquassábit cápita in terra multórum.

De torrénte in via bibet : * proptérea exaltábit caput.

Gloria Patri, &c.

*Ant.* Dixit Dóminus Dómino meo : Sede a dextris meis.

*Ant.* Fidélia.

Psalm cx.

CONFITEBOR tibi, Dómine, in toto corde meo: * in consílio justórum, et congregatióne.

Magna ópera Dómini : * exquisíta in omnes voluntátes ejus.

Conféssio et magnificéntia opus ejus: * et justítia ejus manet in sæculum sæculi.

Memóriam fecit mirabílium suórum miséricors et miserátor Dóminus : * escam dedit timéntibus se.

Memor erit in sæculum testaménti sui : * virtútem óperum suórum annuntiábit pópulo suo:

Ut det illis hæreditátem géntium :* opera mánuum ejus, véritas et judícium.

Fidélia ómnia mandáta ejus : confirmáta in sæculum sæculi : *

facta in veritáte et æquitate.

Redemptiónem misit pópulo suo : * mandávit in ætérnum testaméntum suum.

Sanctum et terríbile nomen ejus : * inítium sapiéntiæ timor Dómini.

Intelléctus bonus ómnibus faciéntibus eum : * laudátio ejus manet in sæculum sæculi.

Gloria Patri, &c.

*Ant.* Fidélia ómnia mandáta ejus, confirmáta in sæculum sæculi.

*Ant.* In mandátis.

Psalm cxi.

BEATUS vir qui timet Dóminum : * in mandátis ejus volet nimis.

Pótens in terra erit semen ejus :* generátio rectorum benedicétur.

Glória et divítiæ in domo ejus: * et justítia ejus manet in sæculum sæculi.

Exórtum est in ténebris lumen rectis : * misericors, et miserátor, et justus.

Jucúndus homo qui miserétur et cómmodat, dispónet sermónes suos in judicio : * quia in ætérnum non commovébitur.

In memória ætérna erit justus : * ab auditióne mala non timébit.

Parátum cor ejus speráre in Dómino, confirmátum est cor ejus : * non commovébitur donec despíciat inimícos suos.

Dispérsit, dedit paupéribus ; justítia ejus manet in sæculum sæculi : * cornu ejus exaltábitur in glória.

Peccátor vidébit et irascétur; déntibus suis fremet et tabéscet : * desidérium peccatórum períbit.

Gloria Patri, &c.

*Ant.* In mandátis ejus cupit nimis.

*Ant.* Sit nomen Dómini.

Psalm cxii.

LAUDATE, púeri, Dóminum : * laudáte nomen Dómini.

Sit nomen Dómini benedíctum : * ex hoc nunc et usque in sæculum.

A solis ortu usque ad occásum : * laudábile nomen Dómini.

Excélsus super omnes gentes Dóminus : * et super cœlos glória ejus :

Quis sicut Dóminus Deus noster, qui in altis hábitat : * et humília réspicit in cœlo et in terra ?

Súscitans a terra ínopem : * et de stércore érigens páuperem :

Ut cóllocet eum cum princípibus : * cum princípibus pópuli sui.

Qui habitáre facit stérilem in domo : * matrem filiórum lætantem.

Gloria Patri, &c.

*Ant.* Sit nomen Dómini benedíctum in sæcula.

*Ant.* Nos qui vívimus.

Psalm cxiii.

IN éxitu Israel de Ægypto: * domus Jacob de pópulo bárbaro.

Facta est Judæa sanctificátio ejus: * Israel potéstas ejus.

Mare vidit et fugit: Jordánis convérsus est retrórsum.

Montes exultavérunt ut aríetes: * et colles sicut agni óvium.

Quid est tibi, mare, quod fugísti: * et tu, Jordánis quia convérsus es retrórsum?

Montes exultástis sicut aríetes: * et colles, sicut agni óvium?

A fácie Dómini mota est terra: * a fácie Dei Jacob.

Qui convértit petram in stagna aquárum: * et rupem in fontes aquárum.

Non nobis, Dómine, non nobis: * sed nómini tuo da glóriam.

Super misericórdia tua, et veritáte tua: * nequándo dicant gentes, Ubi est Deus eórum?

Deus autem noster in cœlo: * ómnia quæcúmque vóluit fecit.

Simulácra géntium argéntum et aurum: * ópera mánuum hóminum.

Os habent, et non loquéntur: * óculos habent, et non vidébunt.

Aures habent, et non aúdient: * nares habent, et non odorábunt.

Manus habent, et non palpábunt: pedes habent, et non ambulábunt: * non clamábunt in gútture suo.

Símiles illis fiant qui fáciunt ea: * et omnes qui confídunt in eis.

Domus Israel sperávit in Dómino: * adjútor eórum et protéctor eórum est.

Domus Aaron sperávit in Dómino: * adjútor eórum et protéctor eórum est.

Qui timent Dóminum speravérunt in Dómino: * adjútor eórum et protéctor eórum est.

Dóminus memor fuit

nostri : * et benedíxit nobis.

Benedíxit dómui Israel : * benedíxit dómui Aaron.

Benedíxit ómnibus qui timent Dóminum :* pusíllis cum majóribus.

Adjíciat Dóminus super vos : * super vos, et super fílios vestros.

Benedícti vos a Dómino : * qui fecit cœlum et terram.

Cœlum cœli Dómino: * terram autem dedit fíliis hóminum.

Non mórtui laudábunt te, Dómine : * neque omnes qui descéndunt in inférnum.

Sed nos qui vívimus, benedícimus Dómino : * ex hoc nunc et usque in sæculum.

Gloria Patri, &c.

*Ant.* Nos qui vívimus, benedícimus Dómino.

*In Paschal time :—*
*Ant.* Alleluia, alleluia, alleluia.

*Then follow the* Little Chapter *and the* Hymn ; *after which is said, with its proper Antiphon :—*

*The* Magnificat.

MAGNIFICAT :*ánima mea Dóminum.

Et exultávit spíritus meus :* in Deo salutári meo.

Quia respéxit humilitátem ancíllæ suæ : * ecce enim ex hoc beátam me dicent omnes generatiónes.

Quia fecit mihi magna qui potens est : * et sanctum nomen ejus.

Et misericórdia ejus a progénie in progénies :* timéntibus eum.

Fecit poténtiam in bráchio suo ;* dispérsit supérbos mente cordis sui.

Depósuit poténtes de sede :* et exaltávit húmiles.

Esuriéntes implévit bonis : * et dívites dimísit inánes.

Suscépit Israel púerum suum :* recordátus misericórdiæ suæ.

Sicut locútus est ad patres nostros :* Abraham, et sémini ejus in sæcula.

Gloria Patri, &c.

*Here follow the proper Collect, and the Commemorations, if any.*

℣. Benedicámus Dómino.

℟. Deo grátias.

℣. Fidélium ánimæ per misericórdiam Dei requiéscant in pace.

℟. Amen.

*If Compline does not follow: after the Pater Noster, which is said secretly, the following ℣. is sung.*

℣. Dóminus det nobis suam pacem.

℟. Et vitam ætérnam. Amen.

*Here follows the Antiphon of the Blessed Virgin proper for the season, if it is to be sung. See p. 468 to 470.*

---

COMMON OF APOSTLES AND EVANGELISTS.

FIRST VESPERS.—*Psalms on Sundays, except the last, which is Psalm* cxvi., Laudate Dominum, *page* 459.

SECOND VESPERS.—1. *Psalm* cix., Dixit Dominus, *page* 448; 2. *Psalm* cxii, Laudate, pueri, *page* 450; *and then the three following:*

Psalm cxv.

CREDIDI, propter quod locútus sum:* ego autem humiliátus sum nimis.

Ego dixi in excessu meo:* Omnis homo mendax.

Quid retríbuam Dómino:* pro omnibus quæ retríbuit mihi?

Cálicem salutaris accípiam:* et nomen Domini invocabo.

Vota mea Domino reddam coram omni populo ejus:* pretiosa in conspectu Domini mors sanctorum ejus.

O Domine, quia ego servus tuus:* ego servus tuus, et fílius ancíllæ tuæ.

Dirupísti víncula mea:* tibi sacrificábo hostiam laudis, et nomen Domini invocábo.

Vota mea Domino reddam in conspéctu omnis populi ejus:* in átriis domus Domini, in médio tui, Jerúsalem.

Gloria Patri, &c.

## Psalm cxxv.

In converténdo Dominus captivitátem Sion:* facti sumus sicut consoláti.

Tunc replétum est gaúdio os nostrum:* et lingua nostra exultatione.

Tunc dicent inter gentes:* Magnificávit Dominus fácere cum eis.

Magnificávit Dominus fácere nobíscum:* facti sumus lætántes.

Convérte, Domine, captivitátem nostram;* sicut torrens in austro.

Qui séminant in lácrymis:* in exultatióne metent.

Eúntes ibant et flebant:* mitténtes sémina sua.

Veniéntes autem vénient cum exultatióne: portántes manípulos suos.

Gloria Patri, &c.

## Psalm cxxxviii.

Domine, probásti me, et cognovísti me : * tu cognovísti sessiónem meam, et resurrectiónem meam.

Intellexísti cogitatiónes meas de longe :* sémitam meam et funículum meum investigásti.

Et omnes vias meas prævidísti :* quia non est sermo in lingua mea.

Ecce Dómine, tu cognovísti omnia, novíssima et antíqua :* tu formásti me, et posuísti super me manum tuam.

Mirábilis facta est sciéntia tua ex me :* confortáta est, et non pótero ad eam.

Quo ibo a spíritu tuo ? * et quo a fácie tua fúgiam ?

Si ascéndero in cœlum, tu illic es :* si descéndero in inférnum, ades.

Si súmpsero pennas meas dilúculo :* et habitávero in extrémis maris :

Etenim illuc manus tua dedúcet me :* et tenébit me déxtera tua.

Et dixi, Fórsitan ténebræ conculcábunt me :* et nox illuminátio mea in delíciis meis.

Quia ténebræ non obscurabúntur a te, et nox sicut dies illuminábitur : * sicut ténebræ ejus, ita et lumen ejus.

Quia tu possedísti renes meos : * suscepísti me de útero matris meæ.

Confitébor tibi, quia terribíliter magnificátus es : * mirabília ópera tua, et ánima mea cognóscit nimis.

Non est occultátum os meum a te, quod fecísti in occúlto : * et substantia mea in inferióribus terræ.

Imperféctum meum vidérunt óculi tui, et in libro tuo omnes scribéntur : * dies formabúntur, et nemo in eis.

Mihi autem nimis honorificáti sunt, amíci tui, Deus :* nimis confortátus est principátus eórum.

Dinumerábo eos, et super arénam multiplicabúntur : * exurréxi et adhuc sum tecum.

Si occíderis, Deus, peccatóres : * viri sánguinum declináte a me:

Quia dícitis in cogitatióne : * Accípient in vanitáte civitátes tuas.

Nonne qui odérunt te, Dómine, óderam : * et super inimícos tuos tabescébam ?

Perfecto ódio óderam illos : * et inimíci facti sunt mihi.

Proba me, Deus, et

scito cor meum :* intér-
roga me, et cognósce
sémitas meas.
Et vide si via iniqui-

tátis in me est :* et de-
duc me in via ætérna.
Gloria Patri, &c.

---

## COMMON OF MARTYRS.

FIRST VESPERS.—*Last Psalm*, Laudate Dominum, *page* 459.

SECOND VESPERS.—*Last Psalm*, Credidi, *page* 453.

---

## COMMON OF A CONFESSOR AND BISHOP.

FIRST VESPERS.—*Last Psalm*, Laudate Dominum, *page* 459.

SECOND VESPERS.—*Last Psalm*, Memento, Domine, *as follows :—*

Psalm cxxxi.

MEMENTO, Dómine, David :* et omnis mansuetúdinis ejus.

Sicut jurávit Dómino : * votum vovit Deo Jacob :

Si introíero in tabernáculum domus meæ :* si ascéndero in lectum strati mei :

Si dédero somnum óculis meis : * et pálpebris meis dormitatiónem,

Et requiem tempóribus meis : donec invéniam locum Dómino : * tabernáculum Deo Jacob.

Ecce audívimus eam in Ephrata : * invénimus eam in campis silvæ.

Introíbimus in tabernáculum ejus :* adorábimus in loco, ubi stetérunt pedes ejus.

Surge, Dómine, in réquiem tuam : * tu

et arca sanctificatiónis tuæ.

Sacerdótes tui induántur justitiam : * et sancti tui exúltent.

Propter David servum tuum :* non avértas fáciem Christi tui.

Jurávit DóminusDavid veritátem, et non frustrábitur eam :* De fructu ventris tui ponam super sedem tuam.

Si custodíerint fílii tui testaméntum meum : * et testimónia mea hæc, quæ docébo eos :

Et fílii eórum usque in sæculum :* sedébunt super sedem tuam.

Quóniam elégit Dóminus Sion : * elégit eam in habitatiónem sibi.

Hæc réquies mea in sæculum sæculi : * hic habitábo, quóniam elégi eam.

Víduam ejus benedícens benedícam : * paúperes ejus saturábo pánibus.

Sacerdótes ejus índuam salutári : * et sancti ejus exultatióne exultábunt.

Illuc prodúcam cornu David : * parávi lucérnam Christo meo.

Inimícos ejus índuam confusióne :* super ipsum autem efflorébit sanctificátio mea.

Gloria Patri, &c.

---

COMMON OF THE BLESSED VIRGIN MARY.

*(The Common of Virgins and Holy Women, and the Vespers for New Year's Day, are the same.)*

First *Psalm*, Dixit Dominus, *page* 448.
Second *Psalm*, Laudate, pueri, *page* 450.

*Third Psalm.*

Psalm cxxi.

LÆTATUS sum in his quæ dicta sunt mihi :*

In domum Dómini íbimus.

Stantes erant pedes nostri :* in átriis tuis, Jerúsalem.

x

Jerúsalem, quæ ædificátur ut cívitas :* cujus participátio ejus in idípsum.
Illuc enim ascendérunt tribus, tribus Dómini : * testimónium Israel ad confiténdum nómini Dómini.
Quia illic sedérunt sedes in judício :* sedes super domum David.
Rogáte quæ ad pacem sunt Jerúsalem :* et abundántia diligéntibus te.
Fiat pax in virtúte tua :* et abundántia in túrribus tuis.
Propter fratres meos et próximos meos :* loquébar pacem de te.
Propter domum Dómini Dei nostri :* quæsívi bona tibi.
Gloria Patri, &c.

*Fourth Psalm.*

Psalm cxxvi.

NISI Dóminus ædificáverit domum : * in vanum laboravérunt qui ædíficant eam.
Nisi Dóminus custodíerit civitátem :* frustra vigilat qui custodit eam.
Vanum est vobis ante lucem súrgere :* súrgite postquam sedéritis, qui manducátis panem dolóris.
Cum déderit diléctis súis somnum : * ecce hæréditas Dómini fílii, merces, fructus ventris.
Sicut sagíttæ in manu poténtis :* ita fílii excussórum.
Beátus vir qui implévit desidérium suum ex ipsis :* non confundétur, cum loquétur inimícis suis in porta.
Gloria Patri, &c.

*Fifth Psalm.*

Psalm cxlvii.

LAUDA, Jerúsalem, Dóminum : * lauda Deum tuum, Sion.
Quóniam confortávit seras portárum tuárum : * benedíxit fíliis tuis in te.
Qui pósuit fines tuos pacem : * et ádipe fruménti sátiat te.
Qui emíttit elóquium suum terræ :* velóciter

currit sermo ejus.
Qui dat nivem sicut lanam :* nébulam sicut cínerem spargit.
Míttit crystállum suam sicut buccéllas : * ante fáciem frígoris ejus quis sustinébit ?
Emíttet verbum suum, et liquefáciet ea :* flabit spíritus ejus, et fluent aquæ.
Qui annúntiat verbum suum Jacob :* justítias et judícia sua Israel.
Non fecit táliter omni natióni :* et judícia sua non manifestávit eis.
Gloria Patri, &c.

*Psalm frequently said as the fifth.*

Psalm cxvi.

LAUDATE Dóminum, omnes gentes :* laudáte eum, omnes pópuli :
Quóniam confirmáta est super nos, misericórdia ejus :* et véritas Dómini manet in ætérnum.
Gloria Patri, &c.

THE CIRCUMCISION OF OUR LORD.

FIRST AND SECOND VESPERS.—*Psalms as in* Common of Virgins, *page* 457.

THE EPIPHANY.

FIRST AND SECOND VESPERS.—*First, Second, Third, and Fourth Psalm, as on* Sunday; *Fifth Psalm,* Laudate Dominum, *page* 459.

S.S. PETER AND PAUL.

FIRST VESPERS.—*First, Second, Third, and Fourth Psalm, as on* Sunday; *Fifth Psalm,* Laudate Dominum, *page* 459.

SECOND VESPERS—*As in* Common of Apostles, *page* 453.

ALL SAINTS.

FIRST VESPERS.—*Psalms as on* Sunday, *except Fifth Psalm,* Laudate Dominum, *page* 459.

SECOND VESPERS—*As on* Sunday, *except Fifth Psalm*, Credidi, *page* 453.

## ASCENSION DAY.

FIRST AND SECOND VESPERS.—*First four Psalms as on* Sunday; *the Fifth Psalm*, Laudate Dominum, *page* 459.

## CORPUS CHRISTI AND FEAST OF SACRED HEART.

SECOND VESPERS.—*First and Second Psalm as on* Sunday; *Third Psalm*, Credidi, *page* 453; *Fourth Psalm*, Beati omnes, *as below; Fifth Psalm*, Lauda Jerusalem, *page* 458.

Psalm cxxvii.

BEATI omnes, qui timent Dóminum,*qui ambulant in viis ejus.

Labóres manuum tuárum quia manducabis:*beátus es, et bene tibi erit.

Uxor tua sicut vitis abúndans,*in latéribus domus tuæ.

Fílii tui sicut novéllæ olivarum,*in circúitu mensæ tuæ.

Ecce sic benedicétur homo,*qui timet Dóminum.

Benedícat tibi Dóminus ex Sion:* et vídeas bona Jerúsalem ómnibus diébus vitæ tuæ.

Et vídeas filios filiórum tuorum,* pacem super Israel.

## CHRISTMAS DAY.

FIRST VESPERS.—*The first four Psalms as on* Sunday; *the Fifth Psalm*, Laudate Dominum, *page* 459.

SECOND VESPERS (and through the Octave).— *The three first Psalms as on* Sunday; *Fourth Psalm*, De Profundis, *page* 238; *Fifth Psalm*, Memento Domine, *page* 456.

# Compline.

*The Reader begins:*

℣. JUBE, domne, benedicere.

THE BLESSING.

Noctem quietam, et finem perfectum concedat nobis Dominus omnipotens.

℟. Amen.

SHORT LESSON.

FRATRES, sobrii estote, et vigilate : quia adversarius vester diabolus tamquam leo rugiens circuit, quærens quem devoret : cui resistite fortes in fide. Tu autem, Domine, miserere nobis.

℟. Deo gratias.

℣. Adjutorium nostrum in nomine Domini.

℟. Qui fecit cœlum et terram.

Pater noster. (*Said secretly.*)

*Then the Hebdomadarius makes the Confession:*

Confiteor Deo omnipotenti, beatæ Mariæ semper Virgini, beato Michaeli Archangelo, beato Joanni Baptistæ, sanctis Apostolis Petro et Paulo, omnibus Sanctis, et vobis, fratres : quia peccavi nimis cogitatione, verbo, et opere : mea culpa, mea culpa, mea maxima culpa. Ideo precor beatam Mariam semper Virginem, beatum Michaelem, Archangelum, beatum Joannem Baptistam, sanctos Apostolos Petrum et Paulum, omnes Sanctos, et vos, fratres, orare pro me ad Dominum Deum nostrum.

*The Choir answers:*

Misereatur tui omnipotens Deus, et dimissis peccatis tuis, perducat te ad vitam æternam.

℟. Amen.

*Then the Choir repeats the Confession:*

Confiteor Deo omnipotenti, beatæ Mariæ semper Virgini, beato Michaeli Archangelo, beato Joanni Baptistæ, sanctis Apostolis Petro et Paulo, omnibus Sanctis, et tibi, pater: quia peccavi nimis cogitatione, verbo, et opere; mea culpa, mea culpa, mea maxima culpa. Ideo precor beatam Mariam semper Virginem, beatum Michaelem Archangelum, beatum Joannem Baptistam, sanctos Apostolos Petrum et Paulum, omnes Sanctos, et te, pater, orare pro me ad Dominum Deum nostrum.

*The Hebdomadarius says:*

Misereatur vestri omnipotens Deus, et dimissis peccatis vestris, perducat vos ad vitam æternam.

℟. Amen.

Indulgentiam, absolutionem, et remissionem peccatorum nostrorum tribuat nobis omnipotens et misericors Dominus.

℟. Amen.

*Then is said:*

℣. Converte nos, Deus salutaris noster.

℟. Et averte iram tuam a nobis.

℣. Deus in adjutorium meum intende.

℟. Domine, ad adjuvandum me festina.

℣. Gloria Patri, et Filio, et Spiritui Sancto.

℟. Sicut erat in principio, et nunc, et semper, et in sæcula sæculorum. Amen.

Alleluia, *vel* Laus tibi, Domine, Rex æternæ gloriæ.

Ant. Miserere.

*In Paschal time:*

Ant. Alleluia.

### Psalm iv.

Cum invocárem, exaudívit me Deus justítiæ meæ: * in tribulatióne dilatásti mihi.

Miserére mei : * et exaúdi oratiónem meam.

Fílii hóminum úsquequo gravi corde: * ut quid dilígitis vanitátem, et quæritis mendácium ?

Et scitóte quóniam mirificávit Dóminus sanctum suum : * Dóminus exaúdiet me cum clamávero ad eum.

Irascímini, et nolíte peccáre : * quæ dícitis in córdibus vestris, in cubílibus vestris compungímini.

Sacrificáte sacrifícium justítiæ, et speráte in Dómino :* multi dicunt, Quis osténdit nobis bona ?

Signátum est super nos lumen vultus tui, Dómine : * dedísti lætítiam in corde meo.

A fructu fruménti, vini, et ólei sui :* multiplicáti sunt.

In pace in idípsum :* dórmiam et requiéscam.

Quoniam tu, Dómine, singuláriter in spe : * constituísti me.

Gloria Patri, &c.

### Psalm xxx.

In te, Dómine, sperávi, non confúndar in ætérnum : * in justítia tua líbera me.

Inclína ad me aurem tuam : * accélera, ut éruas me.

Esto mihi in Deum protectórem, et in domum refúgii : * ut salvum me fácias.

Quóniam fortitúdo mea, et refúgium meum es tu : * et propter nomen tuum dedúces me, et enútries me.

Edúces me de láqueo hoc, quem abscondérunt mihi : * quóniam tu es protéctor meus.

In manus tuas comméndo spîritum meum : * redemísti me, Dómine, Deus veritátis.

Gloria Patri, &c.

## Psalm xc.

Qui hábitat in adjutório Altíssimi : * in protectióne Dei cœli commorábitur.

Dicet Dómino, Suscéptor meus es tu, et refúgium meum :* Deus meus, sperábo in eum.

Quóniam ipse liberávit me de láqueo venántium : * et a verbo áspero.

Scápulis suis obumbrábit tibi : * et sub pennis ejus sperábis.

Scuto circúmdabit te véritas ejus : * non timébis a timóre noctúrno.

A sagítta volánte in die, a negótio perambulánte in ténebris : * ab incúrso et dæmónio meridiáno.

Cadent a látere tuo mille, et decem míllia a dextris tuis : * ad te autem non appropinquábit.

Verúmtamen óculis tuis considerábis : * et retributiónem peccatórum vidébis.

Quóniam tu es, Dómine, spes mea ;* altíssimum posuísti refúgium tuum.

Non accédet ad te malum : * et flagéllum non appropinquábit tabernáculo tuo.

Quóniam Angelis suis mandávit de te : * ut custódiant te in ómnibus viis tuis.

In mánibus portábunt te : * ne forte offéndas ad lápidem pedem tuum.

Super áspidem et basilíscum ambulábis :* et conculcábis leónem et dracónem.

Quóniam in me sperávit liberábo eum : * prótegam eum, quóniam cognóvit nomen meum.

Clamábit ad me, et ego exaúdiam eum :* cum ipso sum in tribulatióne ; erípiam eum, et glorificábo eum.

Longitúdine diérum replébo eum : * et osténdam illi salutáre meum.

Gloria Patri, &c.

## Psalm cxxxiii.

Ecce nunc, benedí-

## COMPLINE.

cite Dóminum:* omnes servi Dómini.

Qui statis in domo Dómini :* in átriis domus Dei nostri.

In nóctibus extóllite manus vestras in sancta :* et benedícite Dóminum.

Benedícat te Dóminus ex Sion :* qui fecit cœlum et terram.

Gloria Patri, &c.

*Ant.* Miserere mihi, Domine, et exaudi orationem meam.

### HYMN.

Te lucis ante terminum,
Rerum Creator, poscimus ;
Ut pro tua clementia,
Sis præsul et custodia.

Procul recedant somnia,
Et noctium phantasmata ;
Hostemque nostrum comprime,
Ne polluantur corpora.

Præsta, Pater piissime,
Patrique compar Unice,
Cum Spiritu Paraclito,
Regnans per omne sæculum. Amen.

### LITTLE CHAPTER.
#### Jerem. xiv.

Tu autem in nobis es, Domine, et nomen sanctum tuum invocatum est super nos, ne derelinquas nos, Domine Deus noster.

℞. Deo gratias.

*Short Responsory.*

In manus tuas, Domine, commendo spiritum meum.

*Choir.* In manus tuas, Domine, commendo spiritum meum.

℣. Redemisti nos, Domine, Deus veritatis.

*Choir.* Commendo spiritum meum.

℣. Gloria Patri, et Filio, et Spiritui Sancto.

*Choir.* In manus tuas, Domine, commendo spiritum meum.

℣. Custodi nos, Domine, ut pupillam oculi.

℞. Sub umbra alarum tuarum protege nos.

*In Paschal time, the above are said thus:*

In manus tuas, Domine, commendo spiritum meum. Alleluia, alleluia.

*Choir.* In manus tuas, Domine, commendo spiritum meum. Alleluia, alleluia.

℣. Redemisti nos, Domine, Deus veritatis.

*Choir.* Alleluia, alleluia.

℣. Gloria Patri, &c.

*Choir.* In manus tuas, Domine, commendo spiritum meum. Alleluia; alleluia.

℣. Custodi nos, Domine, ut pupillam oculi. Alleluia.

℞. Sub umbra alarum tuarum protege nos. Alleluia.

*The* Nunc dimittis.

*Ant.* Salva nos.

NUNC dimittis servum tuum, Domine :* secundum verbum tuum in pace.

Quia vidérunt óculi mei * salutáre tuum.

Quod parásti * ante fáciem ómnium populórum.

Lumen ad revelatiónem géntium,* et glóriam plebis tuæ Israel.

Gloria Patri, &c.

*Ant.* Salva nos, Dómine, vigilantes, custodi nos dormientes : ut vigilemus cum Christo, et requiescamus in pace. (*In Paschal time,* Alleluia.)

(*The following Prayers are omitted on Doubles and within Octaves :*)

Kyrie eleison.
Christe eleison.
Kyrie eleison.
Pater noster, &c. (*Secretly.*)

℣. Et ne nos inducas in tentationem.

℞. Sed libera nos a malo.

Credo in Deum, *secretly (page* 471).

℣. Carnis resurrectionem.

℞. Vitam æternam. Amen.

℣. Benedictus es, Domine, Deus patrum nostrorum.

℞. Et laudabilis et gloriosus in sæcula.

℣. Benedicamus Patrem et Filium cum Sancto Spiritu.

℟. Laudemus, et superexaltemus eum in sæcula.

℣. Benedictus es, Domine, in firmamento cœli.

℟. Et laudabilis, et gloriosus, et superexaltatus in sæcula.

℣. Benedicat et custodiat nos omnipotens et misericors Dominus.

℟. Amen.

℣. Dignare, Domine, nocte ista.

℟. Sine peccato nos custodire.

℣. Miserere nostri, Domine.

℟. Miserere nostri.

℣. Fiat misericordia tua, Domine, super nos.

℟. Quemadmodum speravimus in te.

℣. Domine, exaudi orationem meam.

℟. Et clamor meus ad te veniat.

℣. Dominus vobiscum.

℟. Et cum spiritu tuo.

ORÆMUS.

VISITA, quæsumus, Domine, habitationem istam, et omnes insidias inimici ab ea longe repelle: Angeli tui sancti habitent in ea, qui nos in pace custodiant: et benedictio tua sit super nos semper. Per Dominum.

℣. Dominus vobiscum.

℟. Et cum spiritu tuo.

℣. Benedicamus Domino.

℟. Deo gratias.

THE BLESSING.

BENEDICAT et custodiat nos omnipotens et misericors Dominus, Pater, et Filius, et Spiritus Sanctus.

℟. Amen.

*(Then is said one of the Antiphons of the Blessed Virgin, according to the season. The Antiphon is to be said kneeling, except in Paschal time, when it is to be said standing.)*

## I.

*From Saturday before First Sunday in Advent to the Purification, inclusively:*

ALMA Redemptoris Mater, quæ pervia cœli
Porta manes, et Stella maris, succurre cadenti,
Surgere qui curat populo: tu quæ genuisti,
Natura mirante, tuum sanctum Genitorem:
Virgo prius ac posterius, Gabrielis ab ore,
Sumens illud Ave, peccatorum miserere.

*In Advent:*

℣. Angelus Domini nuntiavit Mariæ.

℟. Et concepit de Spiritu Sancto.

OREMUS.

GRATIAM tuam, quæsumus, Domine, mentibus nostris infunde; ut qui, Angelo nuntiante, Christi Filii tui Incarnationem cognovimus, per passionem ejus et crucem, ad resurrectionis gloriam perducamur. Per eundem Christum Dominum nostrum.

℟. Amen.

*From Christmas-day to the Purification:*

℣. Post partum Virgo inviolata permansisti.

℟. Dei Genitrix, intercede pro nobis.

OREMUS.

DEUS, qui salutis æternæ, beatæ Mariæ virginitate fœcunda, humano generi præmia præstitisti; tribue, quæsumus, ut ipsam pro nobis intercedere sentiamus, per quam meruimus Auctorem vitæ suscipere, Dominum nostrum Jesum Christum Filium tuum. Qui vivit, &c.

℟. Amen.

℣. Divinum auxilium maneat semper nobiscum.

℟. Amen.

Pater noster, &c. *(Secretly.)*

## II.

*From the Feast of the Purification to Maunday Thursday, exclusively:*

AVE Regina cœlorum,
Ave Domina Angelorum,
Salve radix, salve porta,
Ex qua mundo lux est orta.

Gaude, Virgo gloriosa,
Super omnes speciosa,
Vale, O valde decora!
Et pro nobis Christum exora.

℣. Dignare me laudare te, Virgo sacrata.
℟. Da mihi virtutem contra hostes tuos.

OREMUS.

CONCEDE, misericors Deus, fragilitati nostræ præsidium; ut qui Sanctæ Dei Genitricis memoriam agimus, intercessionis ejus auxilio a nostris iniquitatibus resurgamus. Per eumdem Christum, &c.
℟. Amen.

℣. Divinum auxilium maneat semper nobiscum.
℟. Amen.

## III.

*From Holy Saturday till Trinity Eve.*

REGINA Cœli, lætare, alleluia.
Quia quem meruisti portare, alleluia.
Resurrexit sicut dixit: alleluia.
Ora pro nobis Deum: alleluia.

℣. Gaude et lætare, Virgo Maria: alleluia.
℟. Quia surrexit Dominus vere: alleluia.

ORBMUS.

DEUS, qui per Resurrectionem Filii tui Domini nostri Jesu Christi mundum lætificare dignatus es; præsta, quæsumus, ut per ejus Genitricem Virginem Mariam, perpetuæ capiamus gaudia vitæ. Per eumdem Christum, &c.
℟. Amen.

℣. Divinum auxilium maneat semper nobiscum.
℟. Amen.

IV.

*From Trinity Sunday to Advent.*

SALVE Regina, Mater misericordiæ.
Vita, dulcedo, et spes nostra, salve.
Ad te clamamus, exules filii Hevæ;
Ad te suspiramus, gementes et flentes in hac lacrymarum valle.
Eia ergo, Advocata nostra,
Illos tuos misericordes oculos ad nos converte;
Et Jesum, benedictum fructum ventris tui,
Nobis post hoc exilium ostende,
O clemens, O pia, O dulcis Virgo Maria.
℣. Ora pro nobis sancta Dei Genitrix.
℟. Ut digni efficiamur promissionibus Christi.

OREMUS.

OMNIPOTENS, sempiterne Deus, qui gloriosæ Virginis Matris Mariæ corpus et animam, ut dignum Filii tui habitaculum effici mereretur, Spiritu Sancto co-operante, præparasti; da ut cujus commemoratione lætamur, ejus pia intercessione ab instantibus malis et a morte perpetua liberamur. Per eumdem Christum, &c.
℟. Amen.
℣. Divinum auxilium maneat semper nobiscum.
℟. Amen.

PATER noster, qui es in cœlis; sanctificetur nomen tuum; adveniat regnum tuum; fiat voluntas tua, sicut in cœlo et in terra. Panem nostrum quotidianum da nobis hodie; et dimitte nobis debita nostra, sicut et nos dimittimus debitoribus nostris; et ne nos inducas in tentationem; sed libera nos a malo. Amen.

Ave Maria, gratia plena, Dominus tecum; benedicta tu in mulieribus, et benedictus fructus ventris tui, Jesus. Sancta Maria, Mater Dei, ora pro nobis peccatoribus, nunc et in hora mortis nostræ. Amen.

Credo in Deum, Patrem omnipotentem, creatorem cœli et terræ. Et in Jesum Christum, Filium ejus unicum, Dominum nostrum; qui conceptus est de Spiritu Sancto, natus ex Maria Virgine, passus sub Pontio Pilato, crucifixus, mortuus, et sepultus: descendit ad inferos; tertia die resurrexit a mortuis; ascendit ad cœlos, sedet ad dexteram Dei Patris omnipotentis; inde venturus est judicare vivos et mortuos. Credo in Spiritum Sanctum, sanctam Ecclesiam Catholicam, Sanctorum communionem, remissionem peccatorum, carnis resurrectionem, vitam æternam. Amen.

PRAYER AFTER DIVINE OFFICE.

To the most holy and undivided Trinity, to the Humanity of our Lord Jesus Christ, to the fruitful virginity of the most blessed and glorious Mary ever Virgin, and to the whole company of Saints, be for ever praise, honour, power, and glory from every creature; and to us be remission of all our sins, world without end. Amen.

℣. Blessed is the womb of Mary the Virgin, which bore the Son of the Eternal Father.

℟. And blessed are the breasts which gave suck to Christ the Lord.

Our Father. Hail Mary.

## Benediction of the Most Holy Sacrament.

---✠---

*When the Priest opens the Tabernacle, and incenses the Blessed Sacrament, is sung the Hymn:*

| | |
|---|---|
| O SALUTARIS hostia, Quæ cœli pandis ostium: Bella premunt hostilia, Da robur, fer auxilium. | O SAVING Victim, opening wide The gate of heav'n to man below! Our foes press on from every side; Thine aid supply, thy strength bestow. |
| Uni trinoque Domino Sit sempiterna gloria, Qui vitam sine termino Nobis donet in patria. Amen. | To thy great name be endless praise, Immortal Godhead, one in three! Oh, grant us endless length of days In our own native land with thee. Amen. |

*After which follows the* Litany of the Blessed Virgin, *see page* 232, *or some Psalm (the Psalm "* Quam dilecta,*" will be found in page* 480*), or Antiphon, or Hymn appropriate to the Feast, or in honour of the Most Holy Sacrament.*

*If* the Te Deum, *page* 126, *be sung, the persons present stand until the words* Te ergo, quæsumus (We pray thee, therefore), *are sung, when they kneel.*

*Then is sung the Hymn* Tantum ergo Sacramentum, *all present making a profound inclination (not prostration) while the words* Veneremur cernui *are being sung.*

TANTUM ergo Sacramentum
Veneremur cernui:
Et antiquum documentum
Novo cedat ritui;
Præstet fides supplementum
Sensuum defectui.

Down in adoration falling,
Lo! the sacred host we hail:
And o'er ancient forms departing,
Newer rites of grace prevail;
Faith for all defects supplying
Where the feeble senses fail.

Genitori, Genitoque,
Laus et jubilatio,
Salus, honor, virtus quoque
Sit et benedictio:
Procedenti ab utroque
Compar sit laudatio.
Amen.

To the everlasting Father,
And the Son who reigns on high,
With the Holy Ghost proceeding
Forth from each, eternally,
Be salvation, honour, blessing,
Might and endless majesty! Amen.

*Then are sung the following Versicles and Prayer.*

℣. Panem de cœlo præstitisti eis. [Alleluia *tempore Pasch et Oct. Corp. Christi.*]

℟. Omne delectamentum in se habentem. [Alleluia.]

℣. Thou didst give them bread from heaven. [Alleluia *in Paschal time, and Octave of Corp. Christi.*]

℟. Containing in itself all sweetness. [Alleluia.]

OREMUS.

DEUS, qui nobis sub Sacramento mirabili, passionis tuæ memoriam reliquisti: tribue, quæsumus, ita nos Corporis et Sanguinis tui sacra mysteria venerari ; ut redemptionis tuæ fructum in nobis jugiter sentiamus. Qui vivis, &c. Amen.

LET US PRAY.

O GOD, who under a wonderful Sacrament has left us a memorial of thy passion; grant us we beseech thee, so to venerate the sacred mysteries of thy body and blood, that we may ever feel within us the fruit of thy redemption. Who livest, &c. Amen.

*Here the* Benediction *is given with the* Blessed Sacrament, *all bowing down in profound adoration, and beseeching the blessing of Jesus Christ on themselves, and on the whole Church.*

Adoremus in æternum Sanctissimum Sacramentum.

May we for ever adore the most Holy Sacrament.

## Praises of the Holy Name.

BLESSED be God; blessed be his holy Name. Blessed be Jesus Christ, true God and true man. Blessed be the name of Jesus. Blessed be Jesus in the most Holy Sacrament of the Altar. Blessed be the great Mother of God, Mary, most holy. Blessed be the Holy and Immaculate Conception. Blessed be the name of Mary, Virgin and Mother. Blessed be God in his Holy Angels, and in his Saints.

(If these Praises be said by way of reparation for blasphemy, one year's Indulgence is granted for each recital; and a Plenary Indulgence, if said once a day for a month, on the usual conditions. A.)

## Benedictus.

BENEDICTUS Dóminus Deus Israel:* quia visitávit, et fecit redemptiónem plebis suæ.

Et eréxit cornu salútis nobis, * in domo David púeri sui.

Sicut locútus est per os sanctórum,* qui a sæculo sunt Prophetárum ejus.

BLESSED be the Lord God of Israel: for he hath visited and wrought the redemption of his people.

And hath raised up a horn of salvation to us: in the house of his servant David.

As he spake by the mouth of his holy prophets: who are from the beginning.

Salútem ex inimícis nostris,\* et de manu ómnium qui odérunt nos.

Ad faciéndam misericórdiam cum pátribus nostris,\* et memorári testaménti sui sancti.

Jusjurándum quod jurávit ad Abraham patrem nostrum,\* datúrum se nobis.

Ut sine timóre, de manu inimicórum nostrórum liberáti,\* serviámus illi,

In sanctitáte et justítia coram ipso,\* ómnibus diébus nostris.

Et tu, puer, Prophéta Altíssimi vocàberis; \*præíbis enim ante fáciem Dómini, paráre vias ejus.

Ad dandam sciéntiam salútis plebi ejus;\* in remissiónem peccatórum eórum.

Per víscera misericórdiæ Dei nostri;\* in quibus visitávit nos óriens ex alto.

Salvation from our enemies: and from the hand of all that hate us.

To perform mercy to our fathers: and to remember his holy testament.

The oath that he swore to Abraham our father: that he would grant unto us:

That being delivered from the hands of our enemies: we may serve him without fear,

In holiness and justice before him: all the days of our life.

And thou, child, shalt be called the Prophet of the Highest: for thou shalt go before the face of the Lord to prepare his ways.

To give knowledge of salvation unto his people: for the remission of their sins.

Through the bowels of the mercy of our God: whereby the orient from on high hath visited us.

| | |
|---|---|
| Illumináre his, qui in ténebris et in umbra mortis sedent; * ad dirigéndos pedes nostros in viam pacis. | To enlighten them that sit in darkness, and in the shadow of death: to direct our feet into the way of peace. |
| Gloria Patri, &c. | Glory be to the Father, &c. |

## Adoro te Devote.

*Hymn of St. Thomas of Aquin, in honour of the Most Blessed Sacrament.*

ADORO te devote, latens Deitas,
Quæ sub his figuris vere latitas,
Tibi se cor meum totum subjicit,
Quia te contemplans totum deficit.

Visus, tactus, gustus in te fallitur;
Sed auditui solo tuto creditur.
Credo quidquid dixit Dei Filius:
Nil hoc verbo veritatis verius.

In cruce latebat sola Deitas:
At hic simul latet et humanitas.
Ambo tamen credens atque confitens,
Peto quod petivit latro pœnitens.

Plagas, sicut Thomas, non intueor,
Deum tamen meum te confiteor.
Fac me tibi semper magis credere,
In te spem habere, te diligere.

O memoriale mortis Domini.
Panis vivus vitam præstans homini,
Præsta meæ menti de te vivere,
Et te illi semper dulce sapere.

In figuris præsignatur.
Cum Isaac immolatur,
Agnus Paschæ deputatur,
Datur Manna patribus.

Bone pastor, panis vere,
Jesu nostri miserere:
Tu nos pasce, nos tuere

Tu nos bona fac videre
In terra viventium.
Tu qui cuncta scis, et vales,
Qui nos pascis hic mortales:
Tuos ibi commensales,
Cohæredes et sodales,
Fac Sanctorum civium.
Amen. Alleluia.

## Quam Dilecta.

### Psalm lxxxi.

Quam dilécta tabernácula tua, Dómine virtútum!* concupíscit et déficit ánima mea in átria Dómini.

Cor meum et caro mea* exultavérunt in Deum vivum

Etenim passer invénit sibi domum: et turtur nidum sibi, ubi ponat pullos suos.

Altária tua, Dómine virtútum: * Rex meus, et Deus meus.

How lovely are thy tabernacles, O Lord of hosts: my soul longeth and fainteth for the courts of the Lord.

My heart and my flesh: have rejoiced in the living God.

For the sparrow hath found her a house: * and the turtle a nest for herself, where she may lay her young.

Even thy altars, O Lord of hosts: my King and my God.

Beáti qui hábitant in domo tua, Dómine: * in sǽcula sæculórum laudábunt te.

Beátus vir cujus est auxílium abs te : * ascensiónes in corde suo dispósuit, in valle lacrymárum, in loco quem pósuit.

Etenim benedictiónem dabit legislátor, ibunt de virtute in virtútem : * vidébitur Deus deórum in Sion.

Dómine Deus virtútum, exaúdi oratiónem meam: * auribus pércipe, Deus Jacob.

Protéctor noster áspice, Deus:* et réspice in fáciem Christi tui.

Quia mélior est dies una in átriis tuis * super míllia.

Elégi abjéctus esse in domo Dei mei, * magis quam habitáre in tabernáculis peccatórum.

Quia misericórdiam, et veritátem díligit

Blessed are they that dwell in thy house, O Lord: they shall praise thee for ever and ever.

Blessed is the man whose help is from thee: in his heart he hath disposed to ascend by steps, in the vale of tears, in the place that he hath fixed.

For the lawgiver shall give a blessing, they shall go from virtue to virtue: the God of gods shall be seen in Sion.

O Lord God of hosts hear my prayer: give ear, O God of Jacob.

Behold, O God, our protector : and look upon the face of thine Anointed.

For one day in thy courts : is better than a thousand.

I have chosen rather to be an abject in the house of my God: than to dwell in the tabernacles of sinners.

For God loveth mercy and truth: the Lord

Y

Deus: * grátiam et glóriam dabit Dóminus.
Non privábit bonis eos qui ámbulant in innocéntia: * Dómine virtútum, beátus homo qui sperat in te.

Gloria Patri, &c.

will give grace and glory.
He will not deprive of good things them that walk in innocence: O Lord of hosts, blessed is the man that hopeth in thee.

Glory be to the Father, &c.

## Prayer of St. Ignatius of Loyola.

TAKE, O Lord, and receive all my liberty, my memory, my understanding, and my whole will, whatever I have and possess: Thou hast given me all these things, to thee, O Lord, I restore them; all are thine; dispose of them entirely according to thy will. Give me thy love and thy grace, for this is enough for me. Amen.

FINIS.

# Contents.

|  | PAGE. |
|---|---|
| Explanatory Notice | iii. |
| Table of Feasts and Fasts | iv. |
| ———— Moveable Feasts | vii. |
| Eight Plenary Indulgences granted to the Faithful in England | viii. |
| Lay Baptism | x. |
| Instructions and Devotions on Rising | 1 |
| Morning Prayers | 2 |
| The "Angelus Domini" and "Regina Cœli" | 16 |
| Instruction on Meditation | 23 |
| Short Meditations for each Day of the Month | 26 |
| Acts of Faith, Hope, Charity, and Contrition | 72 |
| The Holy Sacrifice of the Mass | 75 |
| Prayers before Mass on Sundays | 77 |
| A Devout Method of Hearing Mass | 86 |
| The Asperges | 106 |
| The Ordinary of the Mass | 108 |
| Prayers after Mass on Sundays | 125 |
| Manner of Serving at Mass | 135 |
| On the Performance of the Ordinary Actions of the Day | 141 |

## CONTENTS.

|  | PAGE |
|---|---|
| Ejaculatory Prayers | 143 |
| Grace before and after Meals | 147 |
| Consecration of Study to Mary Immaculate | 148 |
| Short Visits to the Blessed Sacrament for every Day in the Week | 149 |
| Creed of St. Athanasius | 158 |
| Universal Prayer | 162 |
| Pontifical Indulgences | 172 |
| Notice of Indulgences attached to the Rosary | 175 |
| The Living Rosary | 179 |
| Mysteries of the Rosary | 180 |
| Little Office of the Immaculate Conception *(Latin and English)* | 193 |
| Seven Penitential Psalms | 209 |
| Litany of the Saints *(Latin and English)* | 218 |
| Night Prayers | 232 |
| Short Meditations on Death | 245 |
| On the Choice of a State of Life | 247 |
| Instructions and Devotions for Confession | 250 |
| ——————— for Holy Communion | 273 |
| ——————— for Confirmation | 296 |
| ——————— for the Sick | 306 |
| ——————— for the Dying | 318 |
| Prayers for the Dead | 328 |

Burial of the Dead for Adults *(Latin and English)* - - - - - - - - - 330
Indulgences attached to Devotions for the Faithful Departed - - - - - - - 341

DEVOTIONS IN HONOUR OF THE SACRED HEART OF JESUS:
   Act of Consecration - - - - - - 345
   Litany of the Sacred Heart - - - - 346
   Act of Reparation - - - - - - - 349
   Prayer of St. Gertrude - - - - - 351
   Confraternity of the Sacred Heart - 352
   Devotion to the Agonizing Heart of Jesus - - - - - - - - - 354
   Guard of Honour of the Sacred Heart 355
   Apostleship of Prayer - - - - - 358

DEVOTIONS IN HONOUR OF THE IMMACULATE HEART OF MARY:
   Act of Consecration - - - - - - 192
   Litany of the Immaculate Heart - - 362
   Confraternity of the Immaculate Heart 364

OCCASIONAL DEVOTIONS:
   The "Quarant 'Ore," or Forty Hours' Prayer - - - - - - - - - 366
   Reparation of Injuries done to the Blessed Sacrament - - - - - 367

## Occasional Devotions:

| | PAGE |
|---|---|
| The Way of the Cross | 374 |
| The "Agnus Dei" | 422 |
| Month of May | 391 |
| Scapulars of our Blessed Lady | 418 |
| Devotion of the Ten Sundays in Honour of St. Ignatius | 392 |
| Novena of St. Francis Xavier | 394 |
| Six Sundays in Honour of St. Aloysius | 402 |
| Devotions in Honour of St. Stanislaus | 414 |
| Devotions in Honour of Blessed John Berchmans | 444 |
| Devotion of the "Bona Mors" | 424 |
| [Ordinance] of the "Bona Mors" | 437 |

## Litanies.

| | |
|---|---|
| Litany of the Saints (Latin and English) | 218 |
| Litany of the Most Holy Name of Jesus (Latin and English) | 168 |
| ——— Sacred Heart of Jesus | 346 |
| ——— Loreto (Latin and English) | 13 |
| ——— the Immaculate Heart of Mary | 363 |
| ——— St. Joseph | 306 |
| ——— St. Francis Xavier | 394 |
| ——— St. Aloysius | 403 |

CONTENTS. 487

OCCASIONAL PRAYERS:

|  | PAGE. |
|---|---|
| "O Deus, ego amo te" | 295 |
| "En ego" (after Holy Communion) | 291 |
| "Anima Christi" (*Latin and English*) | 292 |
| Act of Consecration to our Blessed Lady (*Latin and English*) | 18 |
| "Memorare" (*Latin and English*) | 19 |
| Prayer to our Blessed Lady | 19 |
| Consecration of Study to Mary Immaculate (*Latin and English*) | 148 |
| Prayer to Mary Immaculate | 150 |
| Dedication to St. Joseph | 20 |
| Prayer to St. Joseph | 21 |
| ———— to our Guardian Angel | 21 |
| ———— to St. Aloysius, for Purity | 22 |
| ———— of St. Ignatius of Loyola | 482 |
| ———— of B. John Berchmans | 447 |
| ———— before every Important Action | 143 |
| ———— for the Blessing of God on the Choice of a State of Life | 248 |
| ———— to be said by those who wear the "Agnus Dei" | 423 |
| ———— after Divine Office | 471 |
| ———— for the Holy Catholic Church | 440 |
| ———— for the Pope | 440 |
| ———— for Bishops and their Flock | 440 |

CONTENTS.

OCCASIONAL PRAYERS:

PAGE.

Prayer for a Congregation or Family 441
——— for Peace - - - - - - - 441
——— in any Tribulation - - - - 442
——— of Children for their Parents - 442
——— for a Friend - - - - - - 443
——— for the Faithful Departed - - 338
——— on the day of a Person's Decease or Burial - - - - 339
——— on the Anniversary of a Person's Burial - - - - - 339
——— for one lately Deceased - - 339
——— for a Bishop or Priest Deceased - - - - - - - 340
——— for a Father or Mother Deceased - - - - - - - 340
——— for Friends or Benefactors Deceased - - - - - - - 340
——— for a Deceased Friend - - - 443

HYMNS:

Te Deum *(Latin and English)* - - - 126
To the Most Holy Name *(Latin and English)* - - - - - - - - 164
Ad quem diu suspiravi - - - - - 293
O Deus, ego amo te - - - - - - 295

HYMNS:

PAGE.

Veni, Creator Spiritus *(Latin and English)* - - - - - - - - - - 301
Veni, Sancte Spiritus *(Latin and English)* - - - - - - - - - - 303
To Jesus' Heart all Burning - - - 367
Te Lucis ante terminum - - - - - 465
O Salutaris hostia - - - - - - - 472
Adoro te devote - - - - - - - 477
Lauda, Sion - - - - - - - - - 478
Ave, Maris Stella *(Latin and English)* 235
Stabat Mater *(Latin and English)* - 387
Dies iræ - - - - - - - - - - 342

Vespers for Sundays and Festivals - - 448
Compline - - - - - - - - - - - 461
Antiphons of B. V. M., according to the season of the year - - - - - - - 467
Benediction of the Most Holy Sacrament 472
Psalm "Miserere" *(Latin and English)* - 131
—— "Benedictus" *(Latin and English)* 475
—— "Quam Dilecta" *(Latin and English* - - - - - - - - - - 480
Prayer of St. Ignatius of Loyola - - - 482

www.ingramcontent.com/pod-product-compliance
Lightning Source LLC
Chambersburg PA
CBHW032002300426
44117CB00008B/869